THE
PEOPLE
FACTOR

Maudie Evans

THE
PEOPLE
FACTOR

HOW BUILDING GREAT RELATIONSHIPS
AND ENDING BAD ONES
UNLOCKS YOUR GOD-GIVEN PURPOSE

VAN MOODY

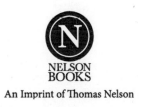

NELSON
BOOKS

An Imprint of Thomas Nelson

Published in Nashville, Tennessee, by Nelson Books, an imprint of Thomas Nelson. Nelson Books and Thomas Nelson are registered trademarks of HarperCollins Christian Publishing, Inc.

Published in association with Eames Literary Services, LLC, Nashville, Tennessee.

Thomas Nelson, Inc., titles may be purchased in bulk for educational, business, fund-raising, or sales promotional use. For information, please e-mail SpecialMarkets@ThomasNelson.com.

Unless otherwise noted, Scripture quotations in this book are from The Holy Bible, New International Version. © 1973, 1978, 1984, 2011, International Bible Society. Used by permission of Zondervan Bible Publishers. All rights reserved.

Scripture quotations marked NKJV are taken from the New King James Version. © 1982 by Thomas Nelson, Inc. Used by permission. All rights reserved.

Scripture quotations marked MSG are taken from *The Message* by Eugene Peterson. © 1993, 1994, 1995, 1996, 2000, 2001, 2002. Used by permission of NavPress Publishing Group. All rights reserved.

Library of Congress Cataloging-in-Publication Data

Moody, Van, 1975-
  The people factor : how building great relationships and ending bad ones unlocks your God-given purpose / Van Moody.
     pages cm
  Includes bibliographical references.
  ISBN 978-1-4002-0502-8
  1. Interpersonal relations--Religious aspects--Christianity. I. Title.
  BV4597.52.M65 2014
  248.4--dc23

                        2013022629

Printed in the United States of America

13 14 15 16 17 RRD 6 5 4 3 2 1

He who walks with the wise grows wise,
but a companion of fools suffers harm.

—PROVERBS 13:20

*To my amazing wife, Ty, and our
beautiful children, Eden Sydney and
Ethan Isaiah: I love you so much!*

*To the Worship Center Christian Church
family: I am honored to serve the
greatest church this side of heaven.*

Contents

Foreword

PEOPLE ARE RELATIONAL BEINGS. WE ARE made to be in relationships with others. In fact, when God created humankind, He quickly observed that it is not good for people to be alone (Gen. 2:18). We all need dual dimensions of relational love in our lives—a vertical love relationship with God and horizontal love relationships with other people. Perhaps like you, I have spent my life trying to manifest and maximize my vertical relationship with God, but my greatest struggles have not been vertical; they have been horizontal—with other people. Sometimes I wish the Lord had simply said in His Word, "Love the Lord your God with all your heart and with all your soul and with all your mind" and not included, "Love your neighbor as yourself" (Matt. 22:37, 39).

Maybe you can relate when I say my biggest relational challenges are with the horizontal connections in my life. Maybe you also love God vertically but have trouble trying to love horizontally—especially when people are unlovely or unlovable, or when they do not want the love you have to offer. Trying to obey God and love people when they do not love you can be especially difficult.

Let's think for a moment about the first human relationship, the one between Adam and Eve. In Genesis 1 and 2, they related to each other in ways consistent with their vertical relationship with God. However, in Genesis 3, the serpent (the devil) entered the picture and both the vertical and horizontal relationships of Adam and Eve were forever distorted. Their loyalty and love for God disintegrated into disobedience, demonstrated by deception and the destruction of their trust, honesty, and holiness. Adam blamed Eve, and she blamed the serpent. Ultimately they tried to put the blame on God, who had given Adam the woman, and who had made the serpent!

As people living after the fall, we are predisposed to handle our relationships in the shadow of distorted humanity. Rather than flesh out those relationships based on our vertical connection with a loving God, we strain and struggle horizontally to love, forgive, and bless the people around us. We are to love others as God loves us, forgive others as He forgives us, and ideally we are to handle others as He handles us. Oh, that dealing with other people could be so simple! The insights and skills we desperately need in the realm of relationships do not come naturally to us. In a sinful, fallen world, we need all the help we can get in the area of relationships. As the Ethiopian said to Philip, "How can I [understand] without some help?" (Acts 8:31 MSG). In this book, help is on its way!

The author of this potentially life-changing book, Van Moody, has wisdom beyond his years, vision beyond his imagination, and commitment beyond his generation. He has an unquenchable thirst for righteousness and a persistent passion for the things of God, and he is in dogged pursuit of godly truth. Van Moody is a gift from God for the times in which we live, and I believe these pages are also a powerful gift to all who will read, absorb, and apply their insights.

This exceedingly helpful book introduces and explains practical principles about the oh-so-challenging arena of earthly relationships. It will help you break patterns of destruction, disrespect, and deception; and it will assist you in assimilating and applying eternal principles of living and dealing with other people in the ever-changing dynamics of today's culture.

Moody suggests that the foundational problem we face in many aspects of our lives is a lack of skill and mastery in the art of relationships. He helps us gain and develop those abilities. In a flowing, attention-grabbing style, he affirms the timeless value of issues that seem to have become relics of the past: integrity, commitment, loving honesty, fidelity, and forgiveness. With remarkable insights and a high level of practicality, he unapologetically grounds his redemptive revelations and directives in "the greatest, most effective relationship book of all time, the manual for all successful lives and relationships: the Bible."

I can't help but speculate what the world would have been like if Adam and Eve had had a book like this, if Cain had had a book like this, or if Abraham and David had had the information and advice available in these pages. In fact, I can't help but wonder what my life would have been like had I had a book like this before now! I am one of a whole host of people who have crashed their lives, endangered their destinies, and ruptured and ruined relationships because I did not have access to a practical grasp of the truths documented in this book. Choices I have made, hearts I have broken, lives I have impacted negatively—all could have been radically redeemed had I had a book like this. There is a long list of men and women who could have benefited from this instructive, insightful, inspirational work. Prepare to be challenged, confronted, and changed. And prepare to have your relational skills sharpened and honed to position you for your next level of success and destiny.

Kenneth C. Ulmer, DMin, PhD
The King's University
Los Angeles, California

Introduction

THERE MUST BE A REASON YOU PICKED UP
this book.

Most people do not read books on relationships if they feel
their relationships are healthy, happy, or easy. So I wonder: What
is it that you want to know about relationships? Have you recently
realized how vital good relationships are to every area of your life?
Has it just dawned on you that you need to learn to do relationships
better? Have you recently attained a leadership position that calls
for more savvy than you have had in the past when dealing with
people? Have you found yourself at a crossroads or a crisis in your
life because a relationship has fallen apart? Or are you looking at
a whole new future because a seemingly great relationship has just
begun and you are desperate to get it right? Whatever your situation, keep reading all the way to the end of this book, because I
believe you will find the answers you need—and so much more.

You have some kind of relationship with everyone you encounter. Some relationships are extremely personal and some are strictly
professional. Some are casual and on-the-surface relationships, and

some are intimate and deep. But every relationship you have influences your life. *There are no neutral relationships.* Each one lifts you up or weighs you down. It moves you forward or holds you back. It helps you or it hurts you.

As a pastor, I have listened to thousands of people share a variety of problems, each one looking for answers and advice. In these face-to-face meetings, people are ready to talk about serious stuff, the rubber-meets-the-road issues in their lives, the circumstances that keep them awake at night. Almost always, these major situations stem from relational challenges. Sometimes the matter pertains to a loveless marriage or a conflict at work. Sometimes the problem is that people truly cannot understand each other or do not know how to communicate. Sometimes what they talk about makes me sick and angry, such as situations involving incest or abuse. Most of the time, I simply need to share with them the lessons no one ever taught me about relationships, truths and insights I have learned along my journey through life by the grace of God.

As a human being, in addition to my role as a pastor, I have come to understand that relationships are the most important area of a person's life. The most important relationship, of course, is a relationship with God, and then relationships with others. I am convinced that everything in life rises and falls on our relationships. They make us or break us. Along these lines, author and marketing guru Seth Godin says: "Who you hang out with determines what you dream about and what you collide with. And the collisions and the dreams lead to your changes. And the changes are what you become. Change the outcome by changing your circle."[1] Clearly, relationships can make the difference between a great life and a miserable existence. They can launch us into heights of excellence and achievement we never dreamed possible, or they can keep us down in the dumps, tethered to mediocrity for all of our days.

Relationships can be our source of greatest joy or our place of greatest pain. In fact, if anything is more painful than physical illness or injury, it is the emotional ache of a human heart. If any situation is as serious as the widespread outbreak of disease or the devastation of natural disasters, it's the epidemic of broken or unhappy relationships that covers the globe today. It exists in every culture and every demographic—maybe even in you. Like the rampant spread of H1N1 or SARS when those diseases were so frightening, the growing destruction that results from bad relationships must be stopped. This is a cause to which I have dedicated my life.

Like you, I have watched while shaking my head over celebrities, politicians, and business leaders who were phenomenally talented but lost everything because they made bad choices in relationships. People such as Tiger Woods, Arnold Schwarzenegger, Ted Haggard, Chad "Ochocinco" Johnson, and Lisa Nowak (a former astronaut and navy captain now serving prison time for attacking a romantic rival) are synonymous with achievement—at least they once were. At one time, these people touched the pinnacle of success in their respective fields. They are educated, trained, practiced, and skilled; they diligently prepared for greatness. They even had an abundance of leadership books available to them. But they all suffered disgrace and bear permanent scars on their character for one reason: relationships. Their stories made the front covers of popular magazines and the headlines of cable and Internet news. But famous people are not the only ones who suffer because of their relationships. It can happen to anyone.

In fact, suffering and struggling because of relationships happens every day in all kinds of ways. Most of the time, these situations do not capture media attention, but they all have stories behind them. The stories are not simply the details of "why so-and-so got a divorce" or "why he left the company" or "why the children have been removed from the home." These accounts are not as much about what took place behind the closed doors of a home or a business as they are about what happened in a person's heart and mind. They are not about who gets the house or where that bruise came from or what she will do if she cannot find a new job. They are about *why* a person cannot stay in a marriage, *why* someone abuses others, or *why* a person is known for not being a team player.

These situations and countless others all stem from the same source: the level of understanding and skill a person possesses about relationships. We simply must know what makes a relationship healthy and what makes it toxic. We have to learn to identify the warning signs of a relationship that is in trouble and gain the ability to leave it wisely, at the right time, and for the right reasons. We need to be able to assess people not for the petty purpose of being judgmental, but for the greater purpose of recognizing the people God has called us to walk closely with on the amazing journey He has planned for our lives. We need to lovingly undertake the important task of evaluating a person's character so we will know if we should allow a deep relationship, keep the acquaintance casual, or avoid the relationship altogether. In addition, we are in desperate need of information to help us improve our relationships and develop the necessary tools to put the information into action.

Years ago, Robert Fulghum wrote a popular book titled *All I Really Need to Know I Learned in Kindergarten.* I understand his point and appreciate his insights. I also learned a variety of important lessons in kindergarten, but as I grew older I realized I needed to build on the basic things I knew about relationships. As my educational path took me through elementary school, high school, college, and graduate school, I recognized the need to raise my relational IQ as much or more than I raised my level of knowledge and skill in other areas.

For example, I learned to add as a young boy, but before long I also needed to know how to multiply. I learned about the concepts of hot and cold as a very young child, but later needed to understand the balance and relationship between those two so I could operate my thermostat and keep my family comfortable. I learned to spell *cat* as soon as I could write, but the time came when I needed to know how to spell *category, catapult,* and *catastrophic.* The fundamental lessons I learned about relationships were vital and provided necessary building blocks; I simply needed to know more.

Just as I needed to raise my relational IQ, perhaps you do too. We seem to be able to easily locate books that talk about specific aspects of relationships, such as improving communication or developing skills to be more effective parents or better spouses. I have also read many books about leadership and business, looking for insight into relationships because I believe the true secret to any leader's success lies not in degrees or pedigrees or corporate smarts, but in the ability to relate effectively to others. To my surprise, most leadership books practically ignore the vital area of relationships, even though that's the area that makes the difference between a terrific leader and a terrible one.

One of the main reasons I have written *The People Factor* is that I could not find in one book the insights and information I needed to take me to the next level of relational skill, not only in one specific area of relationships but in relationships of all types. I did not have a concise, practical resource to recommend to audiences who listen when I speak and ask important questions about the relationship challenges they face. There was nothing to put in the hands of people who left my office after sharing their deep pain over a relationship that would teach them beyond-the-basics lessons that could help them in highly practical ways. Many of these people know the fundamentals of relationships, but they need advice and instruction about how to become more relationally savvy and strategic. So I have written the book I always wanted to read. I have put into print the lessons I wish someone had taught me years ago about relationships. I think it is valuable, even life changing, and I pray you will too.

One reason we really do need to know how to navigate this area is that when God wants to do something in a person's life, He usually does it through a relationship. My wife, Ty, says that she and I are where we are today *because of relationships.* While that is a bold assertion, it is not an understatement. We did not arrive where we are today because an angel came down from heaven and told us to start with a few people what is now a thriving church in Birmingham, Alabama. We have a fulfilling life and a blessed ministry because a series of relationships led us to the place we know God has for us. I have long believed that the biblical purpose of relationships is to add value to people's lives and to help each person or entity involved contribute to the other in positive, life-building ways. That conviction has guided my wife and me as we have developed relationships and made relational decisions.

Any relationship that pulls us away from God, His Word, or His plan for our lives must be put aside. Let me be clear that my designation of "any relationship" does not always apply to marriage. Many principles in *The People Factor* can easily be applied to marriage, but this is not primarily a book about marriage. This is a book about the larger realm of relationships in general. It is important to understand that unlike professional and platonic relationships, marriage is a unique covenant relationship created by God to last until "death do us part." Marriage is an honorable covenant and a great marriage is something worth working for. Nevertheless, there are clear reasons, biblical and other, why some marriage relationships should end sooner rather than later. Abuse of any kind is one of those reasons. If you are or have ever been part of an abusive relationship, please understand that God created relationships to help you, not to harm you in any way.

There is a reason God created Eve from Adam's rib. The rib is one of the closest bones to a person's heart. This suggests that Adam was supposed to protect Eve and to protect her heart. I believe the reason God did not make Eve out of a bone in Adam's hand or foot is that such an action might have indicated that it was permissible for Adam to physically harm or even walk over Eve. I do not believe that God intends abuse of any kind in any relationship, and I would urge anyone who is being abused to exit the relationship quickly and seek professional help.

Two scriptures that clearly affirm the necessity of maintaining godly relationships and walking away from ungodly ones are found among the wise sayings of the book of Proverbs. Proverbs 27:17 teaches: "As iron sharpens iron, so one person sharpens another." Proverbs 13:20 says, "He who walks with the wise grows wise, but a companion of fools suffers harm." Ty and I learned these lessons long ago, and we have used them ever since because we know God uses relationships to lead us to the places and opportunities He has for us.

The same is true for you. You are where you are in life today because of your relationships. If you like where you are, great! But you are in the minority. If you do not like where you are and you hunger for a richer, more fulfilling experience in every area of your life, this book is a great place to start. I guarantee that if you put its principles to work, you will soon be a stronger, happier, healthier person. You will be a better spouse, a better friend, a better boss, a better parent, and a better human being if you will embrace the advice and carry out the instructions in these pages.

The insights and principles you will find in this book are based on the greatest, most effective relationship book of all time, the manual for all successful lives and relationships: the Bible. Everything you could ever need to know to have purposeful, thriving relationships is in the Good Book. It's a Book about a lot of topics, but from start to finish one of its primary subjects is relationships.

The One who wrote the Book is the same One who creates relationships, leads us into relationships that will bless us, and helps us avoid alliances that will hurt us. He knows everything there is to know about the inner workings of people and relationships, and He has put it in His Word. Think of it this way: if you were to buy a car and have something go wrong with it, you would not call a plumber to fix it; you would go to the dealer or manufacturer. The same principle applies to relationships. When you want to know about them or speak with someone who can fix them, you go to the person who started them and knows all about them: God.

One of the tragedies of our contemporary society, I believe, is that we often look for relationship advice in sources that are not truly trustworthy. We may think we can trust them, but much of the material available today does not ultimately lead us into truth, freedom, and maturity. We look to television personalities and people who are "experts" in the world's eyes, but have no vital connection with the Author of every relationship. This book will help you with powerful insights and instructions from the only credible relationship source on earth: God's Word.

I think it's only fair to warn you, though: The principles and practices in this book are not overnight miracles. You will have to apply them day after day, week after week, year after year. You will need to put them to work in your relationships when it is easy and when it is not. But I really believe once you start, you won't ever want to stop.

In each chapter of the book, I have included two specific,

practical tools to help you remember and apply the insights you gain in *The People Factor*. The first one is titled "Relational Reminders" and consists of a brief list of bullet points summarizing the key principles of every chapter. The second feature I trust you will find helpful is a series of questions called "Raising Your Relational IQ." Reading and understanding the material in the book will certainly help you become smarter relationally, but these questions will take you to the next level of relational skill because they provide you with an opportunity to think about your relationships, and to apply the lessons of this book to your everyday life.

Are you eager to get started? So am I. Let's go.

The Critical Laws of Relationships

LIKE IT OR NOT, LAWS GOVERN THE ENTIRE universe. We have laws that ensure order in cities and nations, laws of nature, laws of physics, and laws of supply and demand. Everyone on earth is subject to certain laws, and there are at least two facts we must know about them. First, if something is really a law, it works every time. Just think about the law of gravity—what goes up must come down, and it always does. Second, the breaking of a law carries consequences. Sometimes the consequence is physical injury, sometimes it is prison, sometimes it is a fine or a fee, and sometimes it is a terrible feeling of guilt.

Just as laws regulate societies and teach us what to expect in the physical world or in the realm of mathematics, science, or economics, laws also govern the complex world of relationships. They are true in every relational context, and as too many people have discovered, the consequences for breaking them can be painful. The first step toward building strong, purposeful, healthy relationships is to know what these laws are and understand how to make them work for you, not against you.

Observing laws for the sake of obedience to rules and regulations is called legalism, and it produces a life of dry, boring drudgery. But really grasping the truth about these laws and abiding by them for the sake of a larger purpose leads to a life of fulfillment, security, and joy. I believe many people have miserable lives because they have miserable relationships. Learning to live by the laws of relationships will bring dramatic improvement to your life because it will enable you to make great decisions about new relationships and maximize the ones you already have.

1

You've Got to Be You

THE LAW OF BEING REAL

DID YOU SEE ANY OF THE MOVIES IN THE
Batman trilogy starring Christian Bale? What about *Inception*? How
about *The Avengers* or *Iron Man*? In these films, the main characters wear masks or pretend to be people they are not. Similarly, in
the classic film *Roman Holiday,* Gregory Peck's character, Joe, hides
the fact that he is a newspaper reporter who stands to gain five
thousand dollars for securing an interview with Audrey Hepburn's
character and simply pretends to be her friend. At the same time,
Hepburn's character is a princess masquerading as an ordinary girl.

While secret identities and elaborate disguises offer good enter-
tainment, a person who pretends to be anyone other than him- or
herself will not be able to enjoy genuine, authentic relationships. To
build and maintain deep, substantive relationships, people must
know themselves, be honest about themselves, and share their true
selves with others. They need to be real; they have to be who they
really are, with no pretense and no spin. Of course, they also have

to be free from the dark web of keeping serious secrets, but I have reserved that important topic for another chapter. In this chapter, I simply want to focus on how and why we must be genuine, honest individuals, and to explain the importance of looking for those same qualities in others.

When people in a movie hide their identities, the plot inevitably unfolds to the point where circumstances force them to reveal themselves or where they are found out. By the end of the film, the mysteries of identity have been solved and the story concludes neatly. But real life is not so scripted. In the real world, people do not usually wear costumes or disguises, but many do find subtle ways to make themselves seem better than they really are. I suspect we have all done that at times—some of us more than others—but anytime it happens it sets us up for personal and relational failure. To enjoy success in our lives and in our dealings with others, we need to thoroughly know our true selves and allow the right people to know us completely as well.

SEE THROUGH THE WORDS

Most people are quick to speak and slow to hear. They have no clue how weighty their words can be and no idea how seriously others may take what they say. Perhaps you know exactly what I mean. Maybe a boss said you were due for a raise, but then never completed the paperwork so you could actually get it. Maybe someone said the powerful words *I love you*, then proceeded to treat you disrespectfully or to demonstrate all kinds of selfish, unloving behavior. Or maybe you have encountered simple, common situations such as hearing a teenager say, "Yeah, I'll clean up my room," only to see that room still a mess a week later.

You probably have all kinds of personal experience with people who say one thing and do something else. It is a widespread problem. We often build relationships with people who do this because we do not understand that they really do not know themselves and therefore do not realize the incongruities between their words and actions.

A young man named Jason who grew up around the car business now runs a marketing business for auto parts companies. Several years ago, through a family member, Jason became acquainted with Steve, the semiretired owner of an organization with manufacturing and sales operations all over the world, but with very little marketing support. Jason saw great potential in the company and recognized that Steve had a number of ideas that could benefit his current customers and give him access to an entirely new consumer base, if only a savvy marketer like Jason could communicate them clearly. Jason had the ability and experience to serve Steve and the company well, and he was eager to do so.

Despite being warned by someone with personal experience, "That guy will work you harder than anyone else ever has; he will *eat your lunch*," Jason thought the relationship would provide him with good experience, so he moved ahead with it. Because he had been informed they had a small marketing budget and could not pay him a fair market rate, Jason reduced his fees and made very little money for his efforts on their behalf. Working with Steve became so stressful that Jason's church friends and basketball buddies, who normally did not comment on his business endeavors, noticed that he was under unusual pressure.

During the professional relationship, Steve took unreasonably long amounts of time to respond to important e-mails and declared himself "not available" while on the golf course or at his lake house when Jason needed information to complete his projects on time.

But Steve regularly contacted Jason during Jason's few short vacations. Steve and his wife even invited Jason and his girlfriend to spend a nice, relaxing day with them at the lake, but as soon as the young couple arrived, Steve cornered Jason and spent the next three hours talking about marketing ideas.

Even though Steve did not treat Jason well, the older man repeatedly patted him on the back, told him how much potential he had, and told him what a great job he was doing. He even went so far as to say, "Aren't you glad you're working for me? I know it doesn't pay a lot, but nobody will treat you better than I do!" The chasm between Steve's words and his disrespectful actions puzzled Jason at first because Steve's verbal affirmation was so convincing. Finally, Jason's perceptive girlfriend figured out the problem and explained that Steve honestly believed he respected Jason, and that Steve truly could not see how his behavior was inconsistent with his comments. Assessing the situation correctly, she said, "It's easy. The guy is deceived. He doesn't really know himself. He's probably not even aware of the differences between what he says and what he does."

I have known many people in positions similar to Jason's. They build relationships with others based on the words those people speak instead of the actions they take. At first, they are confused because most people tend to believe what others say, especially when their words are encouraging or empowering. But sometimes people's actions do not support their statements. People often try to rationalize this kind of behavior with comments such as, "Well, he just expresses his love differently than I do. He says he loves me, and I believe him" or "The boss says I'm next in line for a promotion. I don't understand why she keeps giving her nephew all the opportunities that lead to the next level and introducing him to the decision-makers in our company. But she assures me I'll move up in the organization as soon as a good position becomes available."

We must realize that discrepancies between words and actions are serious warning signs. Most of the time, people whose words and actions are not consistent do not know themselves well and therefore are not good candidates for relationships. Having the integrity to back up what we say with what we do is vital, and we must find people who will do this with us. Setting this same high standard for ourselves is equally important.

It Starts with You

You will find a lot in this book about how to deal with other people. The truth is, all the positive traits I encourage you to look for when considering a relationship are traits you would be wise to cultivate in yourself. Likewise, the characteristics I urge you to avoid in others are qualities that would also be detrimental to you. I cannot overemphasize the simple, obvious fact that *you* are a critical component of every relationship in which you are involved. You play a vital role in the success and failure of each interaction in your life. The healthier, stronger, and more mature you are as an individual, the likelier you are to seek friends and associates who are also healthy, strong, and mature, and to develop relationships with those same qualities.

You have an important role to play and a responsibility to give the very best of yourself to every relationship in your life—with your family and friends, with your work associates, with individuals in your community, and with people in social or religious settings. If you want to discover your best self so you can share it with others, start by being transparent, being *real*, about who you are.

If you are going to be real, you must demand honesty from yourself and avoid self-deception. The easiest person in the world to deceive is yourself. Think about it: You can so easily tell yourself you are smarter, more attractive, more creative, more loyal, more honest, or more *anything* than you actually are. And whatever you tell yourself, you believe.

Believing your own personal public relations campaign is easy, but it will not lead to truth, transparency, and integrity. One of the best ways to really get to know yourself is to focus on your behavior rather than your words. People of integrity do what they say they will do; the substance of their hearts is expressed through their actions. Ask yourself the questions below and answer them honestly. (You will have a chance to do this at the end of this chapter if you prefer not to stop now.) This will help you see how you are doing on your journey to becoming a truthful, transparent person and let you know where you may need to improve.

- When I say I will show up for an appointment at a specific time, do I show up on time? *yes*
- If I have signed a credit card application agreeing to pay my creditors each month, do I pay them when payments are due? *y*
- If I have committed to marriage vows, am I keeping them? *N/A*
- Do I honor my commitments to family members (including my children) rather than repeatedly letting them down, expecting them to "cut me some slack" because, after all, we're family? *yes*
- Do I tell the truth in casual conversation rather than being content with little "white" lies? *y*
- Do I demand honesty from myself on my job, even if twisting the truth a little will make me appear smarter or put me in a better position for promotion? *y*

- Do I tell myself the truth about who I really am?
- Am I honest about my weaknesses and flaws? *NO*
- Do I exaggerate my own abilities? *NO*
- Do I tell half-truths? *No*
- Do I flatter people to gain their approval? *No*
- Do I minimize or give damaging reports of others to make *No* myself look good?

These questions can all be answered with one word: *yes* or *no.* Once you have answered them, I recommend that you consider them a little more. Examine your responses and ask yourself *why* you answered yes or no. Think of specific examples and identify the reasons you responded as you did. The more thorough and honest you are willing to be about yourself, the more effectively you can make the adjustments needed for personal growth and improvement. An honest assessment of yourself will help you get to know yourself better than ever before. The better you know yourself, the better your relationships will be.

INVITE OTHERS INTO THE PROCESS

Ophthalmologists will tell you that everyone has blind spots. That's right, having one blind spot in each eye is normal. If you are a living human being, you have visual blind spots. The same is true mentally and emotionally; there are certain things you cannot see about yourself. Your blind spots may be something like pride and jealousy that only reveal themselves in certain situations: a tendency to exaggerate your accomplishments or a habit of "polishing" the truth when doing so benefits you. These are thoughts, attitudes, or actions you probably are not aware of, but other people see them.

These blind spots can become barriers or stumbling blocks on your journey to great relationships.

If you want to take the next step in getting to know yourself accurately, ask a few honest, trustworthy friends for their opinions about you. Friends who are willing to do this can help you see your blind spots, and the right people will do so with candor, but also with love and grace. Be prepared for straightforward answers, but if you are willing to hear the truth, this exercise may yield some lessons that will help you be a better friend, coworker, leader, or family member. Asking an honest, compassionate friend these questions will help you get started and may even lead to more questions that will also give you great insights into who you are.

- What do you think are my best qualities?
- What do you think are my greatest weaknesses?
- Do you believe I consistently tell the truth?
- How well do you think I know myself?
- What do you think is the biggest deception I have about myself?
- Do you feel you can depend on me in an emergency or a crisis?
- In what ways have I earned your respect?
- Do you trust me?
- What one thing do you think I could do to improve my life and my ability to relate to others?
- Do you think I treat other people with honor and respect?
- Do I have a good record of keeping my word and doing what I say I will do?
- Do you believe I am open to constructive criticism and to making personal adjustments when others speak the truth lovingly to me?

Some of the answers your trusted friend gives may surprise you; some may even sting. You may not agree with him or her, but remember: you chose the person who answered the questions because you trusted and respected that person and you wanted honest responses. Be willing to think and pray about what you learn from this exercise and be willing to make the changes needed in order to become a better person in general and a better participant in all your relationships.

KEEPING IT REAL

Once you have had the courage to take an honest look at yourself and to ask someone you trust to help you identify your blind spots, you have what you need to begin a powerful journey of making significant adjustments that will serve you and your relationships well. Only you can know the specific changes needed in your life, but let me suggest several general ways to be a real, transparent person. These are also important qualities to look for in every person with whom you consider having a relationship.

Be straightforward and sincere.

Have you ever walked through a crowd and heard two people making small talk? Maybe the conversation goes something like this:

> "It is so good to see you! How are you doing?"
> "Good to see you too. I'm doing great. How are you?"
> "Oh, I couldn't be better! You know, that outfit looks great on you."
> "What? This old thing? I just pulled it out of the closet in a hurry this morning."

"Well, you look great. Hey, I've got to go, but I hope to see you
again soon."

"Me too! Take care!"

Interactions such as these take place all the time—in hallways
of office buildings, in break rooms, in neighborhoods, at ball
games, at churches—in all kinds of places where people encounter others. Of course, such conversations are fine *as long as they
are honest.* The problem comes when people really are not glad to
see each other and say in their minds, *Oh no. I really didn't want
to run into him today,* while saying with their mouths, "Nice to see
you!" Interactions become insincere when one person says, "That
looks great on you" while thinking, *She must have gained forty
pounds since last time I saw her and that dress makes everything
worse!*

Even in situations that call for the most casual conversation,
we need to learn to be straightforward and sincere, yet loving and
kind. Sometimes, we can do so with only slight tweaks in our language, for example:

- If you do not think someone looks good in a particular
  outfit, but you really like one part of it, you can simply say,
  "What a beautiful scarf," or "I like that tie!" or "What a
  pretty color!"
- If you are not glad to see someone, you can still smile and
  say, "What brings you here today?"
- If you are not doing well, instead of answering, "Fine," when
  someone asks how you are and you really do not want to
  discuss your situation, you can say, "I'm really enjoying
  being out and about on this beautiful day" or "I am so glad
  the weather is finally getting milder!"

I cannot overestimate the importance of being straightforward and sincere. Being able to say what you mean and mean what you say is a vital component of a successful life and healthy relationships. If you have ever encountered people who are insincere, you may agree that lack of straightforward honesty is often the first indication that they might not be trustworthy or are not who they say they are.

According to folk etymology, the Latin words from which we get the English word *sincere* are *sine cera,* meaning "without wax." Apparently, this term comes from an age-old practice common in the production of fine porcelain. Real porcelain pieces can crack during the production process, and dishonest vendors filled the cracks with wax to make them appear as though they did not have flaws in them. Honest vendors, in contrast, displayed signs saying *Sine Cera* to indicate that they sold pure porcelain pieces, not deceptive ones.[1]

A sincere, secure person does not try to cover personal "cracks" or flaws. He or she will respect you enough to be honest and transparent with you and to expect you to do likewise. On the other hand, insincere people try to make themselves appear better than they really are, often because they are afraid of being rejected.

Sometimes people go a step beyond simple insincerity and are downright hypocritical. The Greek root of the English word *hypocrisy,* which is *hupokrisis,* offers a vivid description—an image of a person who pretends to be someone he or she is not and speaks from behind a mask in a theatrical production.[2] In other words, you cannot see who hypocritical people really are because the way they present themselves is deceptive. If you deal with someone who operates this way, hurt and devastation are inevitable.

When you repeatedly sense that a person is insincere or hypocritical, I urge you not to ignore or excuse the behavior, because an individual who cannot be straightforward and sincere is often incapable of other important relational skills. *When people show you who they are, pay attention!* This is one of the most valuable lessons in this book. A vital key to developing great relationships is to identify people who have the capacity for strong, healthy ones. By listening to what they say and watching how they act, you can learn a lot about them. If someone has trouble being straightforward or sincere, be careful as you move forward with that relationship.

> *When people show you who they are, pay attention!*

Don't be afraid to be vulnerable.

Many people believe that being vulnerable, which is a form of transparency and being real, is foolish and ill-advised. They are convinced that being vulnerable leads to being hurt. This is because they see vulnerability as a weakness that leaves a person open to attack instead of viewing it as a strength that makes a person available for intimacy. In fact, the Google definition of *vulnerable* is "exposed to the possibility of being attacked or harmed, either physically or emotionally."[3] Many times, exposing ourselves to the possibility of harm is the very way we expose ourselves to the possibility of receiving the greatest love, acceptance, and level of relationship we can know. The risk is great, but the reward is greater.

Having the courage to choose to be vulnerable takes a strong, secure, stable person. Doing so requires someone who thinks, *I know I could get hurt in this relationship, but I have made my best possible assessment of this person. This individual has proven trustworthy thus far, and I believe the positive aspects of a fulfilling relationship with this person are worth risking potential hurt or disappointment.*

To have winning relationships, we cannot play offense and defense at the same time. Unless we become vulnerable, we will not be able to enjoy intimate, fulfilling interactions with others. Unless we tear down our walls of self-protection, we will never experience the joy of being truly protected. Building fortresses around our hearts will certainly protect us from being wounded, disappointed, or betrayed again, but it will also prevent us from ever giving or receiving in relationships again—and that would be miserable. Without love and relationships, the human heart shrivels and dies. If we want to live instead of simply exist, we must be vulnerable. Once we are able to become vulnerable, we position ourselves to enjoy deep, intimate relationships.

Learn to be intimate.

In today's world, intimacy often gets confused with a sexual act or a sexual relationship. But intimacy is much more comprehensive than physical involvement. In fact, physical intimacy does not necessarily include other, more important kinds of intimacy, such as emotional or spiritual closeness. To gain a true understanding of intimacy, we must move beyond limiting it to the physical realm and broaden our understanding of it.

Simply put, to be intimate means to allow yourself to be known—fully and deeply, in every way. I often explain this concept using the familiar saying that intimacy implies "into-me-see." This means not being afraid to let others see you for who you really are, which is the essence of being real and transparent. It means being honest about your strengths and your weaknesses; it means not trying to hide your flaws and not being bashful about your significant accomplishments. It also means being open about your hopes and dreams, and about your fears and concerns. In addition, being intimate means consistently offering the real you to another person who is also willing to be real and transparent. To be intimate with another human being is to communicate, in many different ways: "This is who I am. This is everything I am and this is all I am— nothing more, nothing less, nothing better, nothing worse."

For various reasons, many people fear or avoid becoming intimate with others, and the refusal to be intimate is an enormous barrier to deep, genuine relationships. Sometimes people are afraid to become intimate because they have done so in the past and they have been terribly hurt or even devastated. This is one reason intimacy in all its forms needs to be given time to develop and grow. Intimacy often increases in conjunction with trust and, in fact, *depends* on trust. I urge you never to let intimacy develop faster than trust in any relationship. It is an extremely effective way to keep your heart from being hurt.

All human beings are created for intimacy and even if we fear it, we crave it. The sixteenth-century English poet John Donne wrote: "No man is an island, entire of itself; every man is a piece of the continent, a part of the main."[4] In other words, no one can go through life alone. We need other people, and the more we let them into our lives and are willing to be involved in theirs, the more authentic and trustworthy our relationships will be.

I have observed that the very best relationships on earth exist between people who are intimate with God. I have also experienced this personally. The more intimate a person is with God, the more intimate he or she can be with other people. The first relationship on earth, between Adam and Eve, struggled in this very area (Gen. 3). When Adam and Eve lost intimacy with God, they also lost real intimacy with each other. One result of their sin was that Adam and

Eve began to hide from God and from each other (Gen. 3:7–10). They once enjoyed nakedness in their relationship with each other, but now they have sewn fig leaves together to hide their nakedness. The great "cover-up" in relationships started with them, and the cover-up was a result of a lost relationship with God.

The important point to understand is that people who are not intimate with God will have an extremely hard time being intimate with others. If you are looking for a terrific spouse, friend, employer, or employee, do not hesitate to bring faith into your search. If a person's relationship with Christ really influences his or her life, it will also affect how he or she behaves in relationships. I know from firsthand experience that people who have genuine relationships with Christ make the best marriage partners, business partners, and friends.

THE BENEFITS OF BEING REAL

Several years ago I reconnected with someone I knew years earlier in my life. I remembered him as a highly intelligent and principled person. When our paths crossed again, I thought redeveloping our friendship would be good because we shared common interests and pursuits. Early in the newly reconnected friendship, I began to see things in this man's behavior that did not match my memories of who he was. As I watched him and listened to him talk about how he made decisions, I realized that he seemed to be a different person than he was when I had known him before. He frequently acted without integrity; he often manipulated and misled people; and he displayed a jealous, competitive demeanor toward me. After giving him the benefit of the doubt on numerous occasions and hoping he was "just going through a phase," I ultimately left that relationship with a heavy heart because I never saw these negative qualities or behaviors in him during our previous association.

No matter how well you have known someone in the past, that person may change over time. People whose motives were pure years ago may no longer operate according to the high standards they once held. Unfortunately, some people's principles and priorities deteriorate over time, so always take time to reacquaint yourself with people who come back into your life after a season of absence or infrequent communication. Look closely to make sure those people are still who you believe them to be, and move slowly as you rebuild relationships with them to make sure their motives remain pure. When people are not transparent, discerning their motives can be challenging; but when people are real, you can identify their motives quickly.

The word *transparency* basically means "nothing hidden." In a transparent relationship, everything is clear. In my years as a pastor, many people who have suffered the pain of hurt or betrayal in a relationship have said to me, "I thought he was a good person, but I was wrong" or "I thought she was reliable, but I found out I cannot depend on her." This almost always happens because the offending person is good at hiding motives. In real relationships, people are not concerned about ulterior motives because of their commitment to transparency. This commitment benefits everyone involved and makes genuine relationship possible.

Being real and transparent in relationships also makes innocence possible and eliminates suspicions. Being real and transparent can restore a childlike innocence and joy to a relationship. Notice that I say child*like* (meaning pure and innocent), not child*ish* (meaning immature). Have you ever watched how children behave in relationships? They can be hurt or angry with a parent one minute and then run to that parent for comfort or help the next. If they like a person, they show it; if they don't, they try to avoid him or her. They express their feelings clearly and sometimes intensely. In addition, most children take people and situations at face value, and they tend to trust easily. They bring everything they have into their relationships, holding nothing back. This is one reason childhood conflicts can often be resolved easily, hurt feelings can be mended, and relationships that struggle for brief periods of time over insignificant matters can be restored quickly. We adults could definitely learn some important lessons from the children around us!

Another benefit of being real in relationships is that it allows unfeigned love to exist between two people. Unfeigned love is pure and without hypocrisy or guile. Love that is tentative and vacillating is not love at all; it is manipulation. It promises fulfillment and acceptance but never truly delivers.

Being real also leads to unquestionable trust and unwavering confidence. Author Gary Smalley, in his book *The DNA of Relationships*, has written at length about the "fear dance" that characterizes so many relationships. What he means is that each person involved has some level of fear, and that both parties tend to act or speak in ways that "push the fear buttons" in each other, causing relational strain instead of strength.[5] Fear proves a lack of trust. If you are afraid of a person or fearful in a relationship, that's a danger sign. It means you do not have the trust needed for an authentic relationship. For great relationships to form, people must reach the point where they trust each other implicitly, and that can only happen when everyone involved is being real.

Transparency and realness often produce a type of confidence that will fear-proof a relationship. If someone has been absolutely transparent with me, fear will find no place to rear its ugly head. And when fear is locked out of a relationship between two people who are willing to be real, an atmosphere of confidence, faith, genuine partnership, and true intimacy will reign.

PUT YOUR WHOLE SELF IN

You may remember the childhood song called "The Hokey Pokey." The last verse goes, "You put your whole self in; you put your whole self out. You put your whole self in and you shake it all about. You do the hokey pokey and you turn yourself around; that's what it's all about!"

Had we all learned as children to "put our whole selves" into the right relationships, many of us could have been more successful in our friendships and acquaintances. Instead, we often live out parts of the Hokey Pokey in our relationships, putting parts of ourselves into them while leaving out other parts. But people need to see those parts in order to enter into a healthy relationship with us. Many of us have tried to cover up or change certain things about ourselves to please others or to make us feel more attractive or desirable; and we have learned firsthand how detrimental that can be to any kind of relationship.

Let me encourage you to know yourself well and also allow the right people to know you well. Put your whole self—your *real self*—into your relationships, so you can participate in and enjoy real relationships in return.

RELATIONSHIP REMINDERS

- Make a priority of getting to know yourself.
- Do your best to avoid self-deception. Assess yourself honestly and ask trusted friends to help you guard against believing you are someone you are not.
- Evaluate people to find out whether or not they

really know themselves, recognizing that if they have deceived themselves, they may deceive you too.

- Remember that actions speak louder than words. Focus on behavior when you really want to assess someone's character.
- Keep yourself real by being straightforward and sincere, not being afraid to be vulnerable, and learning to develop the skills needed for true intimacy.
- Don't tolerate anything hidden in yourself or in the people with whom you are in relationships. Insist on transparency.
- Realize that the benefits of being real are worth pursuing in your relationships, and don't settle for relationships that are not transparent and real.

RAISING YOUR RELATIONAL IQ

1. In what ways do you think being transparent will benefit you and your relationships?
2. In the section titled "It Starts with You," I list several questions that will help you get to know yourself better. I encourage you to take some time to answer those questions now.
3. In the section titled "Invite Others into the Process," I suggest some questions to ask a trusted friend. Whom do you trust enough to answer these questions lovingly and honestly for you?
4. Think about a few people with whom you have extremely close relationships. Are their actions consistent with their words? Do you believe they know

themselves well and allow themselves to be transparent with you? In what ways?

5. In what specific ways do you need to become more straightforward and sincere? What steps can you take to become more vulnerable or to develop skills needed for true intimacy?

6. What parts of yourself do you allow people to see? What parts do you hide? Are you allowing your whole self to enter into your relationships? If not, why?

7. Do you display fear in any of your relationships? Why?

8. What aspect of being vulnerable scares you most, even though you know it brings out the best results in relationships? Will you allow this to hinder you?

2

Healthy Relationships Must Be Win-Win

THE LAW OF MUTUAL BENEFIT

IN 1992 SOMETHING AMAZING HAPPENED IN the world of sports. Most people call the phenomenon "the Dream Team." I'm talking about the United States Olympic basketball team who won the gold medal in Barcelona that year. They were a group of greats—highly skilled, gifted players with a brilliant coach and staff. During regular season games, many of the Olympic teammates were fierce opponents. They were all outstanding, elite athletes as individuals, including Michael Jordan, Larry Bird, Magic Johnson, and Charles Barkley. Each of these men brought exceptional basketball abilities to the team; but more important, each one brought a willingness to learn to play effectively with the others. When they put aside old rivalries, learned to play together, and brought out the best in each other to play for their country, the result was explosive.

This group is often described as the greatest sports team ever assembled. The only losers in the whole Dream Team story were their opponents. The team, and everyone associated with them, experienced "win-win" every step of the way to their memorable victory.

Why was the Dream Team so successful and so wildly popular? I believe it was because they connected in ways that were beneficial to everyone.

BOTH PARTIES NEED TO WIN

For various reasons, many people find themselves trapped in relationships that are bad for them, not good for them. These situations make them feel that they are losing, not winning. This often happens because one or both people in the relationship are emotionally needy or afraid to be alone. They find something in the other person that meets their needs, and they feed off of each other for a while until they become codependent. There can come a point at which one or both people become so miserable they cannot continue in the relationship. They realize the association that once met their unfulfilled needs has become a chore. When these conditions are in place, relationships typically break down, leaving people exhausted and feeling used.

The scenario I have described happens in marriages; it happens to adult children who care for ill or aging parents; it happens in friendships and work relationships; it even happens between individuals and organizations, especially in situations of long-term employment. Whatever the circumstances, this kind of development is damaging to the people involved.

The good news is that relationships do not have to be this way. In fact, healthy relationships do not leave people with a constant sense of losing anything, but with a healthy sense of feeling good about themselves and their friends or associates. When people are in healthy relationships, they can say, "This is good. This relationship is an extremely positive situation for me." Both parties need and deserve to win.

If you have ever been involved in a bad situation and felt like the "loser," even if it has happened repeatedly, things can change! Your relationships can get better. You can know the joy, security, and fulfillment of relationships that add to your life instead of gradually subtracting your energy and enthusiasm, siphoning away the good qualities and abilities you have to offer. Your encounters with the people around you can be refreshing, restorative, empowering, and encouraging, and others will be able to say the same about their experiences with you.

The success of any relationship depends on having two people who *both* give and receive; it requires mutual pursuit and joint benefit. A meaningful relationship is only possible when respect, honor, and values are shared. The very word *relationship* implies the involvement of two entities, and a true relationship is a state of being mutually connected for positive purposes, with positive results for everyone.

The success of any relationship depends on having two people who both *give and receive; it requires mutual pursuit and joint benefit.*

You Can't Run on Empty

Anyone who has ever driven a car knows one thing for certain: it will not go anywhere if it is out of gas. No matter how hard you press the accelerator, it simply will not budge if it does not have any fuel. That same simple principle applies to you. If you do not have the "fuel" you need, you cannot move forward in life, whether that means taking care of yourself and your family, fulfilling your responsibilities at work, or pursuing the destiny for which God created you.

One essential of an enjoyable, purpose-filled, successful life is surrounding yourself with people who can benefit you as much as you benefit them. When both parties in a relationship are pouring good things into each other, no one's tank ever reaches empty, and greatness results. As one person becomes vulnerable and learns to share, the other one does too. No one feels alone, uncovered, or as though he or she has given too much. As one person expresses love and support, the other does too. This whole concept of mutual benefit is a beautiful and life-giving exchange.

But when one person gives while the other one takes, the relationship first becomes lopsided; and then it becomes difficult or even damaging. One person begins to feel drained and the other one does not even notice. Emotional exhaustion, feelings of aloneness, and eventually resentment begin to take root. That's when the situation ceases to be win-win, and one person becomes a tired, frustrated "loser."

So how do you know when a relationship is depleting you and bringing loss to your life? Sometimes it is obvious; you do not need any help at all to figure it out. But sometimes relationships that drain you can be so familiar and so convenient that you stay in them without realizing how dysfunctional they are. On a more serious level, these relationships may include elements of control or manipulation, which cause you to be confused about whether they are unhealthy.

When you are involved in a relationship and wondering if it may be leaving you empty, think about these things. A relationship that depletes you

- is a constant source of discouragement.
- gives you the sense that you want it more than the person you are in relationship with wants it.
- is one you repeatedly try to convince yourself to stay in.
- may make you physically, mentally, or emotionally tired after speaking to or being with a certain person.
- may be comfortable or convenient on a surface level, but it leaves you with questions in your heart about whether or not it's right.
- may seem to be too much work to get out of if you need to leave it.
- is one in which you feel you have little energy to confront problems or challenges. Often, this is because the relationship itself is draining, literally leaving you with little motivation or ability to make necessary improvements.
- taxes your internal resources, such as your joy and peace, and external resources, such as time, money, or possessions.
- is one in which you may be able to be pleasant when with the person, but later regret that time you gave to him or her.
- is one in which you feel a combination of excitement and a sense of dread about being with a certain person, but do it anyway.
- pulls you away from closeness with God and with other people.
- dulls your vision for your life and your future.

Conversely, people in relationships that give to you and add positively to your life

- won't allow you to become complacent.
- equip you with wisdom needed to navigate life and situations successfully.
- offer you unconditional love and acceptance.
- provide a safe place for you to be yourself.
- hold you accountable to your dreams.
- do not compete with you and your accomplishments.
- stretch and challenge you to become better.
- give their time and energy to you when needed.
- always lend a listening ear.
- expose you to more than you have experienced before and open your life to new possibilities.
- are your biggest cheerleaders and are constant sources of encouragement.
- are simply a joy to be involved with.

As you can see from the characteristics of relationships that deplete you and ones that add to your life, relationships can be either disastrous or amazing. Relationships that take from you rarely, if ever, become win-win, but relationships that add to you can move beyond the blessings of simple win-win and become powerful catalysts for greatness in your life today and in the future.

RELATIONAL HEALTH

Many of us were raised to give to others and to "be nice." While being nice is an admirable trait, it can get us in trouble if we overdo it and do not surround ourselves with people who are nice to us in return.

Your life can benefit significantly from being in relationships with people who will serve and sacrifice for you as much as you serve and sacrifice for them. You could gain a lot by having people who will be as honest and transparent with you as you are with them. When these kinds of mutual exchanges take place, both people are happy, fulfilled, and relationally healthy. Individuals who are relationally healthy do not worry about being empty or being alone; they are not afraid to be vulnerable and open in a relationship because they know the other person will also be vulnerable and open. That mutual vulnerability in a safe relationship leads to emotional safety and protection for both people.

In unhealthy situations, people play double Dutch, the old jump-rope game in which players jump in and out of a twirling rope. When a situation lacks relational health, people never fully commit. They are sometimes "in" and sometimes "out" because they do not feel safe enough to stay in all the time. In unhealthy relationships, people frequently feel they do not know what to say. They fear saying something wrong, and they constantly wonder what the other person feels or thinks. These dynamics set up insecurity and drama—they are *not* win-win!

Relational health does not happen outside a win-win situation, but it thrives in an environment of mutual benefit. Just as physical health empowers people to achieve and enjoy things they could not if they were not healthy, relational health also enables people to take their interactions with others to a new level. When both people are free to be who they are, they are safe and secure. That gives both of them the freedom to grow and the power to experience, accomplish, and together enjoy things they could never do on their own.

Beyond Win-Win

Think about advertisements you've seen for amazing new products. Often, near the end of the pitch, an announcer says, "But wait! There's more!" He goes on to promise that if you order right now, you can get two products for the price of one, plus some extra little gadget guaranteed to help you in some way.

I have written about the necessity of win-win relationships and the advantages that can result from them, but I need to say, "Wait! There's more!" You see, some relationships bring "double bonuses" into our lives. These are not inexpensive or gimmicky things, like certain products on TV. These are rare treasures that go beyond win-win and offer even more than mutual benefits do. These are the relationships that maximize our lives. They provide to both our friends and to us an unspeakably powerful and valuable dynamic called *synergy*.

Before I define *synergy*, let me say that I believe it was the key to the greatness of the Dream Team; they moved beyond win-win and into synergy. Simply put, synergy means people, groups, or things come together to produce something greater than any of them could ever produce alone. Synergy is much greater than the combination of their abilities; it is win-win in every way, exponentially. Synergy is to relationships what multiplication is to mathematics. While 10 *plus* 10 equals 20, 10 *times* 10 equals 100.

Relationships that bring synergy to your life will not only be win-win for you, they will add exponential value to you. They will multiply your potential and your impact so your abilities, plans, natural gifts, skills, and everything about your life functions at its optimum.

THE ONLY ATMOSPHERE FOR SYNERGY

At the dawn of biblical history, God established an unwavering and vital truth: "It is not good that man should be alone" (Gen. 2:18 NKJV). This was true for Adam, it has been true for every human being who has lived since Adam, and it remains true for you and me today. In this verse, God committed Himself to make Adam a helper and companion, so He created Eve. I believe God's message to us through this story is, as it was to Adam, "You cannot do it alone." Adam could have easily done what so many of us do, saying, "I am strong; I am smart; I know what's best. I really do not need any help. I'd rather just do it myself." But God knew that an independent attitude was not good, so He put Adam into an interdependent relationship from the start, letting Adam know that he needed Eve and she needed him. They were to exist in a mutually beneficial, synergistic relationship with each other in the context of shared dependence on God.

In Genesis 1:27 we read: "So God created man in His own image; in the image of God He created him; male and female He created them" (NKJV). Immediately, the first thing God said to these two people in the first relationship on earth was: "Be fruitful and multiply" (Gen. 1:28 NKJV). We do not ever see the terms *win-win* or *synergy* in Scripture, but here in the Bible's first chapter, the principle is clearly established. God knew mutual benefit and multiplication could only happen in the context of relationship.

Every living being is designed to grow and thrive. Left to grow and increase by ourselves, the process is laborious and lonely, and the results are often unimpressive. But within right relationships lies an immeasurable amount of accelerated energy just waiting to be harnessed and released—the power that becomes available to us when we connect with others. Synergy is the explosive momentum for growth that occurs once we tap into it. And synergy never happens in isolation; it only exists in relationships.

THE POTENTIAL OF SYNERGY

The wise and ancient king Solomon understood synergy. He wrote:

> *Two are better than one,*
> *because they have a good return for their work:*
> *If one falls down,*
> *his friend can help him up.*
> *But pity the man who falls*
> *and has no one to help him up!*
> *Also, if two lie down together, they will keep warm.*
> *But how can one keep warm alone?*
> *Though one may be overpowered,*
> *two can defend themselves.*
> *A cord of three strands is not quickly broken.*

(ECCL. 4:9–12)

Solomon is referring to good, right, win-win, synergistic relationships. All of us know what happens in wrong, bad, losing, antagonistic relationships. When someone falls down, the other person may not have the ability or desire to help him up, and the relationship can be quickly and easily broken. But God-intended, God-designed relationships are filled with benefits for everyone involved. If you look closely at Solomon's observations, you will see that when you invest your life in the right people and enter into synergistic relationships with them, you step into a realm of protection, provision, and promotion.

Synergy provides protection.

Have you ever had a moment when you realized you were your own worst enemy? Maybe you ended up with a problem because you did not know any better or you did not have all the information you needed. Or maybe you made a bad decision because you took advice from the wrong person.

In a mutually beneficial, synergistic relationship, you could easily find yourself linked with someone wiser and more experienced than you are, someone who can help you avoid decisions and situations that will destroy your future. You could also develop a synergistic relationship with someone less experienced than you are in certain areas, but who has precisely the words of wisdom or advice you need. Regardless of age or experience, a true synergistic friend will stand with you and provide the protection of companionship and prayer. That person can also offer you the protection of important perspectives that guide your decisions, insights you may not think of on your own.

Synergy brings provision, production, and promotion.

Solomon asks: "Also, if two lie down together, they will keep warm. But how can one keep warm alone?" (Eccl. 4:11). I see a broader question here: "How can a person not only keep warm but move forward and grow, alone?" It is not possible! A critical key to seeing increase in your life is refusing to isolate yourself and, instead, joining with other productive, loyal people. So often in life, we end up metaphorically in the cold, broken or stuck because we insist on going our own way and refusing to allow others to help.

When two people working together are headed in the same direction with the same mind-set, both will reach their destinations faster than they will alone, and each will go farther than they could go by themselves. Each can also provide guidance and encouragement to the other along the way. If you want to be most productive, connect with people who will add value to your life and give you the support, wisdom, and help you need. When you reach a high level of productivity in your life, your chances of promotion will increase. Whether that means a literal promotion in your career or an opportunity for greater influence, enjoyment, or responsibility in some other area of your life, productive people are the ones who get promoted.

As you evaluate current relationships and consider new ones, I urge you to look for people who are headed to the same places you want to go and who understand that unity of heart and mind leads to accelerated progress, provision, and promotion.

Synergy enables prevailing power.

Solomon concludes his remarks on relationships in Ecclesiastes 4 with these words: "Though one may be overpowered, two can defend themselves. A cord of three strands is not quickly broken" (v. 12). If you have ever found yourself overpowered or overwhelmed, you know that if you are in a situation alone, you can easily believe it will defeat you. But if just one person comes along to stand beside you and support you, your perspective changes. You begin to believe you can win. When other people infuse their faith, their confidence, their wisdom, or their encouragement into your negative situation, those positive qualities grow exponentially. Soon you feel you have a small army on your side and you find your way to victory.

BEWARE OF NEGATIVE SYNERGY

I hope you are gaining clear insight into the power of win-win relationships and the positive potential of synergy. I also want you to understand the negative aspect of synergy because, as surely as positive synergy will benefit and elevate you, negative synergy can destroy you.

Have you ever noticed that trouble simply seems to follow certain people or that every time two specific individuals get together, something negative happens? I am sure you have. In fact, many mothers seem to have built-in alarm systems that go off when they hear their teenager is "just going out with so-and-so tonight." Or maybe your day is going just fine until certain people ask for a ride home from work. By the time you get them home, they have dumped such a load of trouble on you through their words and emotions that your head is spinning! Or maybe you have a family member about whom others commonly say, "You'll never guess what she's done now," and each incident seems to be worse than the one before.

The reason some people constantly seem to exhaust or frustrate us is that we have negative synergy with them. Sometimes that happens because of their personalities or their choices; sometimes it arises because of something in us. Regardless of the reason, we need to be diligent to avoid negative synergy.

Many people, maybe even you, are in unfortunate circumstances today because of past relationships. I know people who have been to prison because they got involved with the wrong crowd, people who had children before they were ready because they stayed in bad relationships, and people who have struggled economically for years because of unwise financial alliances with business partners who did not have integrity. I have never once heard anyone in any of these situations say, "I just woke up one day and decided to do something that would take my life in a different direction. I just decided to risk going to prison or getting pregnant or losing my life savings." No, what people tend to say is, "I had no idea I would end up like this. I just got into a relationship and I didn't realize how bad it was until it was too late."

Negative synergy is always painful and always lose-lose, but it is nothing new. In fact, the apostle Paul wrote to a group of Christians in Corinth centuries ago regarding a specific matter: "I'm not at all pleased. I am getting the picture that when you meet together it brings out your worst side instead of your best!" (1 Cor. 11:17 MSG). The NIV translation renders this verse, "Your meetings do more harm than good." The best way I know to succinctly define negative synergy is to say that it does more harm than good; it brings out the worst instead of the best in people. Nobody wins in that kind of relationship; everyone loses. This is why building mutually beneficial alliances with people and cultivating relationships that bring positive synergy to your life is so important.

FINDING WINNING, SYNERGISTIC FRIENDS

The only way to build win-win, synergistic relationships is to develop them with the right people. In this section, I want to identify and explain seven qualities of synergistic friends, but first I want you to understand that I use the word *friends* in this context to refer to a wide variety of people to whom you may relate. As you consider these insights, know that they apply to romantic interests, family members, and work associates as readily as they apply to friends.

Winning, synergistic friends encourage greater faithfulness.

The best kinds of friends urge you to obey God's Word and to seek and follow God in every way. They walk with God in such a way that simply being around them and seeing their lives inspires you to develop a deep, personal relationship with Him. They live lives of love and obedience toward God and influence you to do likewise.

Winning, synergistic friends are character driven.

The right kinds of friends do not need a constant flow of discipline from other people because they are self-correctors. They have a depth of personal integrity and Christian character that will not allow them to behave in disingenuous ways. When you spend time around people who live according to high standards, you will want to live by their values, too, and you will have support in doing so.

Winning, synergistic friends will defend you.

If you have ever heard about a situation in which someone you thought was a friend spoke negatively about you in a conversation, you know that such disloyalty can be extremely painful. If a person does not know your heart and trust your character enough to stand up for you when others speak against you, that person does not add value to your life. The right kinds of friends will know you well enough and believe in you strongly enough to defend you confidently when others speak or scheme against you.

Winning, synergistic friends love God more than they love you.

Throughout this book I emphasize the importance of investing your life in people who put God first. Individuals who truly honor

God and spend their lives developing an ever-deepening relationship with Him make the best kinds of friends. They are the people who will speak the truth to you lovingly when you need it, storm heaven on your behalf when you need God's help, and stay loyal to you through life's ups and downs. They are not nearly as concerned about pleasing you as they are about helping you please God.

Winning, synergistic friends urge you to sow.

Scripture is filled with instructions and examples of the blessings of sowing and giving (Job 4:8; Hos. 10:12; 2 Cor. 9:6; Gal. 6:7). Friends who bring synergy to your life understand that sowing is the only way to tap into God's abundant supply. They will encourage you to sow your time, energy, finances, and other resources into worthy people, places, and activities because they want to see you experience the exponential benefits that result from generous, heartfelt giving.

Winning, synergistic friends are committed to your future, not your past.

I like to say there are three kinds of people in the world: yesterday people, today people, and tomorrow people. Yesterday people are the ones who populated your past and will keep you bound to situations that happened long ago. Today people are in your life in the present, and they are satisfied to live today, not looking back, but not really looking forward either. Tomorrow people have their focus locked on your future and are currently investing their time and energy in your relationship toward where you are going, not toward where you have been or where you are today. Look for tomorrow people because they will be the ones to usher you into your destiny.

Winning, synergistic friends help you live a life of gratitude.

Do you know there is one sure, certain, never-fail way to guarantee that you are in the will of God? It is to be thankful. First Thessalonians 5:18 says, "Give thanks in all circumstances; for this is God's will for you in Christ Jesus." The right friends will inspire you not to simply speak words of appreciation when people do nice things for you but to live a life of thanksgiving to God for all He has done, all He is doing, and all He will do. God responds to gratitude, thanksgiving, and praise, and I wholeheartedly believe that godly success and favor will chase you down when gratitude becomes the fragrance of your life. Surround yourself with people who motivate you to be thankful, and see what happens.

PREPARE TO SYNERGIZE

Now that you know some of the qualities of winning, synergistic friends, I trust that synergistic relationships will be part of your life for the rest of your life. I have rarely seen a truly synergistic relationship develop at random, but I have seen a number of them evolve for people who are prepared for them, and I want you to fall into that category.

Have you ever heard about someone who really, really wants a certain opportunity, perhaps a job with a particular company, and then cannot say yes to that opportunity when it finally comes along? Maybe the person has to turn it down because she is not in a position to make a geographical move and the job is in a city across the country. Maybe someone has wanted to buy a franchise with a partner for years, but cannot do so when the opportunity arises because he has not saved enough money to invest in it. Situations like these happen frequently, and they are not only sad, they are also often unnecessary.

Missing great opportunities can be avoided when people simply prepare for the things they are hoping for and working toward. I firmly believe that lack of preparation for the future keeps people chained to the past. No one can move forward into better things if he or she is not ready for those experiences. Without adequate preparation even the best opportunities can become overwhelming and frustrating.

If you are serious about your future and your potential, and if you truly believe that God has more for you than you are currently experiencing, then prepare for it. Part of preparing for your future includes identifying the people who will help you get to your God-ordained destination and support you when you reach it. I strongly encourage you to remember and apply the relationship laws in this book every time you meet someone and see potential for a relationship. Make wise choices about the people in whom you invest your time, energy, and heart. And when you have made a great decision, expect the synergy to take both you and your friend farther than you could ever go alone.

Becoming Better

If I had to summarize the power and benefit of a mutually beneficial, synergistic relationship in a few simple words, I would say this: it makes you better. The right kind of influence from the right kinds of people can make you more creative, focused, diligent, compassionate, and responsible. It can maximize many of your good qualities and help you improve in the areas that need work.

But I have observed that some people are reluctant to enter into the relationships that will be best for them. Most of the time, they resist because they simply do not want to change. They are comfortable where they are; maybe they even feel their current stress level is all they can handle and they do not want the temporary disruptions of life that can accompany a new relationship, even if it could be the best one they have ever had. When people think this way, they chain themselves to their pasts and they prevent themselves from becoming better.

Let me remind you that every relationship in your life will move you forward or hold you back. In other words, each association can make you better or worse; neutral is not an option. But synergy does more than simply move a person forward. When synergy is positive it moves a person farther, faster. When it is negative, it propels a person backward quickly, often with severe consequences. So when you evaluate potential relationships, look not only for those that will help you advance but also for those that can bring synergy to your life.

Whether a relationship is as intimate and as intense as a marriage or as ordinary and necessary as dealing with coworkers, it will make both parties better if it is synergistic. Synergistic marriages will not only create a joyful environment for husbands and wives, it will make them better partners to each other, better parents to their children, better employees or bosses, and better friends and neighbors. Synergistic work relationships will make everyone involved better citizens of their communities, better stewards of their time, and better human beings.

Many people fear change simply because change means *different* and *new*. But to become better, change is necessary. Think of it this way: a person goes into a store and finds the best-looking pair of shoes she has ever seen. The shoes fit, basically. The fashionable lady can hardly wait to wear these shoes, but after she puts them on for the first time and wears them for a while, they begin to rub a little blister on her foot. But she likes the shoes so much that she puts on a bandage and keeps wearing them. Within a week or so, the blister has healed and she can wear them with ease.

A win-win, synergistic relationship works the same way as that new pair of shoes, multiplied by a million. You may have to endure the discomfort of leaving your past behind you, abandoning old ways of doing things, or letting go of relationships that are not beneficial to you. It may not feel good at first. But it is more than worth any short-term twinge of emotional pain. It will catapult you to a new place of greatness and make you part of your very own dream team.

RELATIONSHIP REMINDERS

- Everyone in a relationship needs to win. If one or both parties feel they are losing, they are headed for trouble.
- You can't run on empty; the people with whom you are in relationship must pour into your life as you pour into theirs.
- Relational health grows and thrives in an environment of mutual benefit.
- The next step beyond mutual benefit is synergy, which enables everyone involved in a relationship to do and be exponentially more than they could do or be on their own.
- Negative synergy is as damaging as positive synergy is helpful in your life.

- Find winning, synergistic relationships.
- Make the effort to prepare for synergy and become a better person.

RAISING YOUR RELATIONAL IQ

1. Given the unique circumstances and specific realities of your life, what would a win-win relationship look like for you?
2. If you could write your own script for a great relationship, what benefits would you want to offer other people, and what benefits would you like others to offer you?
3. Has a one-sided relationship ever drained or exhausted you? Think for just a moment about what you could do with the time and energy you would save if you were to back away from that relationship and invest instead in win-win alliances.
4. Of all the people you know, which two or three do you believe have the greatest potential to become synergistic friends?
5. Consider your hopes and dreams, your goals and desires. How could a synergistic relationship help you achieve them in faster, better ways?

3

Be Like-Minded About
What Really Matters

THE LAW OF AGREEMENT

I HAVE AN IMPORTANT QUESTION FOR YOU.
How do you make decisions about relationships? Maybe you have
never thought about it before, but if you take a moment to consider it now, the answer may surprise you. I have found that some
people enter relationships slowly, carefully, and with a great deal
of thought and prayer. While these people do exist, they are rare.
In contrast, most people form new alliances fairly quickly, without thinking much at all about the potential relationship. They
simply meet someone, decide they like or share common interests
with that person, and soon develop a relationship on some level.
Sometimes this approach works amazingly well; sometimes it leads
to disappointment, betrayal, or heartbreak.

One of the smartest moves anyone can make when a potential
relationship surfaces is to ask an ancient question that is as relevant
and vital to a successful life today as it was centuries ago, when the

Old Testament prophet Amos first asked it. "Do two walk together unless they have *agreed* to do so?" (Amos 3:3, emphasis added).

I believe the first and most important question to ask yourself in every relationship is, "Am I in agreement with this person?" To be in agreement is not to simply think in similar ways or share the same opinions on good food, movies, places of employment, sports, or politics. It is not even to enjoy the same activities or want to achieve the same goals. Certainly agreement in these ways can be a plus in a relationship. But I am talking about the kind of agreement that comes from shared core values and beliefs, agreement that goes beneath the surface of life to the issues and attitudes that really matter. To be in the kind of agreement required for a great relationship is to be mutually committed to the values, foundational issues, and matters of character you regard as nonnegotiable.

> *To be in the kind of agreement required for a great relationship is to be mutually committed to the values, foundational issues, and matters of character you regard as nonnegotiable.*

Walking through life in a meaningful way with a friend, spouse, family member, boss, coworker, or romantic interest is only possible when the two of you can build a relationship on the foundation of agreement in critical areas. This does not mean there is no room for diversity or different opinions on certain matters; it simply means you and the person with whom you are in a relationship place the same degree of value on the issues that are truly important.

Understanding the law of agreement and asking the agreement question is best done *before* you enter into a relationship with someone, because doing so may save you heartache and stress. Thinking through important issues of agreement is also important in your current relationships, because that could explain why you feel uncomfortable or pressured in certain situations—and it could help you know if you need to make a change.

Several areas of agreement are necessary to a strong, healthy, godly relationship: faith, generosity (as opposed to selfishness), and capacity for commitment and personal integrity, which is the most critical of all. Being in agreement on the issue of integrity is so important that when I teach on the subject of relationships, I urge audiences to refuse to walk through life with people who do not possess it. Years of study and pastoral care have convinced me that agreement, especially where integrity is concerned, is the first vital step toward healthy, purposeful alliances with people.

Integrity is critical in every type of relationship, whether it is business or personal, casual or intimate. What exactly do I mean by integrity? I mean a personal commitment to what is right no matter what it costs, an unwavering dedication to truth and honesty in every area of life, and a refusal to compromise. I mean the quality that makes a person completely trustworthy. The thing we must know about integrity is that it does not come and go. A person of integrity cannot turn it off and turn it on. Real integrity means doing the right thing when no one is watching. It means walking the walk 24-7, not just talking the talk to impress other people.

In relationships, commitment to integrity must take precedence over mutual comfort or shared enjoyment because integrity is the foundation of a person's life. Everything else rises and falls on this one quality. For a relationship to succeed, integrity is absolutely necessary. If it is present, that person may end up being a high-quality relationship for you. If it is not, the relationship will crumble, and someone will likely be damaged in the process.

Think about it this way. When people decide to buy a house, they often make a list of what they want in a new home. It could include an attached garage, big windows, ample storage space, or high-end countertops. A pool, a nice view, or hardwood floors might also make the list. But one thing everyone wants is a good foundation, even if it is not on a wish list. A firm, solid foundation is nonnegotiable—a no-brainer—because anyone who knows anything about buildings knows that the entire structure is in jeopardy if the foundation is faulty. A well-laid foundation may not be as attractive as crown molding or as fun as a swimming pool, but it is a *lot* more important. It may not be the first thing people look at when choosing a new home, but no one hoping to make a smart house purchase would buy a house without a thorough inspection of the foundation and assurance that it is in good shape.

The same principle applies to relationships. Lots of people can be attractive and seem to be fun, but if they do not have a well-developed sense of personal integrity, I would caution you against buying into a relationship with them. Over time, in the absence of integrity, a relationship will shift, crack, become unsteady, and eventually fall apart.

So how do you know whether a person has integrity? After all, like the foundation of a house, it may not be visible at first glance. It may not show up when you have pizza together or sit around a boardroom table for a meeting, but sooner or later, a situation will arise that will tell you whether someone operates with integrity or not.

FOUR INGREDIENTS OF INTEGRITY

The best way to know whether someone has integrity is to observe that person in a crisis. Nothing seems to shine a spotlight on a person's character more effectively than a situation that causes pressure or conflict, or circumstances that present a person with temptation. But while everyone faces difficulties on occasion, and we never wish them on people, we do not want to have to wait around for them in order to catch a deep glimpse into someone's character. So when you are trying to determine if a person has integrity, look for these four specific qualities. (And by the way, if you are trying to grow as a person of integrity or to raise children or influence staff or coworkers to increase in integrity, these four dynamics are a great place to start.)

- An unwavering commitment to truth
- An absolute refusal to compromise on core values
- A complete dedication to pure motives
- A passionate, consistent pursuit of excellence

An Unwavering Commitment to Truth

Truth must be part of the foundation of any relationship. This applies in every setting, from the bedroom to the boardroom. If you have ever been in a relationship with a person who is not dedicated to truth, you have learned the hard way why agreeing to commit to truth is so vital in relationships.

I enjoy some individuals just as people. I may admire their abilities, respect their experiences, and like their personalities, but I cannot be in relationship with them because they disregard truth. These people do not add value to my life; they add stress and confusion! No one enjoys, values, or feels secure in a relationship filled with lies. But when both parties are committed to being completely truthful with each other, they move beyond the mundane, shallow quality so many people endure in relationships and pave the way for a strong relationship. Jesus says in John 8:32, "The truth will set you free." When people embrace truth, they can expect at least three beneficial results from the freedom it brings.

- They can look forward to a relationship of trust because truth is what builds trust. Truth enables people in a relationship to express who they really are, without hiding secrets or adjusting aspects of their personalities. When people live and relate to others in this way, trust can thrive.
- People who are committed to truth will enjoy true intimacy because trust based on truth makes intimacy possible. The level of commitment to truth in a relationship actually determines the level of intimacy two people can share.
- They can count on being able to fulfill their destinies because trust and intimacy in a relationship set both people free to confidently pursue everything God has created them to do and be.

A successful relationship requires agreement upon standards of truth that surpass individual thoughts and opinions. When challenges, disagreements, or questions arise, both parties must agree to subject themselves to truth, not to good ideas or personal opinions. But in an age where information is everywhere, advice abounds, and lots of theories claim to be true, where does a person go to find the real truth? The same place truth-seekers have always gone: the Word of God.

When Jesus stood before Pilate just before His crucifixion, Pilate asked a question people are still asking today: "What is truth?" (John 18:38). Jesus had already answered that question, though Pilate did not know it. While praying to God in John 17:17, Jesus said, "Your word is truth." God's Word offers divine wisdom and perfect advice for any issue or challenge life presents. Its insights are time-tested and have proven true for generations. We can look for truth in books and magazines, on the Internet, or on afternoon talk shows, but most of the time those sources only offer ideas and opinions. More than we need to know what other people—even so-called experts—say about the situations that affect us, we need to know what God says because He is our only real source of truth.

One of Scripture's clearest pictures of courageous truth telling takes place between Jesus and His impulsive disciple and friend, Peter. Let me give you the background. There came a point in Jesus' earthly life when He knew He had to begin preparing His disciples for His death. He did so in detail, telling them that He would have to go to Jerusalem and suffer greatly under the treatment of the religious authorities there. He made clear to them that He would be killed but raised from the dead three days later.

Peter, with his fiery temperament probably mixed with horror and devastation at the thought of losing his Lord, reacted immediately. He called Jesus aside and began to rebuke Him, contradicting what Jesus had said by declaring, "Never, Lord! . . . This shall never happen to you!" (Matt. 16:22).

In response, Jesus spoke strong and shocking words to Peter, saying, "Get behind me, Satan! You are a stumbling block to me; you do not have in mind the things of God, but the things of men" (v. 23).

How would you like to be addressed the way Jesus spoke to Peter? And would you ever be so bold with a close friend? Jesus was!

Even though His relationship with Peter was valuable and important to Him, He prized truth even more than friendship.

A strange dynamic sometimes takes place in relationships:
people sometimes fail to tell the truth because they think it will hurt
or anger the person with whom they share it. For example, a wife
who spent grocery money on a new pair of shoes tells her husband
a friend gave them to her. An unfaithful boyfriend makes up stories
to hide the truth about his other lovers from a girl who has given
him her heart. Children blame their siblings for the magic marker
scribbles on freshly painted walls or their pets for eating their homework. A retail employee tells her boss she doesn't know why her
drawer won't balance, when she knows she has taken a few dollars
from the register to pay for her lunch. In all these situations and
countless others, people know the truth; they just do not want to
tell it because they know they will get in trouble. They subject themselves to the miserable feeling of knowing they have lied instead of
enduring an hour of being yelled at or a few nights of sleeping alone.

Only small, self-serving, petty people allow themselves to
deceive or lie to others. Strong, healthy, mature people are not willing to compromise the truth to avoid being on the receiving end of
tears, raised voices, slammed doors, or the silent treatment. People
who are unwavering in their commitments to truth have the courage to bear the consequences when they have to tell a truth that
hurts. They know that trust can be rebuilt when truth is present.

When people value truth over everything else, good relationships grow stronger. Bad ones may come to an end; and while that
is painful, it can also be crucial to a person's destiny. People of
integrity are people who love, seek, and cling to truth. They also
require truth from others. If you want relationships you can trust,
coming to an agreement about integrity and truth is not only wise,
it is necessary.

An Absolute Refusal to Compromise on Core Values

One sure sign that an individual is a person of integrity is his or her refusal to compromise on the core values and priorities of life. This is true in the little things, such as not keeping extra change that may be received from a cashier; and in the big things, such as saying, "No. I will not under any circumstances alter that expense report or alter those records!" and meaning it.

As I have read or heard about people who are willing to compromise on important issues, I have made an interesting observation: whatever people compromise their integrity to keep, they ultimately lose. They may get the short-term gratification they desire, but they lose the treasure they already have.

To prove the point that people lose what they compromise to keep, think about some of the major corporate scandals that have plagued American businesses since the beginning of the twenty-first century. For example, a chief executive officer at a large energy company called Enron wanted to keep his job and make his company look good, so he devised a plan to inflate the stock price to keep people from knowing that the company was in financial trouble. Because the reports were not accurate, that man, Jeffrey Skilling, ended up not only losing his job but also going to prison. Many, many former employees were hurt in the scheme, especially elderly people who depended on Enron to provide what had been promised to them during their retirement years.

Much like Jeffrey Skilling, Bernard (Bernie) Madoff was a husband, father, and business executive who traded his freedom and life of luxury for a 150-year prison sentence, all because he was willing to compromise his character. Madoff engineered an elaborate scheme that defrauded thousands of investors of billions of dollars. His deceptive promise of high-yield gains led countless individuals to trust him, but in the end led to the demise of his wealth and theirs. At one point, Madoff and his wife had an estimated net worth of almost $823 million. They lived lavishly: multiple homes in various parts of the world, access to shares in two private jets, and a fifty-five-foot yacht on the French Riviera.[1] Madoff chose to compromise the truth, and the end result was the loss of material possessions; a full-scale investigation of several family members who worked for him; and the suicide of his oldest son, who worked alongside him.[2] All this tragedy and heartbreak happened because of his lack of integrity and his tolerance for dishonest compromise.

Many of us could never imagine compromising in the same manner as Skilling and Madoff. Fabricate records and defraud people out of millions of dollars? Never! But have you ever been in a situation where the right choice was apparent, but a slightly different choice, ultimately the wrong choice, seemed to promise personal gain with few negative consequences for others?

Genesis 3 tells a story much like those of modern-day financial disasters. Adam receives specific instructions from God. Eve, even in the face of temptation, understands those instructions but makes a conscious decision to compromise. Not knowing that their decision will affect their lives and ours, they eat from the tree in the middle of the Garden of Eden. Yes, they chose to be disobedient, but their actions reveal a willingness to compromise their integrity. Their seemingly small decision forever changed the course of history and the human race.

Adam and Eve are often referred to as "the first parents," and in their case, they set a terrific example of what *not* to do. Eve allowed herself to be deceived, and Adam compromised his integrity to please his wife. He allowed his commitment to her to overshadow his commitment to doing what is right. In the end, this compromise destroyed the very thing they were both trying to preserve: true intimacy with God and with each other.

A similar story unfolds for a well-known biblical hero named David. He has a lot going for him, including a powerful position as king of Israel and, at one point in his life, the great honor of being called "a man after [God's] own heart" (1 Sam. 13:14 NKJV). He has killed a fierce Philistine giant with a mere slingshot and led armies to stunning victories on the battlefield. And yet, when he sees a beautiful woman—another man's wife—bathing on her roof, a seed of compromise takes root in his mind. He gets her pregnant because compromise gets the best of him (2 Sam. 11). His life and leadership are never quite the same after that. Even though he pens a stirring song of repentance (Ps. 51), he suffers the consequences of his sin in certain ways for the rest of his life. For example, three of his children died (2 Sam. 12:19; 13:30–32; 18:9), he was never able to deal with the rape of his daughter (2 Sam.13:1–21), and the Lord would not allow him to build a temple because there was too much blood on his hands (1 Chron. 22:7–8).

Adam pleases Eve, but he loses the Garden of Eden. David compromises his integrity with a woman and pleases himself, but he loses his kingdom temporarily, and his family becomes filled with strife. We must understand this fact about integrity: compromise only seems like a good idea at first. Once a person acts on the willingness to compromise personal integrity, the results can be disastrous. This is true for people who compromise and for everyone around them.

A Complete Dedication to Pure Motives

Integrity is so much more than obeying a set of rules. It is not simply *doing* right in terms of behavior, it is *wanting* to do right. It comes from an internal motive, not from external actions. While integrity can be seen in people's actions and heard in their words, it is also evident in people's motives.

Simply put, a motive is a person's reason for doing whatever he or she does. If a student cheats on a test, the motive is to get a good grade without having to do the work necessary to make the grade honestly. That person values good results but does not value integrity. He or she wants to *look* good, but does not want to *be* good.

In relationships, understanding motives is vital. You must know why certain people want to be in relationships with you. Are they in relationships with you because they want access to your connections or because they want to be able drop your name in conversations with others? Do they want to be around you because you make them feel smart, attractive, funny, or desirable? Do they want to use your skills to their advantage? Do they want something—tangible or intangible—that belongs to you and that you may not be willing to give?

If you can say yes to any of these questions, you are in a relationship with a taker. Takers, as opposed to givers, seek relationship for the purpose of getting for themselves, not benefiting you. Under these circumstances, the motivation is selfish, not loving. And that is a recipe for relational disaster. I would go so far as to say that the worst kind of people to be in relationships with are ones with impure motives, especially those who want to take from you without ever giving to you. They may ask you to be loyal and offer disloyalty in return, demand honesty from you while lying to your face, or insist that you love them while they treat you with apathy and indifference. Be very cautious of these people! They are users who will likely take advantage of your commitment to integrity, but they have no intention of making that commitment themselves.

If there has ever been a brazen example of a person with impure motives, it was a man named Judas. We first read about him in the ancient literature of the New Testament, but his spirit and his ways have pervaded every generation and are still at work today. Perhaps even you have encountered one of his descendants. They are far too common, and being in relationship with them is, frankly, a living nightmare.

No one knows exactly why Judas connected with Jesus at first or what his motive was for becoming a disciple. But somewhere along the way, his motive went wrong. Given the opportunity to betray Jesus for a nice sum of money, he did so (Matt. 26:14–16). He wanted worldly gain more than he wanted to be loyal to a friend. His betrayal set in motion the events that led to Jesus' crucifixion and to his own demise. His polluted motive would not allow him to rest until he delivered Jesus into the hands of killers. Once the deed was done, he was so miserable he could no longer live with himself and committed suicide (Matt. 27:3–5).

The story has lots of lessons in it, but the one I want you to notice right now is this: Judas's bad motive overtook the good influences of people around him. He was one of the disciples; he spent a lot of time around a group of men who certainly were not perfect, but they were sold out to Jesus. They were hungry for the things of God, and they dearly loved and deeply respected His Son. They gave up everything to follow Him. But the positive influence of eleven devoted disciples could not quench the bad motive in Judas. Even significant exposure to the Son of God Himself didn't cause Judas to let go of his wrong motives and get his heart right. First Corinthians 15:33 summarizes my point: "Do not be misled: 'Bad company corrupts good character.'" This is a fact of life and relationships: *Bad* tends to out-influence *good*. Everything bad begins with wrong motives.

Trying to assess a person's motives is not easy. It can take time and it requires asking questions. But you must get to the truth. Being associated with a person of impure motives can ruin your life, but being in a relationship with someone who has a pure heart and right motives can be one of the best things ever to happen to you.

A Passionate, Consistent Pursuit of Excellence

If you want to realize God's best for your life and have His best in your relationships, then you must launch out on a lifelong pursuit of excellence and surround yourself with people who hold the same high standards. You need to be around people who challenge you to grow and who refuse to allow you to settle for mediocrity. Surround yourself with others who have sold out to excellence. This is part of having integrity.

Stay away from mediocre people who are satisfied with who they are, where they are, and what they are doing. A casual or common attitude toward life will lead you to a place of disappointment and defeat. Mediocrity is an infectious, contagious disease that will penetrate deep into the crevices of your life and kill any desire for personal improvement. Mediocre people will halt the progress you have made; they will disguise themselves by saying all the right words, but ultimately they are in your life to hinder your future. So require excellence from the people with whom you associate. Ask them to live extraordinary lives and to demand the same of you.

Excellence is a quality that almost always earns respect, and *excellent* is definitely an adjective people want used when they are being described. But wanting excellence is altogether different from achieving excellence. People often say they want excellence in their lives, but they stop pursuing it because the cost is too great. They are not willing to pay the price to obtain the prize. They become discouraged and quit when they realize that excellence requires daily striving for improvement. Excellence demands continual, passionate effort. It is a goal you have to go after all the time. Yes, it takes time and energy, but it is worth the work. It is the only way to guarantee a consistent level of integrity in your life. Going after excellence is easier when you are not alone in the pursuit. Encourage yourself to pursue excellence every day. Make sure the people you relate to are also pursuing it personally and can encourage you as you seek it. That fulfills the biblical purpose of relationships, which is to add value to your life and to the world around you. Excellence certainly adds value!

How to Recognize Integrity

I hope you have realized the absolute necessity of requiring integrity from the people with whom you are in relationship. Sometimes when I teach on this subject, people say, "Isn't it arrogant to require integrity from others? Shouldn't we just accept them as they are and walk through life in relationship with them anyway?"

My answer is this: The kind of requirements you place upon others reveals the kind of person you are. You have to require integrity from those with whom you relate. If you do not, you will end up involved with the wrong people. To try to understand someone's integrity in this way is not arrogant; it simply ensures that the relationship will not be a hindrance or a waste of time. The Bible calls us to love one another. We can love people who do not have integrity, but we cannot allow ourselves to walk closely with them in purposeful relationships.

You can gain insight into a person's integrity by asking some of these specific questions designed to reveal character:

- What is the purpose of this person's life?
- Who is this person trying to please?
- What motivates and drives this person? Are his or her motives pure?
- What standards and values does this person hold?

- To whom is this person committed?
- Does this person tell the truth? Is he or she as honest about the little things in life as about the big things?
- Is this person fiercely unwilling to compromise his or her integrity?
- Does this person set personal high standards and ask others to set high standards as well?

One of the spiritual realities of relationships is this: when God decides to bless you or do something wonderful in you or through you, the enemy assigns people to stop you. This is why understanding agreement and integrity is so important.

You must be able to recognize the individuals God has brought or wants to bring into your life versus the people the enemy sends to you. Failure to discern the difference can destroy your life, but being able to identify those God sends and relate to them in the right way is one of the best things you could ever do for yourself. It will not only bring you a high degree of personal fulfillment; it will enable you to do what God has created and destined you to do, and it will greatly benefit the people and the world around you.

RELATIONSHIP REMINDERS

- Take time to find out whether you are in agreement with a person regarding values and priorities before entering into a relationship.
- Don't waste your time trying to build relationships with people with whom you are not in agreement about the important issues in life.

- Require integrity from the people with whom you are in relationships.
- Learn to look past a person's charisma, abilities, or position in life, and do not allow these superficial things to cause you to think integrity is not important.
- Seek these four qualities in a potential friend, spouse, or significant business associate: an unwavering commitment to truth; an absolute refusal to compromise; a complete dedication to pure motives; and the passionate, consistent pursuit of excellence.
- Don't shortchange yourself by accepting anything less than integrity from people with whom you choose to share your life.

RAISING YOUR RELATIONAL IQ

1. What are the primary values in your life? What are your top priorities? What are the nonnegotiable character traits you need in friends and associates?
2. Think about your closest relationships. In each case, are you and the other person in agreement about important issues such as values, beliefs, and matters of character?
3. Why is agreement on major issues important in your life?
4. Who are the people in your life who operate with the highest levels of integrity? In what ways have they proven their integrity to you?
5. In the section titled "How to Recognize Integrity" I mentioned some questions designed to help you

assess character in others. These questions would also be good for you to answer for yourself as you continue to develop greater character and integrity. Why not do so now?

4

Release Your Past to Embrace Your Future

THE LAW OF LETTING GO

IF YOU HAVE EVER HEARD THE UNMISTAKABLE voice of James Earl Jones, you probably cannot forget it. Perhaps the most powerful statement he has ever uttered on stage or screen is this simple, four-word exhortation: *Remember who you are.*

This line comes from the poignant and joyful musical *The Lion King.* In the story, the young lion cub Simba is destined for greatness, but he struggles with fear in the face of tremendous threats and challenges along the way. Simba is devastated, frightened, and angry when his father, Mufasa, is killed. He blames himself for a while, until he comes to understand differently. At a crucial point on his journey, Mufasa's voice speaks to him and says, "Remember who you are." This helps Simba deal with his pain and he goes on to fulfill his destiny and become a great leader.

Sometimes, remembering who you are is easier said than done. All kinds of factors and influences shape our understanding of our identities, many of them beyond our control. Some things that contribute to our self-images are deeply rooted in our past experiences and relationships. Though the actual words or events that impacted us lie buried in our personal histories, they continue to affect us negatively. They hinder the ability to know and remember who we really are and thwart our efforts to give ourselves fully to the people and relationships God has ordained for our good.

As you begin this chapter, I want you to know that your past does not define you. It may have impacted you, but it does not dictate your present or your future. It may be a reality and a painful memory, but it can be healed and reconciled. It does not have to bind you to its pain or its shame. You can find out who you really are, gain strength to put the past behind you, and move forward into a great life and great relationships.

> *I want you to know that your past does not define you. It may have impacted you, but it does not dictate your present or your future.*

A Man You May Relate To

One of the stories of Scripture nearest and dearest to my heart is the tale of a man who is rarely mentioned. I have never seen his picture in a Bible storybook or heard rousing, inspirational sermons based on his life. But to me, he is one of our faith's great tragic heroes. And he is a man whose life is full of crucial lessons about our relationships with others and with ourselves.

This little-known man's name is Jephthah, and you can read

about him in Judges 11 and 12. From the very beginning of his life, certain unfortunate realities worked against Jephthah, especially in his relationships with his brothers. Though Jephthah's story happened long ago in a place you may have never heard of, you may know from personal experience the struggles he endured and the suffering he faced. He is a symbol of everyone who struggles with strained relationships in the present and is headed for troubled personal and professional alliances in the future because of painful relationships in their pasts.

Jephthah was the son of a distinguished man named Gilead, but he was also the son of a prostitute. In a moment of weakness and terrible judgment, his father visited the harlot, resulting in Jephthah's birth. In contrast, his brothers were all true sons of Gilead and his wife. They did not carry the stigma of being conceived outside the covenant of marriage, and they had no use for Jephthah, who bore the invisible label "Illegitimate." The Bible clearly states that the brothers drove Jephthah away from them, saying, "You are not going to get any inheritance in our family . . . *because you are the son of another woman*" (Judg. 11:2, emphasis added).

No doubt Jephthah was a disturbing reminder of Gilead's infidelity and of the pain and shame his actions caused the family. He was a walking representation of Gilead at his worst, and every time anyone in the family looked at Jephthah, they remembered on some level, consciously or unconsciously, the embarrassing reason for his existence.

The fact that Jephthah's mother was a prostitute leads us to believe she came from a non-Hebrew race or culture because Mosaic Law strictly prohibited prostitution. Because Jepthah's ethnicity was mixed and his brothers were "pure" Israelites, Jephthah was different. Just as certain prejudices unfortunately exist today among various ethnic groups all over the world, biases and unfair judgments were also common in Jephthah's time. No doubt he endured whispers, condescending looks, and perhaps unsavory comments from society in general—and probably worse from his brothers.

The realities that separated Jephthah from the rest of his family—the shame of his conception and birth and the strong possibility that he was racially mixed instead of 100 percent Hebrew—may have given his brothers reason to fear he would follow in the ignoble footsteps of his father, inheriting his weaknesses instead of his strengths. We do not know whether Jephthah ever actually gave them reason to believe he would grow up to be dishonorable or not, but I think the possibility is strong that they feared such an outcome. I know about this dynamic from personal experience.

My parents divorced when I was six months old. Growing up I became aware that my father's Gilead-like behavior caused the separation. The hurt and betrayal of his infidelity led my mother to divorce him. While my father and I share the same name, my mother was determined that I would become a different kind of person than my father. In fact, she often said to me, "I don't want you to be like your father!"

During my childhood, her comment did not really bother me, but as I became more mature and began to develop a relationship with my father, those words began to sting more and more. I realized that those comments came from a place inside my mother, a place of lingering hurt and resentment toward my father. Because my father and I have a strong physical resemblance and share the same name of Van Moody, my mother was afraid I would become just like he was.

The truth about my story is that I did not grow up to be like my father. I did not inherit his particular weaknesses. I know that Jephthah, like me, may have been destined never to make the same mistakes Gilead made, but his family did not know that. They, like my mother, could have easily been afraid this young man would grow up to hurt himself and embarrass the family by behaving as his father did.

I cannot speak for Jephthah's brothers; nor can I know for certain the details of the ways they treated him or thought of him. But I do know that certain things about him, things beyond his control, so bothered them that they banished him from their family and cut off his inheritance. This tells me there was serious trouble!

Some of the problems you have faced in your life may be no fault of your own; they may have *nothing* to do with you and everything to do with the fact that you remind people of someone or something painful. Or maybe the issue is that you represent a difficult time in their past, a failure or a mistake that did not even involve you personally. Maybe a relationship is painful for you because of cultural, racial, or socioeconomic gaps between you and another person. Or perhaps, like me, you carry the weight of someone else's fears that are based not on anything you have done or said, but on your connection to someone else. All these situations are unfortunate, unintentional twists on the phrase "guilt by association"—*and none of them is your fault.*

So What Do You Do?

Any time you are caught in a situation you did not create and cannot escape, you have choices to make. Sadly, Jephthah did not choose well. Scripture refers to him as "a mighty warrior" (Judg. 11:1). He does become a great military leader, and that becomes clear later in Judges 11. But the greatest battle he waged did not happen on the field of conflict; it took place inside of him.

I can only imagine what Jephthah had to fight each day,

knowing that his family never accepted him, did not approve of him, and failed to embrace him. We see no evidence that anyone took compassion on him. We see only indications of the strong negative feelings his family felt toward him. Apparently no one around him "felt his pain" or tried to understand him.

The obstacles Jephthah faced were enormous, as any kind of deep pain in any human heart is enormous. Jephthah's fatal flaw was his failure to deal with his hurt. For the rest of his life, as you will see throughout this chapter, that ache of longing for his brothers' love and acceptance persisted. For some reason, he never found his way to forgiveness toward them and therefore to healing for himself. Holding on to the pain and clinging desperately to his desire for good relationships with his brothers kept him trapped in his past, never fully able to thrive in his present or venture into his future.

Many people are similar to Jephthah and seem to repeatedly sabotage the relationships they desperately long for because they have suppressed the pain of past relationships. They simply do not realize that a conscious or unconscious refusal to deal with hurts from the past does indeed set up a person for failure in the future unless their pain is resolved.

This is one reason I urged you in chapter 1 to know yourself, acknowledge your secrets in safe ways, and make a priority of getting your heart healed. There is no shame or embarrassment in seeking the help you need, but if you refuse to deal with lingering pain from your past, you will endanger your personal destiny and your future interactions with others. I have never met a person who has not sustained some kind of relational wound at some point. Those who move beyond their pain into healing, forgiveness, wholeness, and restoration typically go on to live lives of joy, strength, and impact. Those who don't will suffer in many areas of their lives until they finally realize that their decision to remain wounded has sabotaged potentially great relationships and jeopardized their personal destinies.

As Jephthah's story unfolds in the rest of this chapter, I encourage you to tell yourself this truth: "It doesn't have to be this way for me." No matter what you have endured, God has good plans for you, plans that are well within your reach if you choose to leave your past and all its pain behind you.

Look for Your Blessings in Disguise

How would you feel if your family hated and rejected you so terribly that you had to pack your bags and run away—and you ended up living in Alcatraz? That does *not* sound like a good move! Yet a loose comparison exists between that scenario and what really happened to Jephthah. When he was old enough, the Bible says he "fled from his brothers and settled in the land of Tob" (Judg. 11:3).

Tob (rhymes with *robe*) was not a desirable place to live; nothing about it was ideal. It was a haven for exiles, murderers, mercenaries, and thieves. People from other areas tended to cast aspersions on people from Tob because the land was full of roughnecks and rascals. But Tob was also a place of crucial development and destiny for Jephthah. It may not have been impressive to other people, but it was important in God's purposes for this outcast's life. In Tob, Jephthah got married, established a home, and began to raise a family. He also developed meaningful relationships when he connected with a group of men the Bible calls "adventurers" who gathered around him as friends and related to him as their leader. They became his band of brothers, poised and positioned to give him the camaraderie and support his biological siblings withheld.

In that unlikely place called Tob, Jephthah's life begins to take root and flourish, but he struggles to embrace the good things God gives him because he is so bound to his past. He cannot see that the very things he has always hungered for—the love and acceptance of his family, approval, community, a sense of belonging—have become realities in his life, because he keeps looking for them in the sources of his past.

An interesting note about Jephthah's move to Tob is that in Hebrew, the word *Tob* actually means "good." As an Israelite, Jephthah would have known this. To tell people he lived in Tob would have been like a modern-day person saying, "I live in Wonderful, USA" or "I live in Happy, Mexico." Somehow, the meaning of the name escaped him. His presence in Tob was providential, but he did not know it. Perhaps he could not embrace what his location could have represented to him because he could not let go of the ideal of his family's love. He could not fully settle into "good" because the unhealed wound in his heart still felt it could only be healed in the environment in which it was inflicted—the "bad" of his former family home.

Just What You Always Wanted . . .

The lesson we can learn from this part of Jephthah's story is that if we do not trust God to lead us, we will undervalue the places He puts us. We will think of certain places and experiences as bad, when in reality they are hugely significant to our destinies; they are blessings in disguise. If we don't trust Him and learn to view our circumstances from His perspective, we can completely miss something truly wonderful that God is doing for us. Instead we will spend our time longing for the something from our past that really isn't His will or His best for us at all. I believe Jephthah was so bound to his past and unable to escape the pain of it because he never received the healing his heart desperately needed. He never resolved the issues of rejection, shame, and probably anger that came from the circumstances of his birth and the cruelties of his brothers. His unhealed hurts kept his focus locked onto his past, but God had moved him away from all that and offered him a fresh start in a good place.

Sometimes God causes people or places others may regard as lowly to be the ideal environments to strengthen us, heal us, and lead us into our destinies. All we have to do is to keep our eyes on Him, not on our surroundings or circumstances. We have to choose not to continue grasping for the people and places that have repeatedly failed us and hurt us in the past and to trust completely that God knows what He is doing and is working for our good.

Whatever the pain you have suffered in your past, I promise you God wants to heal it and to lead you into a better life in the future than would have ever been possible had you stayed chained to your past. As He did when He surrounded Jephthah with friends who recognized his potential and looked to him as their leader, He will also provide you with the people or experiences that have been missing in your life for so long. The key, though, is to learn to appreciate the people who love you. They may not seem to be exactly your type. Maybe they come from a different socioeconomic background or a different racial or cultural experience, or perhaps they have not attained the same level of education or influence you have. The fact is, God knows who you need in your life. Regardless of how deeply you want their approval, people from your past who neglect you or treat you badly are not good for you.

So many people ignore the amazing blessings God places right in front of them because they look beyond those blessings in a vain effort to find something they probably will never get from people who have hurt them all their lives. I hope that will not be the case for you. You must know that God is focused on healing and redeeming the pain of your past. I urge you not to overlook the good things He is doing in your life because you are too busy longing for or chasing relationships or experiences that are not in your best interest. I understand that the pain of the past can have a powerful pull on your present, but you may lose some wonderful relationships and opportunities that are just waiting for you today. Live and thrive among the people God gives you, in the place God has placed you.

WHAT TO DO WHEN YOUR "BROTHERS" COME BACK

Scripture gives us reason to believe Jephthah was basically doing well in Tob. Yes, he did fight internal battles with his past, and while I believe they limited him severely, they did not incapacitate him. He was certainly able to fulfill his responsibilities, as we can see by the fact that he was considered a strong leader among his group of friends.

Then, suddenly, the elders of Gilead (Jephthah's family) came roaring back into his life, along with all the pain they represented. They did not come back because they realized how much they had hurt Jephthah in the past; they did not come back to apologize for treating him badly; they did not return because they had matured and recognized that they may have missed knowing a good and decent person and wanted to develop a good relationship with him. They came back because they wanted what Jephthah had: courage and military leadership skills.

The nation of Israel was under attack, and obviously, the brothers had heard about Jephthah's position with his adventurers. They had no use or regard for him while they were growing up together, but now that everything dear to them was threatened, they needed him!

Jephthah responded, "Didn't you hate me and drive me from my father's house? Why do you come to me now, when you're in trouble?" (Judg. 11:7).

They answered, "Nevertheless, we are turning to you now; come with us to fight the Ammonites, and you will be our head over all who live in Gilead" (Judg. 11:8).

Perhaps remembering how they had treated him in years past and wondering whether they were telling the truth now, Jephthah questioned them, basically saying, "Are you sure about this?" (Judg. 11:9). After they promised to *really* give him a position of leadership in their community, he made the disappointing and detrimental decision to go with them. He left behind the good life and the good place God had given him and went back to his place of pain. The story unfolds as one of the most heartbreaking accounts in the Bible; the results of his decision are tragic. In his desire to please the wrong people, he made a rash vow to God, promising to offer to Him whatever came out of his house first when he returned home. Tragically, when he reached his house, his young daughter came dancing out the door of their home to meet him. To keep his vow to God, he had to sacrifice the girl (Judg. 11:32–40). He abandoned quality relationships to go with people who had previously rejected him, and his choice cost him dearly.

I have seen the principles of this ancient story play themselves out in a variety of circumstances, in all kinds of relationships. I have learned from personal experience and by observation a key lesson from Jephthah's story, which I mentioned in chapter 1 and cannot emphasize enough: *when people show you who they are, pay attention.* Jephthah knew who his brothers really were, and early in the conversation he questioned them, asking if they really would make him their leader. But because he had never dealt with the pain of his past relationship with them and still longed for their acceptance and approval, he ignored what he had learned through years of harsh treatment and went with them. He allowed them to use him, even though he had no reason to believe they had changed their minds about him.

I am aware that some people do change and improve over time. Some realize they have not respected or treated you well in the past. Those people apologize sincerely for what they have done to you and express genuine desire to build a healthy relationship with you in the future. People who *really* do mature and feel badly about their past attitudes and actions toward you are happy to prove their change of heart.

Anytime someone from your past comes back into your life and wants *what you have* instead of *who you are*, beware. The test of knowing what to do when your brothers come back is real and happens far too often. I remember vividly how certain people from my past once ridiculed and marginalized me. There was a time in my past when I did not have much—except dreams and goals. Certain people did not accept me and even went so far as to tell me that my dreams would never happen and my goals were too far-fetched. I strongly desired relationships with several of these people, but in their eyes I did not fit in, so they rejected me.

I was forced to move on, and much as He did for Jephthah, God brought me to my "good" place. I am fortunate to have a great wife and family and to lead a large, thriving ministry. But what's funny and sad is, since God has established those things in my life, many of the people who rejected me earlier in life now want to be my friends. They rejected me before, when all I had were goals and dreams, but now that those dreams have become tangible realities, they want to reenter my life.

Maybe you have had a similar experience with people who once ignored or rejected you. When you sense that someone wants your resources, your connections, your abilities, or your influence, put your defenses up and require those people to demonstrate their honorable intentions. If you are one of the millions of people who have had a painful past and then God takes you into a good place, guard it. Do not leave it because people who have never been trustworthy come calling for you. Take the necessary steps to get your heart healed and whole so the wounds of your past do not bind you to the detrimental people of your past. Otherwise, like Jephthah's, your past may have such a tight grip on you that you return to it and end up paying a tragic price.

God has something good for you. Your past does not define you. It's time to remember who you are. Regardless of what you have suffered in days or years gone by, no matter what you have done or what has been done to you, a bright future is available. As you trust Him completely and follow Him wholeheartedly, God will lead you into places, opportunities, and relationships that will heal you and set you free from your past, strengthen and restore you in the present, and set you up for tremendous blessings in the future.

RELATIONSHIP REMINDERS

- Remember who you are.
- You cannot erase your past. It will always be part of your personal history, but it does not have to define you.
- To fully embrace the great future God has for you, you must let go of the pain of your past.

- Suppressing the pain of past relationships can damage your present and sabotage potential relationships in your future.
- God has great things for you, but at times those blessings may not be obvious. Be on the lookout for blessings in disguise.
- When people from your past resurface in your life, take time to find out if they are interested in who you are or only in what you can offer them.
- Actively believe that God has good things in store for you.

RAISING YOUR RELATIONAL IQ

1. When you think of the phrase "Remember who you are," what comes to your mind? The challenge I want to issue you today is not to define yourself in terms of your past. As you think about who you are, the pain of the past is off-limits. So, who are you?
2. When you think about who you really are, the person God has created and ordained you to be, what kind of potential do you have in life, in your career, and in relationships? If you were to fully express who God designed you to be, what would that look like?
3. Have you ever walked away from a potentially good relationship because of something you experienced in the past? How can you keep from doing that again?
4. Who are your "adventurers," the people God has given to you to provide what you've longed for and found lacking in previous relationships?

5. Only you and God know the specific pains of your past, and God wants to heal them. What steps do you need to take to begin your journey into healing? I encourage you to pray about this and seek wise counsel from a trusted friend, minister, or professional. Get a plan for healing and wholeness and stick with it. Stay on the lookout for God to intervene and to lead you in sovereign ways into good places as you trust Him.

5

You Can't Be Friends with Everyone

THE LAW OF SELECTIVITY

THINK ABOUT THE LAST TIME YOU HAD A nice dinner at a new restaurant. Did you order every single item on the menu? Of course not! If you are like most people, you read the menu, found a few dishes you knew you would like, and then chose only one entrée, maybe a salad or an appetizer, a beverage, and perhaps dessert. But you did not ask for one of everything. Eating that much food would have made you sick!

Probably without realizing it, you were practicing the law of selectivity when you made your menu choices. You looked at your options and eliminated some of them immediately because they had ingredients you did not like or could not eat. You narrowed down your choices to just a few things, and when the server came to take your order, you ultimately made a final decision. All kinds of factors may have influenced your choice. Maybe you simply ordered what sounded best; maybe you made a selection that would be low fat or low carb or low sodium because you knew those would be best for your health. Maybe you ordered chicken or beef because you are allergic to seafood; or maybe your friend wanted to share the meal with you so you ordered something he or she would like.

As you can see, people use all kinds of criteria when choosing what to eat at a restaurant. Whatever they order has to pass some kind of qualifying test (such as flavor or health benefit) before being selected. Because people put their choices to a test, they often end up with a meal they enjoy.

The same basic process involved in choosing something good to eat is the foundation of the law of selectivity in relationships. But while everyone expects to sit down in a restaurant and be choosy, most people do not always think to be selective when developing relationships with others. We have been taught to "be nice to everyone," and though that is important, it does not mean we should build close relationships with everyone. In fact, the opposite is true. To use an elementary comparison, we need to view the people in our lives almost as we view items on a menu: as options. Then we need to get to know them to see whether they will be enjoyable and good for us. When we determine that certain people will add value to our lives, then we can choose to enter into relationships with them.

Less Can Be More

For years, it seems our culture has been focused on "more." Anytime we view something as good, we tend to want more of it, expecting that "more" will be better. That is not always the case. Sometimes, as the saying goes, "less is more." Or to say it another way, quantity does not equal quality.

"Less is more" definitely applies to having quality relationships.

Sometimes people feel good about themselves when they have lots of friends. Having a lot of relationships gives some people a sense of self-esteem, acceptance, or worth. The law of selectivity challenges the notion that the more friends we have, the better our lives will be. In fact, this law proves that in order to build effective, thriving, healthy relationships, we need to learn to choose our friends wisely and make sure they qualify to be our friends, acquaintances, employers, or romantic interests. We are smart not to allow casual relationships to develop unless we have strong reasons to believe those relationships can become healthy and valuable.

I have known so many individuals who were terribly hurt because they were connected to the wrong people. They have been lied to, betrayed, or damaged emotionally in some other way, resulting in deep pain. Almost always, once those relationships fall apart—as they inevitably do—these people suffer guilt and regret because they wasted some of the best years of their lives with someone who never really intended to do them good; that person just wanted to "hang out."

I have also encountered people of tremendous promise and potential who stumbled in the pursuit of their purpose because they were in relationships with people who stood in their way instead of encouraging them to greatness. In every situation I am aware of, the people involved wish they had known how to be selective and make better choices in relationships. In some cases, people would prefer to have had no friend or associate at all instead of having someone who hurt them or held them back. Even though they wanted support in their journeys through life, they realize they could have moved forward alone, rather than allowing themselves to be restrained by bad relationships. These people now understand on the backside of heartache that less can definitely be more!

Mature men and women recognize that every relationship requires investment and maintenance, and they focus on the substance of their relationships rather than the number of people they consider friends or associates. They know the truth I have mentioned before: every relationship matters because it can either promote you or it can demote you. Every person you know can have positive or negative impact on you, and knowing how to choose the right people with whom to surround yourself is vital. You are better off having a few great friends than lots of mediocre and detrimental ones.

How Are Your Relationships Affecting You?

To begin to explain the law of selectivity, I have a few questions for you. As you answer them, think about every relationship you have: your family, your friends, a significant other, your coworkers, someone who mentors you or someone for whom you serve as a mentor, neighbors, and acquaintances. Your answers to these questions may or may not surprise you, but I believe they will definitely help you see why the law of selectivity is so important.

- What unpleasant things are you tolerating or putting up with in your life right now as a result of the relationships in which you are involved?
- Are you currently embracing anything you have never allowed in your life before now because of the influence of someone with whom you have a relationship? What is it?
- What once repulsed you that you no longer resist because you are in relationship with a certain person?
- Are your standards now lower than they once were because of the negative impact of someone with whom you are associated?

The reason these questions and their answers are so important is this: The snapshot of your future is taken with the people of your present. Your today dictates your tomorrow. The people who are in your life right now are setting the course of your next week, next month, next year, and possibly even the rest of your life. The relationships in which you're currently involved will affect your thought patterns and the outcome of your life.

> *The snapshot of your future is taken with the people of your present. Your today dictates your tomorrow.*

When you understand how critical relationships are to your life, you can begin to see why the law of selectivity is an absolute necessity. Learning to be selective about the people with whom you walk closely will accomplish at least two valuable objectives for you. One, it will empower you to surround yourself with the kinds of people you need to be around—people who will help you advance toward your destiny, not derail or distract you. Two, it will keep you from wasting your most precious commodity—your time—on the wrong people.

UNDERSTANDING SELECTIVITY

I want to clearly communicate what I mean—and what I do not mean—by the word *selectivity*. Being selective simply means being discerning about the people you allow into the inner circle of your life. It means you are kind, considerate, and friendly to everyone you meet, but you do not want or attempt to develop meaningful relationships with everyone. Being selective about the people who get close to you does not mean being arrogant, exclusive, narrow-minded, judgmental, or biased; it does not mean judging others or believing you are better than they are. It means you can be gracious and respectful to everyone. You can smile, say hello, and express genuine interest in their well-being while keeping the relationship on a surface level instead of going deeper. Using wisdom and being selective means you are careful and deliberate about building relationships because you understand how important relationships are in your life today and to your future. It means you are not willing to let the wrong people influence you in negative ways.

If you are a Christian, you may be wondering how this idea of selectivity lines up with Scripture. "After all," you may ask, "doesn't Jesus command us to love everyone?" Certainly, Christ Himself did love everyone, and the Bible includes several verses instructing us to love one another. We can do this because of the love and mercy of God. At the same time, we do not have to approve of everyone because of the righteousness and justice of God (1 Cor. 5:11). No one is perfect; no one ever has been perfect except Jesus Christ. We need to understand this truth about ourselves and about each other, realizing that there are some people who are good candidates for healthy relationships and some who are not.

SELECTIVITY DEMANDS LOYALTY

Let's say Mr. Jones is the chief executive officer (CEO) of a corporation and he hires Ms. Smith to be chief financial officer (CFO). Those two executives have a professional relationship that utilizes the law of selectivity. Mr. Jones hired Ms. Smith after a lengthy, thorough interview and reference process. He made sure she was qualified for the job both in terms of her skill and experience as a CFO and in terms of being a good fit for his company's goals, priorities, vision, and culture. Ms. Smith, if she's smart, also did her research on Mr. Jones's company, making sure it would provide a positive, beneficial work environment.

Once Mr. Jones and Ms. Smith agree upon the terms of their relationship in an employment contract, both of them have responsibilities. One of those responsibilities is loyalty. Ms. Smith is committed to Mr. Jones's company, which means she is not available to other organizations. She cannot provide financial leadership or advice to a company in her neighborhood or a business run by one of her fellow church members, because she has pledged her loyalty to her current employer. Likewise, Mr. Jones chose to hire Ms. Smith, so he cannot share financial information or ask for input from people who may be excellent financial managers, but are not in a professional relationship with him. Mr. Jones and Ms. Smith chose to work together, and that means they must be loyal to one another.

The connection between selectivity and loyalty is clear in a healthy marriage relationship. When a person chooses a husband or a wife, hopefully he or she is careful, prayerful, and diligent to select a quality human being. Once those two people commit to marry, they cannot have serious romantic relationships or even casual dates with others. Their decision to enter into a long-term, binding relationship requires that they be exclusive and loyal to one another. This same principle applies to any other selected relationship.

It's Biblical

I recognize that this concept of selectivity may be a bit new to you, especially if your culture or your faith has taught you to be inclusive of everyone, no matter what. So let's take a look at what the Bible has to say about it.

In 2 Corinthians 6:14–7:1, Paul wrote:

Do not be yoked together with unbelievers. For what do righteousness and wickedness have in common? Or what fellowship can light have with darkness? What harmony is there between Christ and Belial? What does a believer have in common with an unbeliever? What agreement is there between the temple of God and idols? For we are the temple of the living God. As God has said: "I will live with them and walk among them, and I will be their God, and they will be my people." "Therefore come out from them and be separate, says the Lord. Touch no unclean thing, and I will receive you." "I will be a Father to you, and you will be my sons and daughters, says the Lord Almighty." Since we have these promises, dear friends, let us purify ourselves from everything that contaminates body and spirit, perfecting holiness out of reverence for God.

Paul certainly knew the biblical teaching to "love one another" (John 13:34; 1 John 4:7), but in this passage, he is urging his readers to learn to be selective. He clearly says, "Do not be yoked together with unbelievers." In other words, loving everyone in a biblical way is fine and good, but don't get close to people who are not headed in the same direction you are going and who have different values, goals, and ideals, especially spiritual ones. Do not judge them, but do not pal around with them either.

The main reason people become unevenly yoked is that they approve of attitudes, behaviors, or words they should not. That is where the trouble starts. They do not understand the difference between acceptance and approval. When they move beyond accepting people and expressing appropriate biblical love and they begin to approve of things that take them away from God and His Word, an unequal relationship is sure to follow. As Paul said, "What fellowship can light have with darkness?" He knew the answer, and we do too. None! Refusing to walk closely with someone who would be unequally yoked with you is not harsh. It is a smart way to protect and preserve the character, integrity, and destiny God has placed on your life.

Let me also call your attention to a situation involving Jesus. In Luke 4, He says that no prophet is accepted in his hometown. He mentions that when God wanted to do a miracle through Elijah, He sent him to a widow in a Gentile area called Zarephath, even though there were plenty of widows in the town in Elijah's home country of Israel (Luke 4:25–27; 1 Kings 17:9). The same thing happened with Elisha. His hometown in Israel had plenty of lepers, but only one, a Syrian man, was healed after encountering the prophet (2 Kings 5:1–14).

When Jesus finished making His point about prophets being limited in terms of what they could do in their familiar surroundings, the people around Him were so furious they tried to drive Him off a cliff and kill Him! What did He do? He "walked right through the crowd and went on his way" (Luke 4:30).

The point of Jesus' story in Luke 4 is that sometimes we can be around people we have been around for years, but a time may come when we must be selective even with them in order to move forward with God's plans for our lives. Those people who have known us all our lives may, like the ones in Jesus' day, be the very ones who try to "kill" us—not physically, but they may try to kill our dreams and visions or keep us from reaching the places God has for us. When that happens, we have to be like Jesus and go in a different direction.

Learning from Experience

I once made a big mistake because I did not understand how clearly the Bible urges us to make wise choices in relationships and I was unwilling to be selective. I was in school, preparing for ministry, and I was offered a job at a large, well-known, prestigious church. It was a phenomenal opportunity.

Before I agreed to take the position, I became aware of some issues involving leaders in the church. In simplest terms, I found out that they were not committed to holy living. At that time in my life, I did not yet understand how much the people around me would influence me. Naively, I thought, *I'm my own person. I know the church leaders aren't living the way they should, but that won't affect me. I will be strong in the Lord and I will live a holy life, no matter what the people around me are doing.*

I was wrong! Not long after I started working for that church, I began to struggle with issues I never struggled with before. I started feeling tempted to do things I never even thought of doing before. Thankfully, I realized what was happening before it was too late, but I also learned the lesson that whatever we are around *will* rub off on us. I subsequently had to resign and, as Jesus did, go in a different direction. I either had to do that or buckle under the pressure of my surroundings. I had to make a choice. If we want to stay on the track where God has placed us, we cannot allow ourselves to be around people who will influence us away from it. We must make a decision.

The Grown-Up Way to Find a Friend

Do you remember sitting in a classroom or school lunchroom and writing or receiving a note that said something like: "Do you like me? Check yes or no." Most people can remember that scenario or a similar one. When someone checked yes, a relationship ensued. When someone checked no, it didn't. Things were simple back then! Unfortunately, that simple "yes, I like you" or "no, I don't" approach to relationships we knew as children contributed to thought patterns that do not serve us well as adults. They caused us to believe that the fact that someone liked *us* meant we had to like *them*—and that is dangerous!

As adults, we have to abandon juvenile ways of making decisions, especially decisions about relationships, whether those relationships are platonic, romantic, or professional. We cannot decide to like another person simply because he or she likes us; we cannot take a job simply because someone offers it; we cannot enter into a marriage covenant only because someone proposes. No, any relationship in which we involve ourselves must be one that has passed some tests and one we have deliberately chosen. We desperately need to set standards for the people we allow into our lives. That is the only way to keep the wrong people from influencing us in negative ways and to surround ourselves with the right ones.

So how do you identify people who qualify for relationship with you and make wise selections concerning individuals, groups, or institutions with whom to build relationships? Let me offer five suggestions.

1. A good candidate for relationship is a person with long-term potential.

Adding value to someone's life doesn't happen overnight. It is a process that takes time—sometimes a *long* time. You cannot give to others all the benefits you have to offer in a relationship in a week or a month or even a year. Great, meaningful relationships are not built on a short-term basis, and it's so important to determine as best you can whether you can cultivate a relationship with someone over a period of years.

Historically, before the age of transportation, people tended to live in the same community for years, and families lived in the same area for generations. This gave people opportunities to really know each other. In those days, people did not have the technology and the machines we have today, so they had to work together and help each other. These types of situations, which some might consider hardships, contributed to the development of strong, long-lasting relationships. Today, having relationships can feel like being on a carousel; people weave in and out of your life as they hop on and off a merry-go-round. But a genuine, biblical friend or family member will be there when things are fun and good—and when things are most difficult. I certainly do not wish problems on you, but difficulties and challenges do arise. So when you have a problem or a crisis, take note of the people who are there for you. They are the ones with the potential to be long-lasting friends, and you can learn so much about their character when you see how they support you in a time of trial.

2. A good candidate for relationship is a person of substance.

A person with whom you can build a quality relationship is one who is deeper and broader than you may realize when you initially become acquainted. To find out whether or not people have empires inside them, try asking some of these questions:

- Where are you going in life?
- What is your personal vision?
- What are your greatest passions?
- What are your goals?

- Where do you see yourself in ten, twenty, or thirty years?
- What kind of impact are you trying to make for the Kingdom of God?

People can waste a lot of time and end up being hurt because they do not assess others correctly at the outset of a relationship. Don't be afraid to ask the questions I have suggested and others that are similar. Listen closely to their answers and let them help you determine whether or not you want to take the next step in developing a relationship.

Know this: *people who are not going anywhere in life have already arrived.* I strongly caution you against spending your time and energy on people who have no vision or drive. Look for people of substance, passion, and ambition—people who aren't seeking to make an impression on the world but to make a powerful impact for God's Kingdom. Find people who have the capacity to appreciate the vision you have for your life and the energy to support you in it. Look for people who will challenge and encourage you to become more than you are today, and who will allow you to do the same for them.

3. A good candidate for relationship is a person who is a giver.

People who are ready, able, and worthy of building a good relationship with are generous and unselfish, not people who always want you to do something for them. Understand that giving is rarely about the gift; it is about the heart. Everyone has a different measure of resources. Some people with many resources give very little, while some people who do not have much to give sometimes give almost all they have. In many ways, there are only two types of people in the world: givers and takers. If you are not in a relationship with a giver, you are in one with a taker, and the only way to have a healthy, balanced relationship is to have two givers. A strong, right relationship includes reciprocation, and a great relationship is one in which both people are eager to bless each other.

4. A good candidate for relationship is a person who is "good soil."

Jesus tells the story of a farmer who sowed some seed. He planted it in different types of ground, but as you can imagine, it only thrived when it was in good, rich, healthy soil (Luke 8). One of the key points of the story is this: the farmer planted the seed, but the soil determined the harvest.

In terms of relationships, this means people need to be "good soil" for the investment you want to make in them, which means they need to value what you have to give. I could have avoided so much pain personally had I simply understood that everyone did not appreciate or honor what I had to give them. Understand that you cannot change people. They are who they are. Along your life's journey, you will encounter some people who will take the love, the time, the finances, or the energy you invest in them, but never give you anything in return. The relationship is like a black hole; you pour into a person, and then you wonder what happened to everything you gave.

No matter how attractive, influential, well educated, or connected a person is, always look beyond those superficial matters and see what kind of heart he or she has. Look for a quality human being, and do not enter into a relationship until you are certain that the person is someone of character who can receive and multiply what you have to give.

5. A good candidate for relationship is a person who places a premium on integrity.

One thread running through several chapters in this book is the importance of integrity. In a true biblical relationship, both parties must have no doubt about what they would do if they ever had to make a choice between their integrity and a relationship.

Real friends will confront you, and even walk away from you if necessary, when you compromise integrity. They know that a lack of integrity on your part will eventually destroy them, and you must know that a lack of integrity on their part will ultimately destroy you. That is why people in healthy relationships do not tolerate violations of integrity on any level, for any length of time.

FAILURE TO BE SELECTIVE CAN BE DISASTROUS

I trust this chapter has taught you some important lessons about being selective. I cannot emphasize enough the importance of doing so. You do not have to look hard to find stories that drive home the point that failing to be selective can bring destruction and devastation in widespread ways.

As I was writing this book during the summer of 2011, a news story emerged that saddened and shocked people in the United States and around the world. It was a tragedy of enormous proportion: a storied college football powerhouse, a legendary head coach, a respected university, and a popular assistant football coach who was convicted of heinous crimes against boys who trusted him, and a university administration that turned a blind eye to the violations, some of which took place in their own facilities.

I am talking about the scandal at Penn State, whose assistant coach, Jerry Sandusky, preyed upon innocent, often fatherless young men and damaged them in unspeakable ways. From a relational standpoint, I can see instances in which every critical law of relationships was broken. To put it mildly, the entire scenario was rife with dysfunction, especially relational dysfunction.

The whole situation was tragic. It was heartbreaking for every victim and every victim's family. It is also sad and appalling that anyone would do what Sandusky was found guilty of doing. But at the same time, it seems that something is also wrong with a group of adults, including university administrators and allegedly head coach Joe Paterno himself, who would conspire to cover up such violations just because they wanted to protect their football program and avoid shaming the university.

Just think about how differently the situation would have turned out had Paterno decided to apply the law of selectivity and sever relationship with Sandusky, going public with the abuse as soon as he discovered what Sandusky was doing. Had Paterno taken appropriate action, he would have preserved his legacy. He would have shone a light on a situation that happens far too often in the dark. He would have been able to take a firm, clear stand against child sexual abuse. Had he announced a zero-tolerance policy against abuse by firing Sandusky and turning him over to police, he would have set a standard for other coaches and other football programs. He had the chance to stop Sandusky from harming the lives of many young men. The opportunity was available to put the university in a position to say, "This has happened. We are outraged and we are deeply sorry. We can never undo the damage Jerry Sandusky has done, but we are working to help the victims rebuild their lives. We have fired Jerry Sandusky and we are fully cooperating with authorities to make sure he never has access to little boys again. We urge every university and every sports program in the world to pay attention to the actions of employees, to encourage the reporting of inappropriate behavior, and to institute zero-tolerance policies against the abuse of children."

Coach Paterno passed away in January 2012, at age eighty-five, with his integrity in question and his legacy tainted. Several months later, the once-great coach was disgraced and held in disdain across the United States and around the world. The National Collegiate Athletic Association vacated 112 wins, from 1998 through 2011, removed college scholarships, and fined Penn State sixty million dollars. In addition, the bronze statue honoring him at Penn State came down. When all was said and done, he spent a lifetime building success and earning respect, only to come to an inglorious end because, among other bad decisions, he refused to be selective in his relationships.

When you consider entering into a relationship, remember this story and remember the illustration of the restaurant used at the beginning of this chapter. Just because an item is on the menu does not mean you have to order it. In fact, you can't order everything. Just because a person comes into your life, that doesn't mean you need to build a close relationship. Set your standards high and give people opportunities to qualify for relationship with you. Then make wise selections that will bless and strengthen both you and those in relationships with you.

RELATIONSHIP REMINDERS

- Selectivity in relationships is the best way to keep from wasting your time with people who do not intend to bless you.

- Selectivity is not arrogant or narrow-minded. It is a wise, biblical approach to relationships. The failure to be selective can be fatal to your destiny.
- Require a process of qualification and selection, understanding that the only way to get the right people around you is to disallow the wrong ones.
- Do not give the best years of your life to the worst kinds of people.
- Understand that selectivity demands loyalty. If a person qualifies to be in a relationship with you, that person should be able to depend on you to be loyal.
- Accepting people is not the same as approving of everything they say or do. Acceptance and approval are different.
- When you need to leave a relationship, do not be afraid to do so.

RAISING YOUR RELATIONAL IQ

1. The idea of qualification and selection is foreign to many people because they have been taught to try to have as many friends as possible. Is the idea new to you, and if so, would you give selectivity a try?
2. Why would selectivity in relationships be good and wise for you?
3. After reading this chapter, are you having second thoughts about any of your relationships? What caught your attention and caused you to think?
4. Have you given some of the best years of your life to some of the worst people you've ever known and

suffered because of it? I want to encourage you today and remind you that God is a Redeemer and a Healer, and He can restore the years you have lost (Joel 2:25).

5. Based on what you learned in this chapter, who are some people in your life who may be good candidates for stronger relationships than you currently enjoy with them? From whom do you need to begin to back away?

6

Everybody Has to Give

THE LAW OF SACRIFICE

THE LATE US PRESIDENT JOHN F. KENNEDY
urged in his 1961 inaugural address, "Ask not what your country
can do for you; ask what you can do for your country." These words
are famous and memorable not simply because they are eloquent
or poetic but because they are powerful and noble. When Kennedy
spoke them, they beckoned us to look beyond ourselves to the greater
good of our country. They called us away from selfishness and self-
focus and into an attitude of sacrifice, service, and focus on others.

When we think about what we can do for others instead of
what they can do for us, we get to the very heart of healthy, successful relationships. One of the immutable laws of relationships
is the law of sacrifice, which means everyone involved must enter
into and remain in a relationship with a willingness to give, not to
take. Both parties have to be willing to sacrifice for each other and
for the relationship as a whole.

The only things we should never sacrifice for a relationship are integrity, character, biblical principles, and our walks with God. In truly healthy relationships, people will not ask us to sacrifice such significant aspects of our lives but will appreciate and honor them. Aside from these priorities, everything else is eligible to be placed upon the altar of sacrifice.

The idea of sacrifice is not often popular. It evokes all kinds of feelings, from minor inconvenience to near agony! But the level of discomfort does not really matter; what matters is the value of a relationship. A whatever-it-takes attitude and willingness to sacrifice provide solid proof that one person truly values another person and the relationship they share.

The most significant relationship the world has ever known clearly demonstrates to us the importance of sacrifice in a relationship. I am referring, of course, to the relationship between God and us. The apostle John gave the world one of its best-known scriptures in John 3:16, "For God so loved the world that he *gave* his one and only Son" (emphasis added). Now, *that's* sacrifice! God, the Creator of relationships (Gen. 2:20–25), demonstrates to the entire world that successful relationships require sacrifice. In order to relate with us, He sacrificed something unspeakably precious—His only Son!

John 3:16 is a familiar scripture, but the power of its message is not limited to the words of this verse. John's ministry continued after he penned these words. Years later, under the leading of the Holy Spirit, a much older and more experienced John wrote three more books of the Bible: 1, 2, and 3 John. After reflecting for years on Christ's life and ministry and on the necessity of sacrifice within relationships, John made an earth-shattering statement: "This is how we know what love is: Jesus Christ laid down his life for us. And we ought to lay down our lives for our brothers" (1 John 3:16). In other words, John realized and taught that in order to have successful relationships, we must follow Jesus' example and sacrifice for others.

After all, that is what Jesus did for us. We need to understand that no other relationship can be successful unless we follow His model.

Sacrifice is something God has demonstrated personally and something He requires of us for healthy relationships. It is not pleasant, and it is not easy. This is because certain enemies of sacrifice are wired into human nature and are constantly pulling us to side with them. We must defeat two specific enemies if we are going to sacrifice in ways that honor God and benefit our relationships: comfort and convenience.

One primary reason people fail to maintain their relationships is that they want to pursue comfort. When people become comfortable with others, they develop a sense of familiarity that can easily breed neglect, lassitude, and indifference. They begin to disregard others and to take them for granted. Then they begin to take undue liberties in the relationship, often leading to minor instances of disrespect that become major problems over time.

The second enemy of sacrifice, an accomplice to the trap of comfort, is the snare of convenience. In today's world, we are accustomed to convenience; and if something is inconvenient, we do not always make the effort to attain or enjoy it. In order to have healthy, biblical relationships, we must discard the idea of convenience because godly relationships have nothing to do with whether they are convenient or not. They require investments of time, energy, resources, and commitment, and those things are not always convenient to give.

To avoid allowing comfort and convenience to destroy our relationships, we must develop habits of continually respecting and valuing others, meeting their needs, and sacrificing for people immediately when their needs arise. We cannot wait until a convenient time to help or support them; we should do so when they need us. Many times, if we wait for a "good time" to do something for someone else, we will never do it. Often the inconvenient kindnesses we extend to people communicate most clearly how highly we esteem them and how much we value our relationships with them.

THE FIRST REALITY OF SACRIFICE: RELATIONSHIPS COST

You have probably heard the trite saying, "There's no such thing as a free lunch." I don't know about that, but I do know there is no such thing as a free relationship. One of the basic truths of any good, healthy, successful relationship is that it costs. It requires an investment from everyone involved. A relationship is like a bank account. If you do not put anything into it, you will never get anything out of it.

If your relationships are going to become everything God has ordained them to be, and if both you and the other person are going to help each other reach your full potential, sacrifice will be necessary. The way people prove beyond all doubt that they are serious about a relationship is that they are willing to sacrifice for it. As I mentioned, John 3:16 reveals that Jesus is the ultimate example of sacrifice. Better than anything else a person can do, sacrifice expresses the fact that people are genuine and pure in their desire for a growing relationship. Sometimes sacrifice stings; it is not enjoyable, but it is unavoidable.

If your relationships are going to become everything God has ordained them to be, and if both you and the other person are going to help each other reach your full potential, sacrifice will be necessary.

Before you get discouraged about the high price of godly relationships, know this: the plans and purposes of God in your life have immeasurable and infinite value, and are worth every investment He asks you to make. If you were able to step into your destiny easily without sacrifice and expense, chances are high that you would esteem it too lightly and readily neglect, misuse, or lose it.

Too Much + Too Soon + Too Freely = Disaster

You may be familiar with the story of the prodigal son (Luke 15:11–24). Basically, the story is about a father with two sons. The younger brother received his inheritance and squandered it. He was irresponsible and profligate, so he ended up losing it all. He returned to his father's house destitute, and his father threw an elaborate party for him.

This parable is often used as a story about salvation. The father's joy and generosity toward his wayward son illustrate God's lavish love and willingness to receive people no matter what they have done. But this story also contains some powerful lessons about relationships.

In the relationship between the son and his father, the son turns prodigal because his father gave him things for which the young man did not have to sacrifice. Under usual circumstances, he would not have had access to his inheritance until after his father's death. He would have had to sacrifice time in order to get everything his father left him. But the son did not want to sacrifice, and the father gave him his share of the inheritance at an early age. This created a problem. Because the son did not have to sacrifice for it, he did not value it. Instead, he squandered it. The son's unwillingness to sacrifice and value what was given to him contributed significantly to the unwise behavior that caused him to lose everything.

Note that the relationship between the son and his father did not change until the son began to think differently and was willing to return home and serve his father. In other words, nothing changed until he was willing to sacrifice some things, including his pride, his time, and his stature. Once he made these changes and desired to return home and to live according to his father's standards, his father welcomed him with open arms.

The lesson here is that when God gives us something He sees as valuable in our lives, He often asks us to sacrifice for it because that ensures that we will cherish it and handle it wisely. He knows that the more it costs us, the more highly we will esteem it.

THE SECOND REALITY OF SACRIFICE: HEALTHY RELATIONSHIPS ARE WORTH IT

Sacrifice is an indispensable component of biblical relationships because *the price you are willing to pay for something reveals its value to you.* Sacrifice must take place because a thriving, meaningful relationship requires investment, and investment often involves risk.

When you sacrifice for a relationship by investing your internal and external resources in it, you communicate that it means so much to you that you are willing to give up other things so you can have it. You send the message that the relationship is worth "paying" for. In the early stages of a relationship, you may sacrifice and invest because you see genuine potential in it. Later on, as you begin to realize the value of the relationship and the person in it with you, you become more and more willing to surrender other things because the benefits of the relationship are worth more to you than those things could ever be.

In a romantic sense, when two people fall in love and eventually agree to marry, the woman typically receives an engagement ring. If a man were to say, "I've got twenty dollars in my pocket. Let's go get you a ring," a woman would know immediately that she is not worth much to him. On the other hand, when a man scrimps and saves, skips nights out with his friends, eats nothing but beans for two months, or moves in with his mother for a while so he can buy his fiancée a beautiful, high-quality ring, she knows he has been willing to sacrifice to buy her a stunning symbol of his love. He has proven her value to him.

Sacrifices, of course, go far beyond the realm of finances and purchases. For example, there may be times when a man gives up an afternoon of golf or basketball to go to the mall with his wife because she's looking for something very special and wants his input. Or there may be times when a woman gives up a weekend away with her friends to help her husband care for an ailing parent. In the workplace, a CEO may get up early and stay up late for weeks in order to develop a strategy to save a failing business and to keep employees paid. A minister or church members may give up time with their own families to help and support those who are bereaved or in crisis. No matter what the sacrifice is—and sacrifice means many different things to different people—when people are willing to do it, you can be sure they value that for which they surrender other things.

Early in our marriage, my wife and I had desires and plans, as most young couples do. We lived in south Florida and expected to stay there for quite some time. My wife, Ty, had worked hard to fulfill her dream of earning her doctorate and had gone through the competitive process of looking for a job, finally being awarded a teaching position at a local university. Just as she looked forward to a promising career in academia, and as we settled into a recently purchased house, I sensed God's call for us to move to Birmingham, Alabama, to work with a ministry there.

My wife was amazing! She never said, "But what about all these years I spent getting my doctorate?" She didn't ask, "How could you do this, with college-level teaching jobs so hard to get—and *I just got one?*" She didn't complain. She did not second-guess God. She simply said, "I'm in. I believe this is what God has for you, and I'm with you 100 percent."

She made a massive sacrifice, and it did not go unnoticed. I was humbled and awestruck because I recognized it as proof of her love for me, of her love for God, and of how deeply she valued our marriage.

Vertical and Horizontal

Another incredible but often overlooked principle revealed in 1 John 3:16 is that a person's willingness to sacrifice for others says something about his or her relationship with God. This verse points out that investing in relationships with others and being willing to sacrifice for other people proves that we desire a deeper relationship with Him. This is because, as Christians, our vertical relationship (relationship with God) and our horizontal relationships (relationships with other people) are intricately connected. Just take a look at what Jesus had to say about this point.

When a teacher of the law asked Jesus what was the most important commandment of all, He replied:

> The most important one . . . is this: "Hear, O Israel, the Lord our God, the Lord is one. Love the Lord your God with all your heart and with all your soul and with all your mind and with all your strength." The second is this: "Love your neighbor as yourself." There is no commandment greater than these. (Mark 12:29–31)

Jesus also said,

> If you obey my commands, you will remain in my love, just as
> I have obeyed my Father's commands and remain in his love. I
> have told you this so that my joy may be in you and that your joy
> may be complete. My command is this: Love each other as I have
> loved you. Greater love has no one than this: that he lay down his
> life for his friends. (John 15:10–13)

In an exchange with the apostle Peter, Jesus clearly connected love
for Him with serving others:

> When they had finished eating, Jesus said to Simon Peter,
> "Simon son of John, do you truly love me more than these?"
>   "Yes, Lord," he said, "you know that I love you."
>   Jesus said, "Feed my lambs."
>   Again Jesus said, "Simon son of John, do you truly love me?"
>   He answered, "Yes, Lord, you know that I love you."
>   Jesus said, "Take care of my sheep."
>   The third time he said to him, "Simon son of John, do you
> love me?"
>   Peter was hurt because Jesus asked him the third time, "Do
> you love me?"
>   He said, "Lord, you know all things; you know that I love you."
>   Jesus said, "Feed my sheep." (John 21:15–17)

Mark 10:17–22 provides great insight into Jesus' thoughts on
human relationships as indicators of the health of a person's relationship with God. In this story, a very wealthy and influential
young man asks Jesus, "What must I do to inherit eternal life?"

Jesus responds, "You know the commandments: 'You shall not murder, you shall not commit adultery, you shall not steal, you shall not give false testimony, you shall not defraud, honor your father and mother'" (v. 19).

Baffled, the young man basically says, "I've been doing those things all my life. There's got to be something more."

Then Jesus gives him a powerful directive. Scripture says, "Jesus looked at him and loved him. 'One thing you lack,' he said. 'Go, sell everything you have and give to the poor, and you will have treasure in heaven. Then come, follow me'" (v. 21).

As it turned out, the young man could not bring himself to part with his belongings and bless needy people, and according to Mark 10:22, he "went away sad."

If we take this passage seriously, we see that people really cannot follow Jesus without reaching out to others. The rich young man seemed to have his vertical relationship in place; he had done everything right according to the law. But what was required of him horizontally was to sacrifice everything he had (which was considerable) to benefit others. Only then, said Jesus, could the young man follow and develop a growing relationship with Him.

The same is true for us. We cannot separate our love for God from our love for other people. This principle is clear in His Word: if we want a strong and vibrant relationship with *Him*, we must also have healthy, biblical relationships with *them* (John 13:15; 1 John 4:7).

When you really understand the inseparable connection between loving God and loving people, you can better handle the challenge of dealing with others. Investing in relationships and sacrificing for people can be extremely difficult. People can have a way of finding your very last nerve and getting on it all day long. They can do with great finesse the *one thing* that makes you want to scream. They can be tremendously frustrating and deeply disappointing.

But if you recognize that you are loving God through loving them, if you understand that your love for them springs from your love for Him, then you can do it regardless of their actions.

What I am suggesting here can be difficult to do without a strong relationship with God. Colossians 3:23 says, "Whatever you do, work at it with all your heart, as working for the Lord, not for human masters." This means everything you do is for God, not for other people. It really does not matter who is involved on a human level, because you are acting on a spiritual level. It means you are not doing what you do for your boss, your spouse, your parents, your children, your coworkers, or your friends. It is all for God; it is all an expression of your love for Him. It's not about the "public" around you; it's about your private walk with God.

This applies to every relationship you have—personal and professional. You love the people around you not because they are always lovable but because you are head over heels in love with God. The way people treat you is not the point. The point is that you are accountable to God for the way you act. The proof of your commitment to Him is displayed in your willingness to sacrifice, your willingness to lay down what you want to do and lovingly care for others.

THE THIRD REALITY OF SACRIFICE:
SACRIFICE KEEPS RELATIONSHIPS GOING

Have you ever noticed that some people seem to have really good relationships? They have strong, intimate marriages; they have close, long-term friendships; and they have worked at the same company for years, enjoying the respect of others and making many positive contributions to their workplace.

How does this happen?

The answer is easy: maintaining successful relationships over a period of time requires sacrifice. Those who are willing to sacrifice reap the benefits of such relationships. Those who are not willing, don't.

All relationships—and I mean *all* relationships—need maintenance in order to stay healthy, and sacrifice provides the energy needed to maintain them. In fact, I would even say a relationship that never receives much attention does not even qualify to be called a relationship. A relationship that is not maintained is nonexistent; it is simply an acquaintance.

Occasionally I hear people say, "I haven't talked to her in such a long time, but that doesn't matter. We can just pick up where we left off!" They make comments like this even if they "left off" two years earlier! Similarly, I have heard people say, "So-and-so is my best friend, but I haven't seen or talked to her in months." These remarks may be well-intentioned and sincere, but sometimes they are not true. They are simply excuses for not wanting to sacrifice in a relationship. I realize that on rare occasions, people have invested in each other's lives in significant ways for a period of time, and then something causes a geographic separation or some other circumstance that prevents them from being together or communicating as frequently as they once did. In those instances, *because of a strong relational foundation,* people can maintain their closeness. But generally speaking, a growing relationship requires an investment of time.

For a relationship to be strong, people cannot weave in and out of each other's lives like cars on an interstate. They cannot be lackadaisical or choose to connect haphazardly when doing so is convenient. They cannot go for months and years remembering the last fond conversation or friendly e-mail with no additional communication. Relationships have to be maintained, and they are maintained with steady investments of time and interaction.

In her book *Fierce Conversations*, author Susan Scott makes a powerful observation: "The conversation is the relationship."[1] In other words, people who do not communicate do not really have a relationship at all. I understand that keeping up with people can be time-consuming; that's why it is a sacrifice.

Bishop T. D. Jakes makes an interesting revelation about himself in his book *Let It Go*.[2] He notes that he refuses to take on more relationships than he can maintain. This is a well-known, globally respected leader who could probably have as many relationships as he would like. But he knows relationships that are not maintained are bad for everyone involved, so he wisely disciplines himself to allow only a limited number into his life. This is because he understands that nurturing and tending to relationships is the only way for all parties to grow and be blessed.

If you do not invest time and energy to maintain a relationship, whatever type of relationship it is, it will disintegrate. It does not matter who you are or how excellent those relationships are at this moment. You can have the best marriage or be the best of friends with someone *right now*, but if you stop working on making the relationship better, it will eventually die. If you value a relationship, sacrifice for it and maintain it.

RELATIONSHIP REMINDERS

- Though sacrifice is necessary for relationships, don't ever sacrifice your character, your integrity, your biblical principles, or your walk with God.
- Relationships cost. Be willing to invest in them,

knowing that the relationships themselves are important and that they are vital to your fulfilling God's purposes for your life.

- Anything worth having is worth sacrificing for. The more valuable a relationship is in your life, the more you may have to sacrifice for it.
- You will receive most from the relationships in which you invest most.
- Separating your love for God from your love for other people is impossible. The two work together.
- Great relationships require continual investments of time, energy, care, and communication. You cannot reasonably expect a relationship to thrive or even survive if you are not willing to maintain it.

RAISING YOUR RELATIONAL IQ

1. From your perspective, what is the connection between value and investment? Why does sacrificing for a relationship increase its value?
2. When you are in a relationship, what do you find most difficult to sacrifice? Take, for example, time, other relationships that may be less valuable, finances, or things you want for yourself.
3. Are you currently involved in a relationship that demands more sacrifice than you are making? If so, is the relationship valuable enough to you for you to make the needed sacrifices?
4. Why is your love for God connected to your love for other people? In your everyday life and in your

relationships, how can you demonstrate in practical ways your love for Him by loving others?

5. I mentioned in this chapter that great relationships require continual investments of time, energy, care, and communication. Given the responsibilities and priorities of your life, how many truly great relationships do you think you can reasonably invest in?

7

What You Don't Know
Can Hurt You

The Law Against Secrets

IMAGINE A COURTROOM FULL OF PEOPLE. Because of the crime committed, emotions are intense and drama is high. A person with a shady past and a résumé of suspect activities is accused of something that has harmed people terribly. He wants a chance to defend himself. After all, the prosecution has done their homework. They have grilled their witnesses. The situation does not look good for the defendant. He will do *anything* to avoid spending the rest of his life in prison. He just wants the opportunity to tell his story from his perspective, even though doing so is not a good idea.

The prosecution calls the defendant to the stand. His attorney's heart sinks as she breathes a frustrated sigh.

In this scenario, the defendant's lawyer knows what all good defense attorneys know. She knows he will try to spin the story in his favor, and she happens to know he is guilty as charged. She also knows her client is not quite as smooth as he thinks he is, that somewhere in his testimony, he is likely to try so hard to present himself well that he will probably betray himself. She knows the defendant has one goal: to keep hidden the secrets that lie deep within his heart and mind. She also knows the prosecutor has only one goal: to somehow get the defendant to expose those secrets.

The members of the jury sit neatly in their box, and because doing so is human nature, they also expect the defendant to define himself and describe his activities in the best possible ways. They may be committed to being open-minded, but they know that if he is guilty, he will not admit it; *he will make every possible effort to keep his secrets.* Their job is to find the holes and inconsistencies in his story, to watch and listen to him carefully to see if he stumbles over his positive presentation of himself.

What I have just shared is a fictitious account of a trial in a courtroom. While this story is invented, it communicates enormously important lessons for the relationships of your life.

In times past, what we now refer to as *dating*, or getting to know an individual romantically, was called *courting*—and there is a reason for that. In a metaphorical way, courting people meant placing them on the "witness stand" and allowing them to testify about themselves. If you were the person trying to decide whether or not to proceed in a relationship, you would be seated in the jury box of the relationship in order to determine whether the person was telling the truth or hiding secrets. That kind of "courting" is still necessary today not only in potentially romantic alliances but in every kind of relationship. The ugly truth is that some people have deep secrets that influence every aspect of their lives, their personalities, and their relationships. Often, uncovering those secrets takes time, energy, and sensitivity, but it is a wise and important endeavor.

SHINE THE LIGHT INTO SECRET PLACES

I am sure you can think of stories or movies based on secrets. Sometimes the secret surrounds the location of a buried treasure. At other times it is a complicated, clandestine plot involving international espionage or an illicit love affair. As scripts and stories go, secrets can be intriguing, and trying to discover the truth can be intellectually invigorating. The opposite is true in relationships. Secrets can cause deep anguish, and getting to the truth can be tiring, frustrating, confusing, and even heartbreaking.

Most of us are familiar with the saying, "What you don't know won't hurt you." The problem with that assertion is that *it's wrong.* What we don't know *can* hurt us; in fact, it can destroy us and devastate our relationships. Secrets build invisible walls around us, walls that other people perceive but cannot penetrate. What we don't know also prevents transparency, openness, and intimacy. It forces us to tiptoe around certain subjects, and it will keep us from giving all of ourselves to another person and from fully receiving all the good others offer us. Keeping secrets will exhaust us, perhaps frighten us, and ultimately separate us from people we love and people who love us.

> *Most of us are familiar with the saying, "What you don't know won't hurt you." The problem with that assertion is that it's wrong. What we don't know can hurt us.*

While you cannot take responsibility for finding out the secrets of others, you *can* make sure that secrets do not hide inside you. In fact, one of the best ways to position yourself to be a strong, healthy contributor to every relationship is to make sure you live "in the light," free from the bondage and destructive influence of secrets (1 John 1:7).

This chapter is important because, while it does not focus as much as other chapters on interpersonal dealings with others, it explains one of the biggest barriers to intimacy and one of the most destructive forces in relationships—secrets. It will give you an opportunity to deal with this huge intimacy barrier in yourself so you can be a healthy, strong participant in great relationships. As you read the remainder of this chapter, I encourage you to ask yourself these questions:

- What is it about my thoughts, words, or actions that I do not want other people to know?
- What aspects of my thoughts, words, or actions do I wish God did not know?
- What am I most ashamed of about my past or about my life today?
- What am I most afraid to share with my spouse, potential spouse, or closest friends?

I realize you may not think you have any "deep, dark secrets," and perhaps you don't. But if there is even the *slightest* possibility you do, this chapter can set you free, change your life, and empower you to enjoy a quality of relationship with others you have never known before.

Everybody Can't Go Everywhere

You may remember that the strong, handsome biblical figure named Samson had a relationship with a beautiful and obviously irresistible woman named Delilah. Their interactions are proof positive that secrets can destroy both individuals and the relationships those individuals have with others. At the end of Samson and Delilah's story, in the process of seducing him, Delilah persuades him to tell her the secret of his strength, which is his hair. Later, as he sleeps, she cuts his hair, robbing him of the strength for which he is famous and leaving him weak and helpless (Judg. 16:16–20).

But the damaging effect of secrets in Samson's relationships did not start with Delilah and his hair. Samson had a pattern of establishing relationships that were not based on truth or authenticity. The evidence of this destructive pattern begins in Judges 14.

While visiting a place called Timnah, Samson catches his first glimpse of a woman (not Delilah) and decides immediately that she is the woman for him!

He says to his parents, "I have seen a woman in Timnah . . . get her for me as a wife" (Judg. 14:2 NKJV).

Because this woman is a Philistine, Samson's parents try to talk him out of a relationship with her.

Samson insists, "Get her for me, for she pleases me well" (Judg. 14:3 NKJV).

Samson's parents ultimately agree, not realizing their son's connection with the Philistines, with all its drama and turmoil, is part of God's plan to deliver His people from Philistine oppression.

Then the trouble starts. A seemingly innocent side trip around Timnah one day puts Samson on a precarious path. He decides, unwisely, to visit the nearby vineyards. Most likely the vineyard was a pleasant place—a nice area for people to visit. Most people probably had no reason to avoid it, but going there is a bad choice for Samson because he is a Nazarite, a person specially set apart for the purposes of God. Numbers 6:3–4 states clearly and firmly that a Nazarite must consecrate himself to the Lord:

He shall separate himself from wine and similar drink; he shall drink neither vinegar made from wine nor vinegar made from similar drink; neither shall he drink any grape juice, nor eat fresh grapes or raisins. All the days of his separation he shall eat nothing that is produced by the grapevine, from seed to skin. (NKJV)

As a Nazarite, Samson no doubt understood the commandment. When I read this passage, I cannot see that it leaves any room for misunderstanding or misinterpretation. The message is plain: "Stay away from grapes, from seed to skin!" In pronouncing the Nazarite vow, God includes strict prohibitions against wine, vinegar, grape juice, fresh grapes, and raisins.

Samson chooses to tread on dangerous ground when he goes to the vineyard. He intentionally places himself in the face of temptation. The Bible never tells us whether he ate a grape, chewed on a raisin, or had a few sips of wine in the vineyard; we simply know he was in a place he should not have been.

SECRET PLACES LEAD TO SECRET BATTLES

The next thing we know, Samson has a battle on his hands. I have a hard time believing that Samson gets caught off guard when a young lion roars at him in the vineyard, but Scripture clearly says he is surprised (Judg. 14:5). He knows the vineyard is not an acceptable place for him to be, so he really should not be shocked when he faces a threat as a result of being there.

When people take the risk of going to places they should not go, whether those are physical places like the vineyard in Timnah, emotional places such as jealousy or bitterness, "cyber" places such as pornographic websites, or places of bad habits or bad influences, trouble is always at hand. A battle is guaranteed to break out.

When Samson first compromises his Nazarite vow, he begins to lose everything God has for him. Not only that, but eventually he loses the presence of God Himself. Judges 16:20 tells us that "the LORD had departed from him" (NKJV). I do not think his life had to end that way, but at the same time I see clearly that he took his first step down a personally destructive path when he went to the vineyard.

Most people know instinctively what is off-limits for them. I suspect you know what is safe for you and what is not. Samson did, but he went to the vineyard anyway and nearly lost his life to a hungry lion cub. While he was aware that the vineyard was no place for him to be, he did not realize a vital truth that applies to everyone: secret places lead to secret battles.

When the young lion threatened Samson, the Spirit of God intervened and empowered him. God's action spared his life, but that did not keep Samson's problems from being multiplied. He not only had the issue of his morally illegal trip to the vineyard, but he also had a serious fight on his hands. When he killed the lion, he broke a second part of his Nazarite vow, touching a dead body (Num. 6:6). He must have suffered silently, because Judges 14:6 informs us that he did not tell his parents about the lion; he kept the matter a secret.

The worst thing about visiting secret places is that you cannot come and go without consequences. Secret places do lead to secret struggles, and a moment of secret sin can produce a lifetime of regret. Secret battles are the ones you fight in the loneliness of your own heart. Because they are secret, no one knows about them, so no one can help you win them.

Deal with It

In the pastorate, I have encountered far too many people who wage silent wars inside themselves. I tell them, "Whatever you won't deal with will ultimately deal with you." What I mean by that is, secrets gnaw on the fabric of your heart, erode your character, and steal your focus away from the people and things that truly need your attention. Once you get away with a small secret for a while, you begin to think you can get away with bigger things. At the same time, the enemy of your soul is at work bombarding your brain with all kinds of thoughts, such as:

- *As long as no one knows about this, it won't hurt anyone.*
- *You got away with this last time; you'll get away with it today.*
- *It really isn't all that bad. Just think about what other people do!*
- *Frankly, you will never be able to break this pattern, so you better just find better ways to hide it.*
- *If your spouse knew about this, he [or she] would leave you.*
- *If your boss knew about this, he [or she] would fire you.*
- *This is your best source of comfort or relief in life. Aren't you entitled to it?*

If these thoughts sound familiar, I hope you will realize you are not alone. Many, many people have secrets, some extremely shameful and painful. Certainly, some people's lives have been blessed in ways that enable them to avoid secrets, but as a pastor, I can assure you: more people have secrets than you think. Sometimes, the people you view as least likely to have anything to hide have the most to cover up. They have simply become experts at doing it.

I do not know whether you have a secret or not. That is between you and God. But I do know three key truths about secrets. First, if you do have a secret, you don't have to keep it. Second, if you have a secret, it *will* damage you and your relationships. Third, the minute you begin to deal with a secret, God will step in to help you, set you free, and lead you into a better life than you have ever known.

In my years of ministry, I have had the unfortunate opportunity of seeing secrets destroy the relationships and futures of several great people. On too many occasions I have had front-row seats as lives were devastated because of secrets. One instance stands out more than all the others.

John was blessed with a beautiful wife who loved him dearly, and he owned an extremely successful business. The growth and success of his business allowed him to hire and place both of his children in top positions in his company. But John had a terrible secret. Despite his wife's love, loyalty, and beauty, he had a mistress. Because of the financial burden of trying to take care of his family and the needs of his mistress, he took money illegally from his company and placed his children's careers in jeopardy. In the end, because of his mistress, his loving, faithful wife of so many years divorced him. His children—brokenhearted and shocked that their father had so little integrity—disowned him. His secret relationship with his mistress led to the destruction of everything he cared about.

Your Purpose Is Bigger than Your Problem

The best motivator I know to help people deal with secret places and win secret battles is this: *your purpose is bigger than your problem.* No matter which secret places you have visited or what secret struggles threaten to overwhelm you, you still have an awesome purpose and destiny. Regardless of your problem, God still loves you, still has a great plan for your life, and stands ready to help you and heal you.

I fully believe the best thing you can ever do for yourself and for your relationships, whether they are personal and intimate, professional, or social, is to expose your secret places and win your secret battles in wise, healthy ways. I want to remind you of a man I mentioned in chapter 3, a great and mighty warrior, a powerful poet and king: David. David's accolades and accomplishments were many. His psalms stir the hearts of faith-filled men and women to this day. But his sin was heinous. If anyone ever had a secret, David did, and it was not long before everyone around him knew it too.

To summarize the situation, let me simply say David was in the wrong place at the wrong time. One spring night, when the Bible says kings were supposed to be at war (2 Sam. 11:1), David instead stays in his palace, goes up to the roof, and catches sight of his beautiful neighbor, Bathsheba, bathing. He lusts, he acts on his lust, and she becomes pregnant.

In an attempt to hide his sexual sin, David calls Bathsheba's husband, Uriah, home from the battlefield, hoping he will sleep with her and people will think her child belongs to her husband. But Uriah is an honorable soldier and refuses to sleep with his wife that night because doing so is not right while his fellow soldiers are fighting an intense battle. Knowing he will soon be discovered because Uriah does not cooperate with his scheme, David sends Uriah to the front lines of the conflict, where he will certainly be killed. He does indeed become a casualty of war.

One of the great truths about David is not that he never had a problem or a struggle. Obviously, he did. A great truth is that he was humble and courageous enough to take responsibility for his sin, confess it to God, and admit it others. In Psalm 51, David's anguish and feelings of guilt are evident; his words are raw and intense. He deals with his secrets honestly and openly, admitting his wrongdoing, asking God to cleanse him completely, begging for a "clean heart," and beseeching God to allow him to continue in His presence, not to leave him or to take His Holy Spirit from him.

Once David deals with his secrets, he never fully escapes the consequences of them, but God does begin to turn his life around in certain ways. His life is not perfect; he does not get to do all the things he wants to accomplish for God or for the nation of Israel, but he goes on to live long and to complete an effective reign over God's people. Despite his sins, David's purpose was bigger than his problem. He had a tremendous call of God on his life—one he would not have fulfilled had he not acknowledged his sin, repented sincerely, received God's forgiveness, and been willing to move forward.

If there is a secret in your life, I urge you to believe that your purpose, too, is bigger than your problem. I pray you will realize in the most powerful ways how deeply and thoroughly God loves you and how much He wants to bring you out of every dark place you have been in and set you on a path of greatness. I trust that knowing God's love and believing He has great things in store for you will give you the courage to confront the secrets that have worked against you until now.

Different kinds of secrets must be dealt with in different ways. If you have a secret, do not think it won't hurt you or the relationships important to you. Understand that the secret is a part of who you are and that it works for your destruction in ways you may not realize. Take a step today to deal with that hidden shame, that addiction, that embarrassing physical or mental illness, those emotional patterns that are so destructive, that memory of something someone else did to you, or that past action you so deeply regret. Find people who are trustworthy (including clergy, physicians, or mental health professionals if necessary) and begin to shine a light on that dark place in your soul. I know the thought of sharing a secret may be frightening, but when you have found someone with whom you can safely share, take the risk. Doing so may save your marriage, your family, or your job. And it will definitely be a big step toward a brighter future for yourself and toward healthy relationships with others.

DON'T HESITATE TO PUT SOME PEOPLE ON TRIAL

At the beginning of this chapter, I noted that allowing a defendant to testify during legal proceedings is generally *not* a good idea, because the members of the jury expect that person to tell the story in a way that tries to prove he or she is innocent. Thankfully, many of us never have to take the stand in a courtroom, and we do not typically put other people on trial in a formal kind of way. Nevertheless, we would be wise to question and investigate the individuals with whom we consider entering into relationships more thoroughly than we often do. I say this because we can easily discover people's obvious characteristics. Are they outgoing and talkative or shy and reserved? What are their interests and activities? What are their favorite foods and colors? Early in relationships, we feel free to continue interacting with people as long as we do not see any blatant warning signs or causes for concern. Most of the time, it is not the obvious issues in people that cause the most trouble in relationships; it's the hidden things.

Some of the most profound hurts in my life have come from

people I failed to investigate thoroughly enough—people who had secrets. Just before writing this book, I entered into a relationship with a certain person thinking I really knew him. On the surface he appeared to care for me, my family, and my dreams. What I did not see was that at the core of his life festered secret jealousy and bitterness. As far as I could tell, he was rooting for me, but I did not know that behind the scenes he was undermining much of what I was trying to build. His secret was so well hidden, and I was so mistakenly convinced he was on my team, that someone else had to tell me what he was doing before I realized the truth. While the reality of the truth was extremely disappointing and hurtful, I had to admit to myself that I had not investigated this individual thoroughly enough and should not have entered into the relationship.

Many other people have stories similar to mine. While I think most people would really like to be able to trust others, a lot of us have lived long enough to understand that trust must be earned. Let me encourage you not to hesitate to put some people on trial before moving to a deeper level of relationship. Go ahead and ask personal questions. Initiate discussions about attitudes or behaviors that concern you. At the appropriate time and in an appropriate way, which only you can know, do not be afraid to ask people what their secrets are.

People with serious secrets may not be forthcoming with answers, but take notice of the way they handle the question. Does it seem to make them nervous? Does their body language change? Do they immediately switch to another topic of conversation? Do they laugh at you or become defensive? These types of responses may indicate that something negative or potentially damaging lurks beneath the surface and needs to be investigated more fully.

People who do not have anything to cover up or be ashamed

of do not usually give the impression of trying to hide something. When you suspect a secret, trust your instincts. You may be wrong; but you may be right. If you are correct, you will save yourself tremendous potential heartache or damage later on. If you uncover a secret, you can help a person deal with it constructively. Or, you may realize an issue is so severe that you must exit the relationship for your own good.

Though we do need to make some effort to find out whether the people we are in relationships with have things hidden under the visible level of their lives, we are limited in our ability to unearth other people's secrets. We do, however, have complete control over our own lives and the way we handle things we choose to do. We can create and keep our personal secrets, or we can live openly and transparently with our trusted friends and colleagues. We can set ourselves up for disappointment and harm, which may impact people we care about, or we can position ourselves for great relationships by being honest about our temptations and failings instead of trying to excuse them or hide them.

RELATIONSHIP REMINDERS

- Some individuals harbor deep secrets that affect every area of their lives, their personalities, and their relationships.
- Uncovering people's secrets usually takes time, energy, and sensitivity, but doing so is worth the effort because secrets can cause great pain in relationships.
- Secrets form an enormous barrier to intimacy and are extremely destructive forces in relationships.

- When people risk going to places they should not go, trouble is at hand.
- Whatever you won't deal with will ultimately deal with you.
- Your purpose is bigger than your problem. Keep believing God has something great for you and that dealing with your problem is a necessary step toward it.
- Don't be reluctant or hesitant to investigate people thoroughly before developing relationships with them.

RAISING YOUR RELATIONAL IQ

1. What is your secret?
2. How has your secret negatively affected your personal life and your relationships?
3. Are any of your current relationships in jeopardy because of your secret? If so, explain the problem and elaborate on why your secret is destroying the relationship.
4. Can you safely share your secret with one or two trustworthy people? Who are they? Do not hesitate to seek professional help if you need to do so.
5. Take a look at 1 John 1:7, 9. How do these verses encourage and strengthen you on a personal level when you think about sharing your secret?
6. Have you properly assessed the people in your life to know if they have secrets? If not, describe an appropriate situation in which you might take the first step.

8

The Most Valuable People Aren't Always the Most Visible

THE LAW OF TRUE VALUE

I ALMOST BLEW IT! BIG-TIME.

I married a beautiful, smart, gracious, God-loving, family-centered woman, but before I asked her to be my wife, I have to be honest: I almost messed up everything! Ty was my friend long before I fell in love with her. While we were both single, we spent time together and we enjoyed a good, healthy, platonic relationship. She was a constant source of prayer, support, encouragement, and friendship for me. She even listened to my dating woes and endured my ramblings about the kind of wife I thought I wanted. I appreciated her, respected her, and regarded her as a great friend—while I kept looking for a wife who met superficial criteria I now know to be totally unimportant!

The longer Ty and I remained friends, the more I began to realize she was exactly the person God had for me. She had every quality I needed, but I had spent so much time searching for something else that I completely overlooked the values and gifts that make her who she is. Now I thank God every day for saving me from the personal disaster that would have resulted had I not married Ty. I do not think I would be half the person I am without her. Her faith, encouragement, prayer, and support have been vital to my life and purpose.

Unquestionably, my wife is the most valuable person in my life, but there was a time when I completely overlooked her. I learned then what I want to share with you in this chapter—that the most valuable people in our lives are not always the most visible ones. We do not always recognize how important certain people are, especially if they prefer not to be in the spotlight but choose to love and support us in unseen ways.

> *The most valuable people in our lives are not always the most visible ones.*

THE WILLIAMSPORT WONDER

Even people who do not keep up with Little League baseball or often watch sports turned their attention to Williamsport, Pennsylvania, and tuned in to the 2012 Little League World Series. It was a contest full of great stories, including the one about an inspiring team from Uganda—the first ever from Africa—who won the hearts of players and spectators everywhere and took home the sportsmanship award.

These ball games truly are a *world* series. Unlike the major-league event that happens every fall in the United States and only involves American teams, the Little League games draw teams from across the globe. The heavy favorite in 2012 was the team from Japan; no one familiar with the series really expected anyone else to win. So the question became, who would win the US title?

The winning team came from Goodlettsville, Tennessee, a little-known, hardworking, historic town just north of Nashville. They had only had an official Little League team for two years. Their manager is a firefighter who built a pitching mound in the backyard of his firehouse and whose father serves as his assistant coach. They were not expected to win it all, but with great attitudes, terrific sportsmanship, courage, and refusal to quit when they were down by ten runs at one point—not to mention some out-of-the-park grand slams and stellar pitching—the team won a hard-fought battle for the US title game 24-16 over Petaluma, California. Sports writers dubbed it "the Williamsport Wonder."

My wife and I have a friend in the Goodlettsville area. She told me about the overwhelming excitement and pride the community felt and the way they banded together to support their hometown players. After the series, when the team arrived home by bus at Goodlettsville City Hall in the sweltering heat of an August afternoon, more than a thousand people erupted in cheers and waved homemade banners congratulating their young heroes.

One thing that caught our friend's attention was the fact that the mayor of Goodlettsville had several opportunities to speak to the team and the crowds who gathered to celebrate them. Every time, he applauded and congratulated the boys, but he never failed to also mention their parents, who sacrificed tremendously for their sons' amazing victory.

The mayor knew something the boys might not have realized in the midst of their appearances on ESPN and ABC, their phone call from the president of the United States, and their congressional resolution. He knew they could never have won a single game without dedicated parents and guardians who took them to practice, encouraged them, fed them, cared for them, and washed their uniforms. Perhaps some of these parents gave up a family vacation or rest and relaxation during the summertime to make the trip to Williamsport instead. Some parents gave brief television interviews, but they never spoke of how hard *they* worked to get their sons into the national spotlight. They just talked about the team and displayed appropriate parental pride and joy in their young men.

I even heard about one mother, not from the Tennessee team, whose boss threatened to fire her if she used her earned vacation days to watch her son play and her husband coach for their West Coast team. She went to the series, and she lost her job. That was the sacrifice she chose to make, but few people knew about it until the games were over and her story hit the media.

These dedicated, enthusiastic Little League parents made the dreams of their sons, the coaches, and their community come true. Generally speaking, they were not highly visible, but they were indispensably valuable.

A Birther of Destiny

Just as it seems the Goodlettsville Little League team was destined to win the national championship in 2012, you also have a destiny. God has a great purpose for your life, and whether you are old or young, that purpose can be fulfilled. It may require hard work, good thinking, and some sacrifices. It will most likely mean that you need the right relationships in your life—relationships of true value. This was certainly the case for a man named Moses. One of the most famous stories about Moses is about God speaking to him from a burning bush. In that moment, God gives him a huge assignment and calls him to the weighty task of delivering His people, the children of Israel, from more than four hundred years of Egyptian bondage (Ex. 3:1–10).

Moses is a great hero of the Christian and Jewish faiths—a man who gains God's trust and who has even been called God's friend. When Moses died, God Himself reached down and buried him (Deut. 34:6). Even though Moses clearly had a remarkably intimate relationship with God, he also had a lot of problems. Moses did not immediately embrace everything God asked of him. He was not strong and courageous in the face of his call as Israel's deliverer; he was fearful, intimidated, and afraid he would not be able to speak. He asks God to send someone else to complete the task (Ex. 4:13). Clearly angry, God suggests that Moses' older brother, Aaron, accompany him (Ex. 4:14). Knowing Aaron will go with him and speak to the Egyptian Pharaoh on his behalf, Moses ultimately says yes to the challenge.

After Moses accepts the call and heads toward Egypt with his family, something curious happens: the Lord shows up to kill him (Ex. 4:24). What on earth could have happened for God to so trust and favor Moses one day, then prepare to take his life so soon afterward? The answer is clear: Moses failed to obey one of God's vital commandments. He did not circumcise his young son Eliezer.

I cannot overemphasize the importance of circumcision. This ritual was the sign of God's covenant people, and as we can see from God's strong response toward Moses' failure to do it, it was highly significant. Perhaps Moses was so busy on his trip to Egypt that he simply forgot to circumcise his son, which means he ignored the covenant. Or maybe, as some scholars suggest, Moses became ill as a precursor to the death planned for him. Whatever his reason for not performing the important procedure, it was a massive mistake.

But Moses' wife, Zipporah, saw what was happening and inter-vened. She circumcised her son and touched Moses' feet with the foreskin. This action saved Moses' life, putting him in a position to fulfill God's call and ensure the deliverance of an entire nation. Without Zipporah's sensitivity to the situation and willingness to do what needed to be done, Moses would have no doubt been killed. Instead, according to Exodus 4:26, the Lord "let him go" (NKJV) and spared his life.

The point of this story is that relationships of true value help position you and prepare you for your destiny. Before God could use Moses in a mighty way, he needed to prove himself faithful over his own household; he had to be trustworthy in little things before he could be trusted to do great things. Zipporah knew this and she helped him. Especially if experts are correct and Moses was indeed ill and weak, then Zipporah literally intervened to do what he may have been physically unable to do.

I wonder how many believers would immediately remember Zipporah's name if asked to identify Moses' wife. She is rarely men-tioned as one of the leading ladies of Scripture, but she is vital to her husband's destiny and to the destiny of her nation. She has never been highly *visible*, as women such as Ruth, Esther, Deborah, and Mary have been as biblical figures, but she is unspeakably *valuable*!

A PERFORMANCE-ENHANCING PERSON

As the story continues, Aaron and Moses begin a series of conversa-tions with Pharaoh. Throughout their interaction, Pharaoh makes the Israelites' labor in Egypt increasingly difficult, and the people, who had viewed Moses as their deliverer, begin to doubt him. Finally, God puts Aaron in the forefront. God speaks to Moses, giving him directions about what to say to Pharaoh. Moses tells Aaron what to say, and Aaron says it.

What arrests my attention about this scenario is that we do not see Aaron demonstrating any real moral support or encouragement to Moses. He simply does his job, and that is to boost Moses' performance—to help him do what needs to be done.

Think about Aaron in comparison to the brief but powerful insights Moses' story provides into Zipporah's role. Scripture does not offer much for us to read about her, but we know that she was part of Moses' life, adding value to him at the most critical times. While Aaron was in Moses' life to help him perform, Zipporah was in his life to help prepare him for greatness. Without her, Moses would never have been able to stand in front of Pharaoh to ask for the release of God's people. He would never have moved beyond the moment when he was almost killed.

Moses' story reminds me of so many modern-day scenarios. For example, have you ever heard about young women or men who work hard to put their spouses through medical, law, or business school? These dedicated husbands and wives put in long hours and overtime to supplement their meager budgets because they know their sacrifices now will lead the couple into a prosperous future. Sadly, some of those well-educated husbands and wives receive these impressive degrees, land amazing jobs, and finally start making a little money, only to meet someone new as a result of the new career—someone more stunning, exciting, and seemingly much more ambitious than the current spouse, who worked to support them as much as possible and put them through school.

Or what about professional athletes whose wives sacrifice, uprooting their lives and their children every time a new team comes calling? Then, when that athlete finally gets a big break, he forgets about the people at home and abandons them for a well-built, attractive cheerleader or fan. Later, when injury takes the athlete out of the spotlight and down on the pay scale, the cheerleader or fan loses interest. The athlete takes his shattered dreams and empty life somewhere else and sells real estate or used cars. That promising player could have had a safe, secure, loving relationship to go home to, had he only valued those who helped him reach stardom in the first place.

These kinds of scenarios play out far too often, and they are always heartbreaking. One person stands by another and helps make his or her dreams come true, only to be abandoned later for someone "better" or "more appropriate" for the dreamer's new status. But the supportive spouse was extremely valuable—much more valuable, in fact, than the dreamer ever realized.

We must understand that the people who sacrifice for us and support us when we are first starting out, when no one knows our names, while we are still struggling to make our dreams come true—those are the people who will most likely be there when we hit a rough spot on life's journey. Why? Because those are the people who are truly valuable to us.

OH, BROTHER!

Of all the siblings listed in Scripture, Moses and Aaron may be the best-known Old Testament pair. When the two brothers are mentioned together in Scripture, it's often in a less complimentary way toward Aaron. The text infers that, aside from being able to speak clearly, Aaron really was not very valuable to Moses. Granted, there was the time when Aaron and Hur held up Moses' arms because that's what was necessary for the Israelites to gain victory over the Amalekites (Ex. 17:10–15). But that day, the lives of all Israel were at stake. Aaron not only helped Moses but he also saved his own life and the lives of his fellow Israelites. If he could not come through in a desperate moment such as that one, then he and Moses were both in big trouble.

While Aaron was extremely visible in the nation of Israel because of his role as high priest, he was not particularly valuable to Moses. If we look at the arc of his service to Moses and to the Israelites and examine the big picture of Aaron's life, we can see he did rally in an important moment. But over the long term, he caused problems for his brother.

In one of Scripture's most intimate stories about the relationship between God and a human being, God invites Moses into His presence on Mount Sinai. There, He speaks to Moses, giving him the Ten Commandments and offering direction and guidance about a number of matters pertaining to the Israelites. This had to be an awesome experience for Moses.

One reason God handles the situation on Mount Sinai as He does—covering the mountain with smoke and allowing the people to hear him speaking to Moses—is so the people will trust Moses wholeheartedly (Ex. 19:9). God wants them to know they have a faithful, trustworthy leader. But instead of patiently waiting for him to come down from the mountain, they grow anxious and frustrated, even saying, "As for this fellow Moses who brought us up out of Egypt, we don't know what has happened to him" (Ex. 32:1).

Having lost hope in Moses, the people demand that Aaron make them an idol. The biblical story includes no protest from Aaron at all. He does not resist making the idol in the form of a golden calf, nor does he remind the people that they are not to have any gods before the Lord or to worship idols. He simply says, "Okay. Give me your gold jewelry and I'll make you something."

God becomes angry at the sight of the Israelites worshipping this calf, so He sends Moses down the mountain to confront them, interrupting what must have been his greatest-ever time of communion and delight with God. This, to me, is one of the most heartbreaking moments in the Bible and of Moses' entire tenure of leadership. Not only does Moses lose his intimate fellowship with God, he must also acknowledge that his own brother cannot be trusted to keep the Israelites faithful to their God or to protect him during this vital time of communion and revelation.

Another sad reality of this story is that I am convinced Moses really thought he needed Aaron. He must not have realized that he had other great people around him, such as Zipporah and her father, Jethro, who gave him excellent leadership advice (Ex. 18:13–24). Instead of keeping Zipporah close to him, we read in Exodus 18 that he sends her back to her father. Though the text does not state exactly why he does this, one point seems clear: he still does not value her. He continues to lean on Aaron.

Thinking about Moses, Zipporah, and Aaron, I wonder how many of us are in relationships we do not need because we think we cannot do without them. How many of us allow ourselves to be hindered and frustrated by people who are very visible, but not really very valuable in our lives?

THE VISIBLE AND THE VALUABLE

You may remember the television series *The Andy Griffith Show*. Griffith played Sheriff Andy Taylor of Mayberry, and Don Knotts played his eager but awkward, not-so-bright deputy, Barney Fife. Barney loved his uniform and his badge; he relished the authority and exposure he received as an officer of the law—but the fact is, he wasn't good at it! He often botched simple operations and served to exasperate Andy much more than he ever really assisted him. Yet when there was a spotlight to be shone, Barney made his way into it. Barney was extremely visible, but despite his position as Andy's deputy, he hindered Andy's work much more than he helped it.

The person of true value in Andy's life was his Aunt Bea. She was the one who opened her home to him, fed him, and cared for him—a widower—and for his young son, Opie. Andy could not have done what he did in the town of Mayberry had Aunt Bea not acted behind the scenes. She was not the center of attention, but she played a critical role in his success.

Though Andy and Mayberry hark back to a time long past, similar scenarios involving visible people versus valuable people continue to unfold today. I have mentioned the US Champion Little League team. But think also about a CEO of a large company. This person may have a CFO or an executive vice president who is well educated, well-spoken, well dressed, and highly visible. But it may be the assistant who has provided twenty years of faithful service who *really* keeps the CEO going. Beyond that, it may be the wife of thirty years who keeps him grounded, motivated, and healthy.

We all have certain people in our lives who are or want to be visible, and we all have those who are truly valuable. My wife, Ty, like many pastors' wives, is acquainted with a lot of people. She sees many of them often. But one of the most valuable people in her life is a friend who lives several states away from us. The two of them cannot get together frequently, but every time they talk, they both end up refreshed and encouraged. These two women rarely make personal appearances in each other's lives, though they do sacrifice in order to see each other from time to time. Ty's long-distance friend has demonstrated the qualities of a person of true value over a long period of time, and her lack of visibility in our lives in no way translates to a lack of value or importance.

The key to success in relationships and in life is to know the difference between those individuals who are simply visible in our lives and those who are genuinely valuable. So how do you recognize people of true value? Let me offer a few important observations about this from Moses, Zipporah, and Aaron.

People of true value seek to please God, not to gain others' approval.

One of the biggest problems Aaron causes is the construction of the golden calf—an idol—for the Israelites to worship while Moses is on Mount Sinai, receiving the Ten Commandments from God. On every level, this is an appalling, disastrous, altogether *wrong* thing to do!

When Moses angrily questions Aaron about this offense toward God, he whimpers a pitiful excuse: "The people made me do it" (Ex. 32:22–23).

This is outrageous! Aaron would become the high priest of Israel; he is Moses' right-hand man. He is a leader. In fact, while Moses is on Mount Sinai, he is the only visible leader of the nation. And he allows the people for whom he is responsible to pressure him into abandoning the God he serves and to lead them into idolatry and sin.

When we think about all the trouble Aaron causes, we see that he does so simply because he compromises his integrity and his principles in the midst of pressure from the people. But if we remember Zipporah, we see that she serves God's purpose instead of stirring up problems for Moses. When she circumcises Eliezer, she honors God. We never see in Scripture that Zipporah is a people pleaser, as Aaron is. She is a God pleaser who honors His covenant and helps Moses—His chosen leader—fulfill His plan.

People who add value to your life will honor God above all.

They will not bow to peer pressure. They will be secure enough in who they are that they really do not care whether others approve of them, as long as God is pleased.

People of true value bring fulfillment, not frustration, to those with whom they are in relationships.

Aaron is *not* helpful. More than anything else, he is a source of frustration to Moses. Ultimately, he also causes frustration for the children of Israel because instead of encouraging them to worship the God who loves them and is leading them to a good place, he helps them worship an idol that has no power at all. Anytime people put their hope in something that does not deliver, frustration results, but that's exactly what Aaron both allows and facilitates.

When Moses finds out what Aaron has done, he is furious! He throws down the Ten Commandments and then has to return to Mount Sinai to get them again. The first time, God writes the commandments for him with His own finger. The second time, Moses has to etch them in stone himself, which costs him and the nation of Israel a lot of time.

Zipporah, in contrast, definitely helps Moses. She helps save his life, she helps ensure his family's faithfulness to God's covenant, and she helps position him to be fulfilled as a leader. Because of her role in Moses' life, she not only propels him to his destiny, she also helps fulfill God's plan for the entire nation of Israel.

For some reason, no matter how much frustration Aaron causes Moses, Moses stays in close relationship with him. Many people today make the same mistake. It happens in businesses (especially family businesses) and work environments; it happens in churches and social settings. Sometimes frustrating people are allowed to stay in certain situations because "they've always been there," or sometimes they have something to offer—perhaps financial resources—that others believe they cannot do without. The fact is, people who have a habit and a history of causing trouble will not provide rewarding relationships for you or help you fulfill your destiny.

I will address in a later chapter some of the ways to get these people out of the forefront of your life and into a more appropriate place. For now, just know that one of the best things you can do for yourself and the people around you is to minimize trouble by sidelining the frustrating people who want to attach themselves to you.

People of true value take joy in helping prepare others for greatness instead of taking pride in their own accomplishments.

After Aaron completes the golden calf, he builds an altar to it. Not only has he turned his back on God and led the people to do likewise, he seems proud of it. We do not see in Scripture how Zipporah responds to the ways she helped Moses, but we also do not see any evidence of her gloating, taking credit for keeping Moses alive, or celebrating her lifesaving action. The text seems to infer that she simply does what needs to be done and goes about her business. Zipporah perceives God's call of greatness on Moses' life, and she does everything in her power to help him answer it well. We do not know for certain, but I suspect she finds great fulfillment in doing so because of her genuine love for God and her obvious love for her husband.

Most people who are truly valuable in your life will not stop to call attention to all they have done for you. Sure, they may be aware of it, but they do not dwell on what they have done; they focus on what you are doing. They are happy to help you reach your goals and live your dreams. They do not repeatedly remind you of how much they have helped you, but they take as much joy from helping you get to your destination as you take in being there.

RELATIONSHIP REMINDERS

- The most visible people around you are not always the ones who add the most value to your life.
- Sometimes, people you may take for granted or be tempted to overlook are the ones who save your life or launch you into your destiny.
- You can absolutely depend on people who are truly valuable to be there for you during critical times in your life.
- The most visible people in your life may not help you very much; they may actually hinder you.
- People of true value seek to please God, and they bring fulfillment, not frustration, to your life. They will also take joy in preparing you for greatness instead of taking pride in what they do for you.

RAISING YOUR RELATIONAL IQ

1. Who are the most visible people in your life?
2. Who are the most valuable people in your life? Why is each one valuable to you?
3. Who has done something significant for you, as Zipporah did for Moses? Have you thanked that person? Do you continue to honor him or her in your life by being loyal?

4. One of the sad facts of the story of Moses and Aaron is that Moses truly thought he needed Aaron, when in reality, he probably didn't. With enough confidence in God and the right people around him, he could have succeeded without Aaron's help. Is there anyone in your life you *think* you need, but who really is causing frustration and sending your destiny on a detour?

5. When you think about the characteristics of truly valuable people, how do you think you may need to improve your relational skills so you can be valuable to others?

9

Is That Person *Really*
on Your Side?

THE LAW OF LOYALTY

ON JUNE 27, 1880, IN TUSCUMBIA, ALABAMA, not too far from where I live in Birmingham, a baby girl was born. Her senses of sight and hearing were intact at birth, but before she reached the age of two, the child had contracted an illness that has never been officially identified except to be called "brain fever." This condition left her completely deaf and blind for the rest of her life. Her name was Helen Keller.

I have mentioned Helen Keller in numerous messages over the years, primarily because she overcame enormous obstacles to accomplish great things, such as graduating from Radcliffe College and authoring twelve books. She made amazing contributions to society in spite of her handicaps. If I ever need an illustration about overcoming adversity, Helen Keller provides one! Her accomplishments were many, and she received several prestigious awards, including the Presidential Medal of Freedom.

Unable to see or hear, Helen Keller could never have impacted the world as she did without a great deal of assistance. The person who helped her most was her teacher, Anne Sullivan, who was also visually impaired but not completely blind. Sullivan arrived at Helen's house to become her full-time teacher in 1887, gave her a doll as a gift and proceeded to write "d-o-l-l" in the palm of Helen's hand. That one word was the beginning of a relationship that lasted forty-nine years.

The relationship between Helen and Anne was not always pleasant, especially in the beginning. The play *The Miracle Worker,* and the movie by the same name, tell their story and depict Helen as a temperamental child, given to rage at times because of her frustrations with her physical limitations. Sullivan persevered and remained loyal to her pupil, and Helen remained loyal to her teacher.

Sullivan accompanied Helen from Alabama to various schools for deaf and blind students in the northeastern United States. After Helen's graduation from high school, Sullivan continued with her to Radcliffe, continually helping Helen and ensuring that she received the best possible education. After Sullivan married, Helen continued to live with her teacher and Sullivan's husband.

As Helen gained national and international prominence, the two traveled throughout the United States and to more than forty countries. When Sullivan's health began to fail in her later years, she hired a housekeeper, whom she trained to be Helen's new caregiver. Sullivan died in 1936, with Helen at her side.

The story of Helen Keller and Anne Sullivan is a remarkable account of loyalty. Though I can imagine that the challenges and frustrations must have been intense at times, Sullivan never left Helen for an easier job. In addition, she made sure Helen reached her full potential, not simply learning to read or write but earning a college degree and gaining worldwide acclaim for her amazing accomplishments.

Loyalty is an incredibly powerful force for good in any relationship. In contrast, betrayal is one of the most hurtful and most negative things that can happen between two people. When loyalty is present, as it was with Helen Keller and Anne Sullivan, a relationship can soar to incredible heights. But when loyalty is lacking, the results can be devastating. To illustrate the damage a lack of loyalty can do, I would like to share some additional insights about a man I mentioned in chapters 3 and 7, King David.

Loyalty is an incredibly powerful force for good in any relationship. In contrast, betrayal is one of the most hurtful and most negative things that can happen between two people.

THE FIRST STEP IN THE WRONG DIRECTION

In chapter 7, I summarized the story of David's adulterous encounter with his beautiful neighbor Bathsheba. Let's review the story here. When Bathsheba becomes pregnant after David sleeps with her, David calls her husband, Uriah, home from battle, hoping everyone will think her child belongs to him. But Uriah acts honorably and does not sleep with her during a time of war; instead he sleeps at the entrance of the palace (see 2 Samuel 11:9). When David finds out Uriah does not sleep in his own bedroom with his wife, he makes a disastrous decision: he sends Uriah to the front lines of the battle, where he will surely be killed. And that's exactly what happens.

I submit to you that, surprisingly, it is not David's illicit relationship with Bathsheba that precipitates his downfall. It is his relationship with her *husband*, Uriah, a skilled warrior and dedicated member of David's army—a man whom David betrayed and had killed. While David's sin with Bathsheba is significant and cannot be overlooked, his sin against Uriah ultimately causes him to suffer even more than his actions with her. If we can understand who David was in relation to Uriah, and vice versa, we can gain vital insight into not only the dynamics of loyalty within the relationship between those two men centuries ago, but also within the relationships that shape our lives today.

It Is Bigger than Bathsheba

Among the unsavory stories in the Bible, David's first encounter with Bathsheba typically emerges as shocking and offensive to some people who hate to see a biblical hero fall. To others, David's story is comforting, because they know too well what it's like to love God but to allow a moral failure along life's journey. All kinds of things have been written and said about David and Bathsheba, but not much has been said concerning David and Uriah. For our purposes in this chapter, this relationship teaches us the most valuable lessons about loyalty, ourselves, and others.

When thinking about David, we must never forget that he was the king. People looked up to him, admired him, and respected him. Some men, a group called "David's mighty men" even risked their lives for him and his cause (2 Sam. 23:8). This band of brothers performed great exploits on behalf of David's administration. We learn from 1 Chronicles 11:41 that Uriah was one of these mighty men. He, like the others, was profoundly loyal to David, but later we learn that David was not at all loyal to him.

Just as Brutus did to the Roman emperor Julius Caesar when

he betrayed and killed him, David violated the brotherhood by the way he treated Uriah. In this case, David the leader was the treacherous, ungrateful man, while Uriah, his faithful soldier, proved to be the loyal one.

A MURDER IN THE FIRST DEGREE

In the United States, when a person is charged with first-degree murder, the charge relates to willful, premeditated killing. In contrast, though they do not carry the weight of an official legal charge, we also hear about "crimes of passion," meaning actions taken spontaneously as a result of intense emotion. The difference between David's sin with Bathsheba and his sin against Uriah is that his actions against Uriah were premeditated and deliberate, while his behavior with Bathsheba came about as a quick reaction to a sight that stirred his passion. For this reason, I believe God's judgment toward David had more to do with what he did to Uriah than with his affair with Bathsheba. Let me explain.

In 2 Samuel 12:9–15, when God pronounces judgment on David through Nathan the prophet, Uriah is mentioned three times while Bathsheba is never named; instead she is referred to as *wife* twice. This highlights her relationship to Uriah more than her individuality. David's sin certainly involves her, but the biblical account is more focused on her *as she is connected to Uriah* than on her tryst with David.

The fact that Uriah is mentioned by name three times in only a few verses demonstrates the literary device of repetition, used throughout Scripture to indicate emphasis or importance. Often in the Bible, certain stories, subjects, and ideas of importance are mentioned more than once.

In another account of David's life, 1 Kings 15:5 praises him, saying, "David had done what was right in the eyes of the LORD and had not failed to keep any of the LORD's commands all the days of his life—*except in the case of Uriah the Hittite*" (emphasis added). This verse does not even mention his sin with Bathsheba; it focuses entirely on the incident with Uriah as David's great transgression. This passage, and the 1 Samuel passage with its use of repetition and its mention of Bathsheba only in her role as a wife, lead me to believe God was more displeased with David's attitude and behavior toward Uriah than with his alliance with Bathsheba.

HAVE YOU EVER MET A DISLOYAL LEADER?

Without question, David was a terribly disloyal leader where Uriah was concerned. Unfortunately, leaders today can still be just as disloyal as David was. Great pain and disappointment can result when you have come to trust someone in a position of leadership in your life and then discover that person has not been loyal to you. When you do what Uriah did and give your loyalty to someone who does not appreciate it or who even abuses it, the wound can be deep.

Everyone—from a stay-at-home mom to a CEO—relates to leaders on some level. I pray you have had great leaders in your life who have affirmed you, recognized your potential, and helped you become all you can be. I also know that, sadly, some leaders pursue positions of influence and authority for the wrong reasons, and they end up hurting the people who look up to them. If you have ever suffered because a leader was more loyal to himself than to those he was called to serve, I hope you will find healing, strength, and encouragement in the insights I would like to share about David in this section.

David was a gifted and excellent leader in many ways. I want to emphasize the fact that I appreciate and celebrate David's many good qualities. In no way do I desire to cast aspersions on a truly great man of God as I point out some specifics of his unrighteous behavior toward Uriah. I do so in an attempt to learn from his life. The fact is, in spite of the strong leadership skills David displayed during many critical moments, he was a leadership failure where Uriah was concerned. This happened not because of a lack of leadership abilities and acumen, but because a vein of disloyalty ran through this otherwise great leader's heart.

This situation with David is still common today. Maybe you know what I mean. For example, perhaps your son's coach is brilliant with x's and o's and the execution of smart plays. Perhaps he pats team members on the back when they do well and maintains a positive attitude on the field and in the locker room. But underneath the facade, he is more loyal to winning championships and gaining accolades for himself than he is to the well-being of his players. Or maybe the CEO of a midlevel company has outstanding skills as a business leader, and maybe she even knows how to inspire loyalty among her employees. But the truth is, she has a manipulative heart, wanting to be well thought of in her industry so she can continue to reach new heights on the corporate ladder. She is not nearly as loyal to her employees as they are to her; she is only loyal to herself and to the acclaim, perks, benefits, and feelings of power she can enjoy as long as others do what she wants. She uses others to make her look good so when the time is right, she can move to a more prestigious position.

The problem with disloyal leaders—whether they are leading teams, businesses, families, churches, or civic organizations—is that disloyalty is not always easy to identify. It can be much more subtle than blatant dishonesty or an obviously disrespectful attitude. Often when disloyalty is a problem, people simply feel that something about the leader "just isn't right."

Speaking the language of loyalty is easy. A leader may have no trouble making comments such as, "We'll all benefit from meeting our quotas this month, so get out there and sell, sell, sell!" Or, "If you hit a home run, the whole team wins, so go knock it out of the park!" These kinds of comments are fine when they are genuine and when they are motivated by an authentic desire for the good of a group. But when a leader really could not care less about the group and simply wants to use everyone involved to help reach his or her personal goals, that's troubling. Interacting with a disloyal leader almost always causes pain, and the best way to keep ourselves from being hurt and used is to learn to identify them.

Throughout Scripture, one of the ways God teaches us the lessons we need to know is through stories. While the story of David and Uriah does not highlight David's good points, it does provide critical insights that will help us choose wise, loyal leaders and avoid those who would be disloyal. Maybe that's why the Bible includes it.

Before pointing out some of the warning signs of disloyal leaders, I want to say that I am well acquainted with a number of secular leadership teachings and programs. I recognize that the world rarely emphasizes the importance of being loyal to the people you serve. Perhaps you are a leader in some arena and the idea of the value of loyalty simply has not significantly impacted your thinking or your style as a leader. If, as you read the remainder of this section, you realize that you have been like David in certain ways, be encouraged. Allow these insights to be catalysts for change, not tools for feeling guilty. Put them to work and let them make you a better leader than you ever have been before.

A disloyal leader holds others to a standard he is not personally willing to meet.

When David inquires about Bathsheba, one of his servants

tells him she is married (2 Sam. 11:3); yet David still sends for her and has sex with her in the royal palace. I have to wonder how this affects the servant. He clearly sees that David is committing adultery. David knows the Mosaic law concerning adultery (Lev. 20:10). He is aware that sleeping with another man's wife is a sin against God, and he willfully disobeys. Maybe he does not remember the Mosaic law in the heat of his passion, but I have to believe that because he had walked with God for a long time, he knows he is in rebellion.

When David asks his servant to get Bathsheba, he expects the servant to obey him, but he himself does not obey the commands of God. This kind of double standard is common in people who are disloyal. They expect others to follow "the rules," but do not abide by those same rules themselves.

When I planted the church I now pastor, my wife and I decided we would be the top givers, financially speaking. This is not always easy for us. There are certainly people in the church who earn more than we do, but we do not want anyone to outgive us because we know that we cannot expect the people who enjoy and participate in the church to give at a higher level than we do. When I teach on finances, tithing, or giving, I do so knowing that I am not asking anyone else to do what my family and I are not doing. This is the only way I know to lead with integrity—to lead by example. In the case of Bathsheba, we see David's character when he refuses to subject himself to the same standards he expects others to maintain.

A disloyal leader does not fight for or with those who support and fight for him.

We know from Scripture that David was a warrior. In his day, standard practice for a king was to fight *for* and *with* his people. That was expected of David; it was what he had always done. In fact, earlier in David's life we read that he fought alongside his men, as a good military leader would have. He was so loyal to them that when they brought him water to drink without having any for themselves, he refused to drink it out of solidarity with them (1 Chron. 11:15–19). Obviously, the connection he had with his men was strong; his loyalty at that time was unquestionable.

When David met Bathsheba, his troops were engaged in a major conflict. This key battle was against a formidable foe, the Ammonites, in their main city, Rabbah. While his men were entrenched in enemy territory, fighting fiercely for him and for his kingdom, David seems to have been lazing around the palace. For some reason he was no longer loyal to many of the things he valued, accomplished, or upheld in his past. For all practical purposes, the soldiers' leader, King David, had abandoned them.

I can only imagine how alone David's army must have felt. They were accustomed to having their strong and wise king in their midst, right there with them in the fight. But he was not there.

Some of the most painful times in my ministry came in the early years, when I tried my best to be a great member of a team, when I worked and fought to accomplish someone else's vision, and that leader abandoned me. I know how heartbreaking those dynamics can be, and I am sure Uriah and the other soldiers were hurt by David's absence while they risked their lives for him.

A disloyal leader is more concerned about self-interest than corporate purpose.

If ever a corporate purpose is at stake, it is during a time of war. In the battle with the Ammonites, Israel's purpose was certainly threatened, and the need for triumph was great. In 1 Samuel 21:5 David expressed the importance of the soldiers' abstaining from sex during military campaigns. Clearly, in times past, he believed abstinence was important to the cause of victory, but once Bathsheba enters his field of vision, he decides not to follow this directive because he wants her. As soon as he sees this woman who pleases him, his own desire trumps the best interest of his soldiers and his country.

Loyalty does not sacrifice people for personal gain. But David does. He basically says, "Forget about consecration and holiness; I want her."

A disloyal leader feels no sorrow over the loss of someone significant and shows no appreciation for that person's past contributions.

When David receives word of Uriah's death (2 Sam. 11:24), he expresses no sorrow or remorse. In addition, David fails to communicate even the slightest bit of appreciation for all Uriah has meant to him, his kingdom, and his cause. David's callous and indifferent response is typical of people who have lost their loyalty; they seem completely unaffected when they lose someone valuable.

In my early days in ministry in Birmingham, an older, wiser friend of mine named John told me a story I never forgot. He had started a business several years earlier and felt extremely blessed to have a young couple named Renee and Carl on his team. They had the gifts, abilities, enthusiasm, and work ethic he needed in his start-up venture, and they were eager to help him. For a few years they were quite active and visible to everyone in the neighborhood where his business was located.

The problem started small, but over a period of time, they became argumentative and resistant to the direction in which my friend and his other employees had agreed to go as an organization. Later they became jealous, underhanded, and even angry. Eventually, John and his board saw no choice but to fire them.

Coincidentally, the weekend the board decided to terminate their employment was the same weekend John had planned an anniversary celebration for their vendors and customers. During that event, John announced Renee and Carl's departure, acknowledged their valuable contributions to his business, and affirmed them. He was genuinely grieved over the circumstances; he knew he could not keep them on his team, but at the same time he did not want to overlook the good they had done in previous years. They were instrumental in what John's business had accomplished, and he wanted them to know their help and support had not gone unnoticed. He also gave them an extremely generous financial severance package because he truly appreciated them and wanted to bless them.

Thankfully, I have not endured many situations like the one John went through with Renee and Carl, but I did learn a vital lesson from the way he handled them. Like all organizations, our ministry depends on people to help us fulfill our vision and reach our goals. Most of these are volunteers. And as happens in other groups, people come and go. Sometimes they cannot continue as ushers or greeters or small group leaders because of geographic moves, returning to school, job changes, or family responsibilities. So every year in November, we give our volunteers a chance to "sign up, re-up or resign." In other words, people who have not volunteered before can join the team, and those who served during the previous year can renew their commitments or resign if necessary. At our annual event for volunteers, we make sure to salute and applaud those who are stepping down, expressing our appreciation for all they have done for us.

My point in sharing these stories is to say that loyal leaders are saddened to lose those who have been important to them and are quick to express appreciation to those who have helped and supported them. In contrast, only people who are disloyal on some level can watch others leave without a trace of sorrow and without recognizing past benefits of a relationship. David's apathy toward Uriah's death clearly proves that his heart was not loyal to Uriah, though Uriah had been extremely faithful to him.

DANGER: DISLOYALTY AHEAD

As a good soldier in David's army, I am not sure what Uriah would have done had he realized David was not loyal to him. I do not know whether he would have left the army and found another job if given the chance, or whether he would have continued in military service with a greater awareness of the character weakness of his commander in chief. I do believe Uriah did not know the truth about David's attitude toward him, which makes his situation all the more tragic.

Unfortunately, all of us can have disloyal leaders in our lives from time to time. In addition to that, people in general can be disloyal. We cannot always avoid them, but we can learn to recognize them so we can deal with them appropriately. Let me explain a few traits of disloyal people so you can see them for who they are, keep from developing strong relationships with them, and avoid being hurt by their disloyalty.

Disloyal people want what they want so badly they do not care who gets hurt as they pursue it.

We have to remember that David knows Bathsheba is Uriah's wife before he sleeps with her. He has no doubt that she is a married woman. Even though he acts rashly in a moment of passion, enough time has elapsed between the moment he first saw her and the time she arrives at his palace for him to calm down and think rationally about what he wants to do. He had to have known his alliance with Bathsheba would hurt Uriah deeply if he ever found out about it. David has an opportunity to stop himself, to not go through with his intentions, but because his desire has completely mastered him, he does. Clearly, he is so determined to have what he wants that he totally disregards and disrespects Uriah.

Bathsheba was not only the wife of David's faithful warrior, she was also the granddaughter of Ahithophel, one of David's favorite counselors. But after many years of Ahithophel's devoted and dependable service, David still dishonors this trusted advisor by violating his granddaughter. Incidentally, I believe this is part of the reason Ahithophel sided with David's son, Absalom, when he later revolted against David.

When people want what they want so badly that they do not care who they hurt, they are trouble. We first see an example of this in Genesis, when Cain kills his brother Abel and then asks, "Am I my brother's keeper?" (Gen. 4:9). Cain felt no responsibility for his brother; he was loyal only to himself. His question about being his brother's keeper is answered in the example Jesus set through His life and in His teachings about loving one another (John 13:34, 35; 15:13; 1 John 3:16).

David's disregard for human life, and specifically for Uriah, is appalling but not surprising, given the fact that the king was not loyal. Disloyal people often display a lack of care and concern for others in small ways before they do it in big ways. When you encounter people who do not think it matters when others are wounded, watch out. They may soon be the ones to inflict pain, and you may end up getting hurt!

Disloyal people violate the principles for which you stand.

When David tries to get Uriah to come off the battlefield in order to sleep with Bathsheba, the faithful warrior refuses to sleep in his home because of the principles that are valuable to him—honoring God, being a good soldier, staying focused, remaining in solidarity with the brotherhood of fighters, being loyal, and other qualities (2 Sam. 11:11). At that time, David was not embracing any of those values. His behavior completely opposes the code of honor by which a soldier, and especially a leader, needs to live during time of war.

As best we can tell, Uriah was a godly man, but if we look closely at David's behavior, we see that the king violated a number of God's commandments. Specifically, he coveted his neighbor's wife, he committed adultery, he bore false witness, and in the end he killed Uriah. The worst thing about all these infractions is that he did not even seem concerned. He had embraced a completely different value system than he once had followed and lived by a code of conduct altogether foreign to Uriah and others.

We need to understand that once a person denies the principles of God, he or she will easily violate other principles crucial to healthy, loyal relationships. When a person dishonors God, it sets in motion a natural progression that quickly leads to dishonoring other people. This is the reason David seemed so nonchalant about having Uriah killed.

If you are in relationship with someone who does not respect and honor God, you cannot expect that person to respect or honor you. If you want loyal people in life, first look to see if they are faithful to God.

Disloyal people are not willing to give everything
for a cause that is vital to you.

As one of David's mighty men, Uriah was clearly willing to die for
David's cause. I feel sure he had made peace with the fact that he could
have been killed in battle, because soldiers in his day were well aware
of the risks they faced. He would not have been regarded so highly had
he been reluctant to give his all for his king. He made David's priorities his priorities and was willing to give his life for them.

Today, with the exception of those in military service, police
officers, firefighters, and perhaps several other dangerous careers,
few people have to make deliberate decisions to sacrifice their own
lives for others when they commit to a professional or personal
relationship as Uriah did. The lesson we learn from David and
Uriah's story is that people do, however, have different priorities at
times. Often, differences in priorities lead to disloyalty. Uriah was
only concerned about advancing David's cause, but David reached
a point where his top priority was Uriah's murder. David was so
coldhearted that he gave the letter of instruction for Uriah's death
to Uriah himself, to deliver to his superior. Tragically, Uriah was so
loyal to David, and he so trusted a person who clearly was not loyal,
that he participated in his own execution.

If you are loyal, like Uriah, I urge you to deal with disloyalty
when you recognize it in the people around you. Otherwise, you
may unknowingly participate in something that is ultimately
harmful or hurtful to you.

LOOKING FOR LOYALTY

We have focused so much on disloyalty in this chapter that it would
be worthwhile to list some characteristics of people who are loyal.

I have personally been blessed to have a number of extremely loyal people in my life, and I strive to be as loyal as possible to others. Let me share a few qualities you will find in people who are likely to be loyal to you.

- Loyal people honor and abide by the standards they set for the people around them.
- Loyal people fight *for* and *with* those who are dedicated to their causes or visions. They assume just as much risk, or more, than others do.
- Loyal people elevate the purpose and interests of a family, group, or organization above self-interests.
- Loyal people grieve genuinely over the loss of friends and supporters and truly appreciate the contributions those people have brought to their lives.
- Loyal people care more about others than about their own goals, projects, or pursuits.
- Loyal people affirm and support your values and principles.
- Loyal people are willing to invest as much as possible in the things that are important to you.

RELATIONSHIP REMINDERS

- One of life's greatest gifts is a truly loyal friend, family member, or colleague. The presence of loyalty will provide tremendous encouragement and support, while a lack of loyalty can be devastating.
- David's biggest problem was not his relationship with Bathsheba but with Uriah. One sin often leads to

another, and sometimes the second one has worse consequences than the first.

- Disloyal leaders set standards for others that they themselves are not willing to meet, and they refuse to support those who support them. Unfaithful leaders value personal agendas over corporate purposes. They don't appreciate people who contribute to them or mourn the loss of these people when they are gone.
- Disloyal people are willing to hurt others to get what they want. They will violate your principles and will not wholeheartedly invest in things that are vital to you.
- Be able to recognize disloyalty and deal with it. Treasure the loyal people God brings into your life.

RAISING YOUR RELATIONAL IQ

1. What kind of leadership position do you hold? Are you a leader in your home, at work, in your church, in a civic organization, or in some other way? Do you see yourself as more like David or more like Uriah?
2. In what ways do you relate to people in positions of leadership—at work, at home, on a team, in a class, in a religious institution, on a committee, or in other ways? Are those leaders demonstrating qualities of loyalty or disloyalty?
3. I often say, "Leadership rises and falls on relationships." After reading this chapter, why do you think that is true?
4. Have you ever been disloyal to someone, intentionally or unintentionally? How did you feel about it?

Have you pursued God's forgiveness and determined to be loyal from now on?

5. Has anyone ever betrayed or been disloyal to you? What was that experience like, and what did you learn from it?

6. One of the saddest parts of David and Uriah's story happens at the end, when Uriah unknowingly takes his own death warrant to his commander. Have you ever been in a situation in which your loyalty did you more harm than good? How can you better recognize disloyal people in the future? How can you be loyal in appropriate ways to the people in your life?

7. Who are the most loyal people in your life? What qualities do they exhibit to prove their loyalty to you?

10

Changing Places

THE LAW OF CONSTRUCTIVE TRANSITION

I WAS SO EXCITED! I COULD HARDLY BELIEVE how tremendously God had blessed the small seed of a ministry my wife and I planted in Birmingham, Alabama. We had been there only nine months, having started a church with just a few families. And now, a relatively short time later, we had a chance to buy a building!

We prayed and prayed about the purchase, wrestling with our decision, well aware that it would be the biggest leap of faith we had ever taken in ministry. We sought wise counsel from people who knew us, loved us, and had prayed along with us. They all supported us. Except one.

I had enjoyed many years of rich, rewarding relationship with one of my friends and mentors, Pastor Sanders. I respected his opinion greatly and was eager to share with him the story of how God had brought us so quickly to the opportunity to buy our very own church building.

He thought it was a bad idea. Based on his years of experience, he felt we were taking on too big a challenge too early in the life of our ministry. He knew the potential pressures and difficulties I as the pastor could face as we absorbed such a huge financial commitment. Even though I was committed to proceeding with the purchase, he thought we were moving too fast and tried his best to talk me out of it.

The excitement drained out of me like air out of a balloon. I was at a critical crossroads. I *knew* in my heart that God was leading us to purchase the property; I *knew* He had given me the faith to take such a big step. But this man I looked up to, this man who had added so much value to my life as a pastor and a preacher, this man who had advised me so well in the past, was dead set against it.

I was in a tough place. I knew what God was leading me to do; I also knew my friend and mentor thought I was making a massive mistake. I could hardly bear the thought of disappointing Pastor Sanders, but I could *not* disobey the Lord's clear direction. I knew what I had to do.

I went with God.

We bought the building and began renovating it, and the church grew as more and more people came and filled the place to overflowing.

I'll bring the story of my relationship with Pastor Sanders to a conclusion later in this chapter, but for now I simply want to make this point: there are moments in life when your best relationships can become your biggest problems. Sometimes, in order to move forward with God, you must change the way you relate to certain people in your life. This does not mean ending a relationship; it simply means restructuring it in a healthy, loving way so you can continue to be friends or associates with a certain person, but with different dynamics than you had before.

There are moments in life when
your best relationships can
become your biggest problems.

DON'T EXHALE TOO SOON

Much of this book deals with how to identify, invest in, and maintain the right relationships. Here I want to encourage you not to relax and settle into those relationships too quickly once they come into your life, because while they may be truly great relationships, they may also reach a point where they need to be redefined in positive ways or constructively transitioned. By "constructive transition," I mean a change in the place or significance a person holds in your life. Perhaps instead of remaining a best friend or confidant, someone becomes a friend in the broader context of your life. Perhaps he or she was once a mentor but becomes a colleague or a peer. These kinds of beneficial adjustments do not mean ending a relationship; they simply mean changing the dynamics of the relationship or moving a person into a new role or position in your life.

The fact that a relationship might change is no reason not to feel secure in it or to enjoy it. Knowing it might need to be adjusted should not cause you to be tentative or to fail to give yourself wholeheartedly and appropriately to another person. The point about not exhaling too soon is that you are constantly changing and evolving, and your life is continually unfolding. As God leads you into greater things, certain relationships may need to adjust in order for you move ahead. So maximize and enjoy the relationships He gives you, realizing that the roles you and the other person play may evolve over time.

SOMETHING NEEDS TO CHANGE!

What would it take for a relationship to reach a point where it calls for constructive transition? The time for that type of change comes when a major, serious, perhaps even life-changing situation arises, and you realize that a significant person in your life is effectively standing between you and your destiny. I am not talking about a difference of opinion or an occasion in which you and someone else "agree to disagree." I don't mean an instance when you say "tomayto" and they say "tomahto." I am talking about reaching a point where you are firmly established in a clear understanding of God's will for your life, and someone with whom you have walked very closely for a long time cannot see it and will not support you in it.

In another section of this chapter, I will elaborate on *why* some people cannot see what you need to do when you need to make a change, but here I simply want to make sure you understand that constructive transition is *not* a casual shift in a relationship. It is a deliberate choice that must be made for the sake of furthering God's plan for your life. It is done carefully and compassionately, with the goal of maintaining a great relationship with new and different roles for both people.

Anytime you enjoy a close relationship with someone, especially when both of you are walking with God, you are likely to share with each other what He is doing in your life and where He is leading you. Sometimes God tests your love and trust for Him by allowing someone important to you to withhold support or encouragement, or to disagree completely with what you believe He is leading you to do.

Relationships can definitely continue to move forward after a disagreement or a set of circumstances in which one person becomes a hindrance to the other. Because such situations do arise as people grow and develop, we would be wise to value, honor, and make the most of great relationships without relying on them or relaxing in them to the point that we allow them to derail us from God's purposes and plans for our lives.

PETER TAKES A BACK SEAT

I believe the Bible's best example of constructive transition takes place in the relationship between Jesus and Peter. Throughout Jesus' earthly ministry, Peter was part of His inner circle, His closest group of companions. Jesus had twelve disciples, but His deepest, most intimate relationships existed with the small group of Peter, James, and John. Of those three, Peter was arguably the most prominent and the one closest to Him.

In Matthew 16:15, when Jesus asks the very important question, "Who do you say I am?" Peter is the only one of the twelve who actually knows. He answers correctly, "You are the Christ, the Son of the living God" (v. 16).

Jesus then gives Peter an outstanding commendation. Of all twelve disciples, Peter is the only one who receives this level of blessing:

> Blessed are you, Simon son of Jonah [Peter's first name was Simon], for this was not revealed to you by man, but by my Father in heaven. And I tell you that you are Peter, and on this rock I will build my church, and the gates of Hades will not overcome it. I will give you the keys of the kingdom of heaven; whatever you bind on earth will be bound in heaven, and whatever you loose on earth will be loosed in heaven. (Matt. 16:17–19)

Jesus bestows tremendous blessing, privilege, and authority on Peter, but just a few verses later, the entire dynamic of their relationship changes. As Jesus attempts to prepare His disciples for His immediate future, including His suffering and death, Peter begins to rebuke and challenge Him, basically saying, "No! I'm not going to let that happen!" (Matt. 16:22).

Matthew 16:23 says, "Jesus turned and said to Peter, 'Get behind me, Satan! You are a stumbling block to me; you do not have in mind the things of God, but the things of men.'"

These negative words are almost as strong as the positive words Jesus has just spoken to Peter in Matthew 16:17–19, so we have to wonder what happened. How could Jesus change His tone toward Peter so dramatically and so quickly? Why did He feel He had to do so?

We need to understand that Peter's resistance to Christ's suffering and death, while understandable, put Jesus in a difficult place relationally. He has just shared with the disciples God's plan and will for His life—and Peter vehemently says, "No!" This presents Jesus with a difficult relationship task: He has to transition His relationship with Peter because if He does not, that relationship will prevent Him from reaching His destiny.

If we were to read this story in its original language, we would make the fascinating discovery that the word for *turn* in New Testament Greek (when Jesus "turned" and spoke to Peter in Matthew 16:23) implies a turning *away from*, not a turning *toward*. This is significant because the essence of transition is to stop going the way we had been going, turn, and move in a different direction. When Jesus says to Peter, "Get behind me," He is instructing him to change places, to take a new position in His life. He can no longer walk beside Jesus because he is not in agreement with what God is requiring Jesus to do. He can no longer occupy the place he once did in Jesus' life; he has to step back so Jesus can move forward.

After this powerful interaction, Jesus clearly remains in relationship with Peter, but He cannot keep Peter, once His great friend and comrade, as close to Him as He once did. Because Peter does not want Jesus to endure everything He will have to suffer and cannot align himself with God's plan, Peter participates in some of the events leading up to the crucifixion, but he ultimately denies ever knowing Jesus (Matt. 26:58, 71–74). As some other disciples do, Peter ends up watching the crucifixion from a distance.

If we look at Jesus and Peter's relationship throughout the New Testament, we see that it was *real*. It had its good times and its hard times, its bitter sorrows and its great joys. One of the most important points about their friendship is that it endured everything the two went through together, and I am convinced this is because they successfully navigated seasons of constructive transition.

THE FIVE *AH-HAHS* OF CONSTRUCTIVE TRANSITION

Do you remember my story about Pastor Sanders? I promised to share the rest of it, and I will, but not yet. Let me first ask if you can relate to the thoughts, emotions, and challenges I experienced as I wanted so desperately to obey God, when doing so meant going against the advice of a trusted friend and mentor. Perhaps you have been in a similar situation. Maybe you sensed God leading you to move to another city, but your parents wanted you to stay in the town where you were raised. Maybe you wanted to start your own business, but your spouse wanted you to stay in a job with a steady paycheck. I hear of all kinds of scenarios in which people believe God is clearly leading them to take a certain course of action, and people they love stand squarely in their way.

How do you navigate this kind of situation? I believe there are five key insights, *ah-hah* moments, that will help you understand and manage relational transitions constructively.

1. Realize that everyone cannot see and understand as you do.

Many times when God begins to lead you in a particular direction, He has been preparing you for a change for quite some time. You will perceive what He is doing and where He wants to take you in a deeply personal way. You may be able to see how the place you are going is exactly the right next step for you, and you may have the wisdom you need to go through the various steps of the journey. But because this is something God is doing in *your* life, the people around you cannot always sense or discern where and how God is leading you. They may not even recognize the general direction in which He is moving you during this particular time. When these dynamics enter into a relationship, I believe they are huge indicators of a need for transition.

Now, back to the story about Pastor Sanders. After we purchased the building and moved in, I later invited him to minister to our church family. After the service, when the two of us met in my office, he began to weep and apologized profusely for trying to keep me from buying the place. He said repeatedly, "I just couldn't see it. I just couldn't see how it could turn out so well for you."

Pastor Sanders and I maintained a good relationship, one we share to this day. He has always been immensely valuable to me, but there was a moment in our relationship when I chose to relate to him differently than I always had because he did not have the vision from God that I had. He was not privy to the many hours of prayer I had spent concerning the building. He did not know everything I was sensing from God, and he did not perceive the genuine faith God had given me for the project. His discouragement was not personal; it was based on lack of perception. He was not against *me*; he simply could not see what I saw.

Maybe you watched the movie *Moneyball*. In it, baseball team manager Billy Beane hires assistant Peter Brand, who proposes a nontraditional approach to assessing new players. Others mock and even become hostile to Beane and Brand, but the unorthodox duo ignore the naysayers and move forward with their strategy, not giving in to the pressure of the people around them. Eventually, people recognize the value of their methods. Ultimately, the Boston Red Sox adopt their way of doing things and win their first World Series since 1918. This is just one of many examples of people who press forward and do what they know they need to do, even when others attempt to dissuade them. Beane and Brand understood their approach and saw where it could take them; the people around them did not.

Next time people close to you try to talk you out of doing something you *know* you need to do, go easy on them. Chances are, they may be voicing opposition simply because they have not been with you through the entire thought process that led to your decision, and they have not been listening in on the many prayers you have prayed as you sought God's will for your life. I will admit that there are difficult people in the world; some will oppose you because they are jealous or resentful or bitter. But I am talking about people with whom you are already in meaningful, valuable relationships—people who do want the best for you but who do not always understand what that "best" is.

2. Know that building blocks can become stumbling blocks.

Whenever a person moves from helping you to hindering you, it indicates a need for transition. In the story of Jesus and Peter, Peter is called a "rock" or a "stone," reflecting the Greek meaning of his name. The "stone" who had just been so honored and blessed (Matt. 16:17–18) became Peter the stumbling block, who was *not* a blessing to Jesus (Matt. 16:23). In the beautiful old King James Version of the Bible, the phrase, "you are a stumbling block" is rendered, "thou art an *offence*" (emphasis added). This is interesting because when the Greek word for *offence* is used, the phrase means, "a stone lying right across the road I must travel."[1] Peter had gone from being a building block to being a stumbling block in Jesus' life.

We must remember that Jesus felt and acted in His humanity, as well as His divinity, while He was on earth. He felt the same emotions we feel and experienced the same types of temptations we face (Heb. 4:15). For this reason, I am certain He felt sorrow over needing to alter His relationship with Peter, but had He not done so, He would have found moving forward in His destiny extremely difficult. I also feel sure Jesus was deeply hurt when Peter denied him; anyone would be wounded by such words. Remember: Jesus was human, and He had human emotions.

Shifting His relationship with Peter could not have been easy for Jesus. They had been together a long time and shared many significant and powerful experiences. So, when Jesus had to reposition Peter, He also had to trust that He would be okay without His friend. He knew He was facing the brutal agony of crucifixion, and He knew He would have to go through it without strong, fiery Peter by His side. This must have been terribly sad and indescribably difficult for Jesus, but it was also necessary to His destiny and the fulfillment of God's plan.

When I was in college, like many young people, I had more than one goal. I definitely wanted to get a quality education, but I also wanted to join a fraternity, specifically the fraternity in which my father and several of my mentors held membership. The fraternity experience taught me a lot about manhood, scholarship, and perseverance. It also provided me with a lot of fun!

When I finished college and began preparing for the ministry, I began to realize I could not continue to hang out with my fraternity brothers and do the things we had done as college students. Frat-boy fun was not appropriate for a young minister, so I had to reposition my relationships with some of my brothers. Being part of the organization with them had been a building block for me in college, but continuing to socialize and stay in the same kind of relationships we had always enjoyed would be a stumbling block in ministry.

When a person or a situation is a building block in your life, take full advantage of it. But also realize that same situation or relationship could become a stumbling block later. Be aware of changes in the relationship and be sensitive to circumstances in which this could happen. If and when it does, realize that the time has come for a constructive transition.

3. Understand that people usually have positive motives.

I would like to make one more comment about Pastor Sanders. When he opposed my plan to purchase the building now known as the Huffman Campus of our church, he did so with a pure heart, with wisdom based on experience, with genuine love for me, and with a true desire for me to have God's very best in my life. As I noted, he simply did not see how such a big commitment really was God's best at that time. His motives were sterling, and I will always appreciate that. But I am also glad our relationship transitioned for a season because that was the only way for me to obey God.

By the time I encountered the situation with Pastor Sanders and the building, I had had another experience that gave me courage to move forward. It had happened years previously, but its lessons never left me.

While I was in graduate school, I lived with my father. I did that by choice because my parents divorced when I was a baby, so I had never lived with him during my growing-up years. As a young adult, I really wanted to develop a relationship with my dad. During the course of my studies, God opened some amazing doors for me. I was part of the World Council of Churches in Germany for a while and then worked at the Vatican. When I returned from Europe, my father was excited because he had so enjoyed the time we lived together; we had truly grown to love one another, and he looked forward to continuing to build our relationship. I would have enjoyed spending more time with my father, but God had other plans for me.

When I received a job offer in Florida, I knew God had opened the door to a great opportunity and was clearly leading me to take it. My father knew it, too, but he did not like it. He did not want me to move away, and through tears, he asked me to stay. He was not trying to block my destiny or to pull me away from God's will. He was simply a grateful man who treasured the chance to build a meaningful relationship with his son somewhat late in life, and he could not bear the thought of losing what we had.

But I had to go, and though I didn't want to leave him either, I moved to Fort Lauderdale, Florida, and ultimately met my wife there. Had I allowed my father to influence me too heavily, I might still be single! I had to go with God, which meant I also had to allow my relationship with my father to change.

The same principle holds true with Peter and Jesus. Peter was not angry with or opposed to Jesus when he so strongly begged Him not to go to the Cross; he loved Him. He did not intentionally speak against God's plan, but he did not want his friend to suffer or experience the grueling death he knew Jesus would face. Chances are, the same dynamics are at work when people seem to be standing in your way. Most of the time, they are not being difficult; rather, they are speaking up because they truly love you and want the best for you. The challenge for you in situations such as these is to understand and receive their love, but also to put everything about the situation in perspective and move forward as God leads you.

4. Be confident that the relationship can remain intact.

In the situation with Jesus and Peter, events do not move immediately from Jesus' instruction "Get behind me" (Matt. 16:23) to His crucifixion. Some time passes, and during that period, Peter stays with Jesus and the other disciples. He is present for the teachings Jesus offers, the stories He tells, and the miracles He performs. He has a place at the Last Supper and, along with James and John, he provides companionship to Jesus during His dark hours in the Garden of Gethsemane.

The fact that Peter remains a visible part of Jesus' life after the relationship shifts proves to me that relationships can endure transition. Relationships do not have to end just because roles or dynamics change. Jesus repositions Peter, but He does not send him away; nor does Peter leave. They both accept Peter's new role because even though they had a major misunderstanding, the relationship is never severed; it simply changes for a season.

Often, in today's culture, people lack the levels of loyalty we have seen in previous generations and view relationships as optional or temporary, not as highly valuable potential destiny makers. When friends, family members, employees, or coworkers no longer serve their purposes, people discard them. This happens in marriages when divorce takes place, and it happens in corporate settings when people retire or change jobs. Sometimes, under those circumstances, relationships that have lasted for years suddenly disappear. Whatever was valuable about them seems quickly forgotten, and everyone involved moves on to the next set of friends, lovers, or colleagues.

I submit that a relationship does not necessarily have to be "on" or "off." It does not have to be hot or cold. There are times and seasons when it is perfectly acceptable for a relationship to simply exist. I have made the point in this book that relationships require regular investments of time, energy, communication, and care, but I also know that once relationships are built and their value is established, allowing them to rest or be restructured at certain times because one person is moving ahead is okay. It is definitely better than letting them go!

I remember how I felt when I was single and some of my friends were married. We were still friends, but I had to accept the fact that they now had different priorities, different values, and different areas of focus in their lives. We could not do the things we used to do, and they did not need to commit to doing anything without first checking with their wives. I had to respect that. They had to respect that I still wanted to engage in a spur-of-the-moment basketball game or a spontaneous trip to our favorite pizza place, and they needed to understand that I would do those things without them. We all had to adjust to new dynamics, but that did not mean we were not still friends.

In this day when you can "unfriend" a person in about a millisecond, know that "friend" and "unfriend" are not your only options in real life, outside the social media realm. When you encounter a situation in which your response to your destiny means you cannot stay friends with someone under the conditions you have always known, that is not necessarily a time to abandon or bring closure to a great relationship; it's just time for a little constructive transition.

5. Remain hopeful about the possibility of restoration.

Just as my relationship with Pastor Sanders is now completely restored, any relationship that goes through constructive transition has the potential to be restored. Sometimes both parties return to their previous roles. But more often one or both people enter into situations that are part of God's plan for their lives, and what gets restored are not their former positions in the relationship, but the level of synergy and intimacy they once knew.

The keys to restoration are shared values and shared vision. When one person still "just can't see" and does not understand the situation, chances are high that the transition needs to remain in place. If one or both people want to go back to the same activities and same type of relationship they had before, it probably will not work. But if they both grow and understand who they are and what they can share in the present, restoration is possible.

At the end of the Gospels, in the last chapter of the book of John, a powerful and tender interaction takes place between Jesus and Peter. We can tell from the content of their conversation that their relationship has been restored and that Peter is once again in a place of prominence in Jesus' life. In fact, the heading of this portion of Scripture in the *NIV Study Bible* is "Jesus Reinstates Peter."

After His death and resurrection, Jesus appears to His disciples. He has reached the end of His earthly ministry and has enjoyed one last meal with the disciples, His friends. He says to Peter, "Do you truly love me more than these?"

Peter responds, "Yes, Lord . . . you know that I love you."

Jesus instructs him, "Feed my lambs" (John 21:15–16).

A similar conversation takes place two more times. Jesus gives him three chances to verbalize his love and to acknowledge that his values are the same as His. Peter takes them all. No doubt, the relationship is restored.

BE CAREFUL AND CONSTRUCTIVE

Every relationship I have mentioned in this chapter is a relationship of value. Relationships that are valuable, meaningful, and real need to be handled with care and caution. When you find yourself in a situation that calls for constructive transition, I encourage you to remember that making the needed adjustments in the relationship may be difficult for both you and the other person. Even when you know you must move ahead, do so with sensitivity. Remember how valuable your friend or associate is to you, and keep in mind that a healthy transition not only paves the way for you to fulfill your destiny and to do God's will, but it also enables a relationship to remain intact and opens the possibility of restoration.

RELATIONSHIP REMINDERS

- No matter how close or important a relationship is, you may reach a point at which you must adjust it in order to obey God.
- Constructive transition is rarely easy, but it is necessary to reach the next level of success and purpose in your life.
- Remember the five *ah-hahs* of constructive transition: everyone cannot always see what you see and

understand what you understand; building blocks can become stumbling blocks; people usually want the best for you; transition doesn't have to mean the end of a relationship; and restoration is an option.

- When a positive, genuine relationship reaches a point where transition is needed, it is a tender time for both parties. Handle the transition with gentleness and compassion, with the goal of effectively changing places while keeping the relationship intact.

RAISING YOUR RELATIONAL IQ

1. Has someone valuable and important in your life ever stood between you and your destiny or tried to talk you out of following God's will for your life? How did you feel? How did you respond?

2. Have you ever hindered anyone from pursuing God's plan because you did not understand everything that person understood? How do you wish you had handled the situation differently? If you have not already done so, would you follow Pastor Sanders's example and apologize?

3. In your personal life, are you willing to believe that people who seem to try to keep you from doing what you need to do may genuinely love you but may not completely understand your situation? Are you willing to believe they have positive motives? This willingness to believe the best will pave the way for relationships to remain intact and possibly be restored at some point.

4. Think about the significant, valuable relationships in your life. How can you be a building block instead of a stumbling block for those people?

5. Is there a relationship in your life that needs a constructive transition right now? Based on the understanding you have gained in this chapter, how will you move forward with that?

PART 2

How to Make the Most Difficult Choices

THE MOST DIFFICULT CHOICES IN RELATIONSHIPS often involve whether or not to remain in someone's life, or allow someone to remain in yours, when problems arise. In Christian circles, we frequently take a naive approach to relationships, urging people to love one another, as Scripture admonishes, while failing to understand and acknowledge how complicated loving others can be. If we believe God leads us into relationships with people, we also tend to think those relationships must last for the rest of our lives. To the best of my knowledge, the only interpersonal relationship bound by solemn vows and the promise "until death do us part" is the covenant of marriage. In other types of relationships, we may find that we have lifelong friends or we may discover that certain people are part of our lives for a specific purpose during a certain period of time. We may also end up in relationships we wish would last for years but that end prematurely for various reasons.

In this section of the book, I hope to help you understand some of the most common and valid reasons certain relationships must come to a close and to help you know how to bring closure in loving, gracious ways. In the following chapters, you will learn from Abraham and Lot that helping some people simply is not worth what it costs to those who try to assist them. Paul and John Mark demonstrate what happens when a relationship starts out well and is filled with promise but one person gets upset and chooses to leave. Ruth, Orpah, and Naomi highlight the differences between covenant partners—people who come into your life to stay—and halfway friends—people with whom you have relationships for a specific reason or for an appointed season.

I pray you will have as many relationships that help you, not hinder you, as possible. But when you find yourself in a place where you must bring a relationship to an end, I hope you will remember this section of the book and be equipped to do it well.

11

You Can't Take Him with You

KNOWING WHEN AND HOW TO END AN UNHEALTHY RELATIONSHIP

ANNMARIE WAS A YOUNG DESIGNER DETERMINED to become famous in the fashion world. When she was invited to join the team of one of the industry's best-known designers in New York City, she was ecstatic. The opportunity was everything she had hoped for and exactly what she needed to take the next step toward her dream.

Her direct supervisor, Cynthia, had been in the fashion business for years and was highly regarded for her cutting-edge sense of style, her artistic eye, and her ability to groom promising young designers for future success. AnnMarie felt working for Cynthia would provide her with everything she would need to later start her own label.

But AnnMarie had a problem. She developed an arrogant attitude because she was too impressed with herself and her abilities. Her teachers and fellow students frequently complimented her designs and thought she displayed amazing talent, and she agreed. The trouble started not when she discovered she could learn from Cynthia but when she decided Cynthia could learn a few things from her.

Cynthia, like others, recognized AnnMarie's talent immediately. She knew her new team member had tremendous potential, and she wanted to help her develop it but did not appreciate AnnMarie's tendency to criticize designs Cynthia had created. AnnMarie did not take hints from her coworkers or direct instructions from Cynthia to keep her opinions to herself and adopt a posture of learning instead of evaluating her boss's work. Feeling her design instincts were not appreciated, eventually AnnMarie became so frustrated that she resigned her job, leaving behind a truly wonderful opportunity and a great mentor.

But It Was *So* Good

I hope you, like AnnMarie, have been blessed with some truly good relationships and opportunities in your life. Sometimes those valuable relationships last a lifetime—but not always. When they do not last as long as you had hoped, the situation can be disappointing and painful. It can also be confusing because you often wonder how a relationship that once was so right could turn into something so wrong.

The fact is, good relationships can go bad for a variety of reasons. This does not mean they are not genuinely good for a period of time; it simply means they will not be good forever. Sometimes people, like AnnMarie, cost themselves great relationships because they are arrogant, jealous, or immature. Sometimes they fail to see or understand the true value of the relationships they have been given. Regardless of the many reasons for a separation, we sometimes need to ask or allow someone who has been a valuable or even vital part of our lives to leave the relationship because a once-positive association has become negative.

> *Regardless of the many reasons for a separation, we sometimes need to ask or allow someone who has been a valuable or even vital part of our lives to leave the relationship because a once-positive association has become negative.*

A RIGHT RELATIONSHIP GONE WRONG

Centuries ago, a man found himself in a situation in which a good relationship went bad and did not last. You can read the entire story in the book of Acts, but I'll summarize it here.

A vicious persecutor of Christians, named Saul, had an amazing encounter with God that blinded him for several days and changed his life forever. He converted from a staunch Pharisee to a sold-out follower of Jesus Christ. He dedicated his life to evangelism, starting churches, and helping individuals and groups of believers follow Christ with ever-increasing passion and maturity.

Because of Saul's past, many Christians were leery of him after his conversion, perhaps wondering whether or not it was genuine. But a man named Barnabas took Saul under his wing and helped him get started in what became a powerful, world-changing ministry. Barnabas's name actually means "encourager" or "Son of Encouragement" (Acts 4:36) and for many years he proved to be a true encourager and a supportive colleague in ministry and friendship to Saul, who later became known as the apostle Paul.

The time came when, after a season of fasting and prayer, the early church in Antioch commissioned Paul and Barnabas to the work of the ministry. They set sail for the island of Cyprus, and Barnabas's cousin, John Mark, accompanied them. Scripture specifically says John Mark went with them for the purpose of helping them (Acts 13:5). Paul and John Mark likely became acquainted through Barnabas, and the three men spent much time together. John Mark was clearly present during the early days of Paul's ministry and proved valuable enough to be invited to join Paul's first missionary journey.

When Paul and Barnabas left Cyprus and traveled to Perga in the region of Pamphylia, the positive relationship between Paul and John Mark turned negative; their association ended—and it ended badly. According to Acts 13:13 in *The Message*, "That's where John [Mark] called it quits and went back to Jerusalem."

For years, scholars have studied and debated what caused the breach between Paul and John Mark. A number of dissertations have addressed this issue, offering various theories about why they did not remain friends. No solid conclusions have been reached, but we can make two points with certainty. First, John Mark was the person who left Paul and Barnabas. Apparently he abandoned them of his own volition; it was his choice, not theirs. Second, only Paul, John Mark, and perhaps Barnabas and a few people close to them at the time knew what actually happened. I certainly do not know the details of the rift, but I am sure the dynamics they faced centuries ago were not much different from some of the circumstances you and I may face in relationships today.

HOW TO KNOW WHEN A
RELATIONSHIP IS GOING BAD

Because the separation of Paul and John Mark has sparked so much interest among Bible scholars over the years, several predominant theories have emerged about why John Mark left. I want to highlight a few of them because they hold important clues to why this relationship may have fallen apart so long ago. These theories offer important insights into how you can know if a once-good relationship in your life is beginning to turn bad and needs to move toward a close.

A relationship is going bad when someone cannot accept a change in your status.

All new believers need someone to help and encourage them in the faith and to support them as they discover and fulfill God's purposes for their lives. For Paul, this person was Barnabas. At the beginning of Paul's experience as a follower of Christ, Barnabas was clearly the leader—the experienced Christian who could help Paul get established in his new way of life and in the ministry to which he was called. Barnabas was the one who introduced Paul to the apostles in Jerusalem, allowing him to build relationships that became extremely important in later years. He also recruited Paul (still called Saul at that time) to the work of the ministry in the early church at Antioch and verified to others the quality and integrity of his work.

In the early stories of their association, the Bible lists Barnabas's name first, giving him a place of honor in the story of their mission of mercy in Jerusalem and on their evangelistic tour on Cyprus (Acts 11:30; 13:2). Then suddenly the biblical accounts no longer mention "Barnabas and Saul," but refer to "Paul and his companions" (Acts 13:13). Clearly, Paul has not only changed his name from Saul, but the change in the order of their names infers that Paul has also taken the lead over Barnabas. This is a significant shift because it reflects Paul's new position in ministry, emphasizing his leadership and growing influence.

When Paul's status changed and he moved from being a follower to being a leader, John Mark may have been jealous or resentful on Barnabas's behalf. As long as Barnabas was in charge, John Mark could have felt special or secure because of their family relationship and their history together. But when Barnabas appeared subordinate to Paul, John Mark seemed to have a problem. Interestingly, we see no indication that Barnabas resisted or resented his change of position. It may not have bothered him, but did seem to upset John Mark. It's possible that John Mark was content to be in a relationship with Paul as long as Paul did not overshadow Barnabas, but when the roles changed, John Mark didn't like it.

These dynamics still happen today. There are people with whom you can have a great relationship as long as you remain at a certain station in life, but when God begins to open doors for you and your status changes, they begin to get nervous, back away, or find reasons not to spend time with you. Your change in status may be something like a raise or promotion at work, a new level of visibility or influence, a new home or car, or some other elevation in status. Changes in status can take place in many ways, and when someone in your life cannot support you through them, rejoice with you, or stay steady in your life, you know that relationship is beginning to sour.

Early in my ministry, I had an opportunity to meet a well-known Christian leader. For several years, I had prayed diligently for God to put me in relationship with key people who could mentor me and help me become everything God wanted me to be. After a while, I had an unshakable sense that this man was one of those people. I truly believed God wanted to connect the two of us so I could learn from this man and receive important impartations of his wisdom.

When I heard this man was coming to Birmingham on a book tour, I asked my staff to pray with me for an opportunity to meet him. Enthusiastically, they did. I went to his book signing and had a chance to share with him the tremendous impact he had made on my life. Then I took the risk of asking if he would consider mentoring me. He said yes!

Over the following weeks and months, this leader took a personal interest in me and in our ministry. He intentionally shared lessons he had learned, let me know how I could avoid mistakes he had made, and generally poured wisdom and insight into my life as a person and as a pastor. It was exactly what I needed, and I was enormously grateful for such a God-ordained opportunity.

As the relationship continued, I began to implement this man's advice in the ministry. Then something strange happened. Some of the same staff members who prayed with me for the chance to relate to this leader began to resent his influence. Over time, this man invited me to travel with him and introduced me to several people who became important in taking my ministry to the next level. The relationship was—and remains to this day—a genuine blessing.

This relationship opened doors of opportunity I could never have opened on my own. It gave me exposure and visibility I never could have arranged without this man's help. It changed my status in ministry in ways that have been 100 percent positive.

But some people on our staff could not see the full picture of the benefits the relationship offered. They did not understand the truth of the saying, "A rising tide lifts all boats." In other words, as growth took place for me, opportunities for growth and promotion also existed for them. Instead, some of the staff resisted implementing his suggestions—not because the suggestions were bad but because the people were insecure. They did not want an "outsider" telling them what to do, even though his advice was excellent. Eventually, their fears and issues became clear: they were uncomfortable because they were afraid this man was taking over the ministry. I began to hear rumblings and questions such as, "So is he running the ministry now?" and "Is he going to fire us?"

Those questions could not have been more ridiculous. This man is known as a person who places a high value on loyalty and who has retained some of his own staff members for more than thirty years. Anyone who knows him well realizes his primary desire would have been to help me develop the team I already had, not to eliminate or replace anyone. That was my first experience with seeing how a change in status can affect relationships negatively, but it has not been my last.

Maybe you have had a similar experience. If not, you probably will as you continue to pursue your destiny. Some people will seem to be good friends or coworkers as long as you can give them a ride, lend them money, or keep their children after school. But when something happens and you have to say no to a request because something has changed for the better in your life, especially if you have been granting favors to your friends for a long time, you may be in for a surprising response. They may suddenly lose interest in being your friend or they may find someone else with whom to develop a relationship.

No matter how your status changes, take notice of the way people around you respond to it. Those who support you and celebrate with you are demonstrating the qualities of a true friend. Those who resent the positive developments in your life are likely to cause trouble.

A relationship is going bad when someone cannot accept a change of direction in your life.

In the early days of his ministry, Paul focused on preaching to and teaching the Jews, but later he began addressing the Gentiles with a message of grace instead of legalism. John Mark was a loyal follower of Paul's as long as Paul preached to the Jews, but when he changed the direction of his ministry, the relationship between Paul and John Mark may have changed as well. Some schools of thought believe John Mark opposed Paul's "libertine" views toward the Gentiles (not requiring them to be circumcised), as did other conservatives from Jerusalem, and many believe he was part of the group who opposed Paul in Acts 15. Clearly John Mark was not a dedicated member of Paul's team. He only wanted to associate with Paul as long as Paul's ideas aligned with his.

A tragic, modern-day story of a person whose life changed direction is Marvin Gaye, the singer-songwriter who gave the world songs such as "I Heard It Through the Grapevine" and the first recording of "How Sweet It Is (to Be Loved by You)."

Marvin Gaye's father was a minister, and young Marvin first developed his musical abilities in the context of the church. As Marvin grew older and as people realized what an amazing gift he had, he began to branch out into secular music and became highly successful. I should say *many* people viewed him as successful; his father did not. While there were reportedly several sources of disagreement between the two men, some reports say the tension between them originally started because Marvin's father did not approve of his foray into secular music. Over time, that conflict escalated and became much more complicated, eventually resulting in Marvin's death. His father killed him, shooting him at close range, in front of Marvin's mother, in the home Marvin had given to his parents.[1] For years, the relationship between Marvin and his father had shown signs of going bad. Most likely, both men would have been better off giving each other some space, even if that meant ending their relationship.

The story of Marvin Gaye and his father is an extreme example of what can happen when one person cannot support a change of direction in someone else's life. It reveals the importance of being in relationships with people who can embrace and accept you when you move in a direction they may not understand or condone.

In his book *Good to Great*, Jim Collins uses the metaphor of a bus to represent a company or organization and writes of the importance of having the right people on the bus.[2] In other words, the right people need to get together, get in their places, and move in the same direction in order for an entity or institution to become great. I believe whether the bus is a marriage or family, a church or ministry, a business, a civic organization, or some other group of people, if everyone is not headed toward the same destination and going in the same direction, the whole vehicle is in jeopardy.

You may have several buses in your life. For each one, having the right people in the right places and moving in the same direction is critical. These people and the great relationships you enjoy with them will continue to travel with you even if the bus of your life changes directions.

A relationship is going bad when a person cannot remain consistent and loyal in the face of stress or challenge.

When Paul, Barnabas, and John Mark left Cyprus on Paul's first missionary journey, they knew they were headed into a dangerous place—a city called Perga in the region of Pamphylia, an area known for being riddled with bandits. No doubt their safety was in jeopardy, but Paul and Barnabas faced the daunting uncertainties with valor. John Mark, however, abandoned them in Perga and went back to Jerusalem.

Many scholars speculate that John Mark left because he was frightened, perhaps by the prospect of being beaten or physically harmed in Pamphylia. To put it succinctly, he lacked courage. Or, as playground bullies from my childhood days would say, he was a scaredy-cat!

In Acts 15, Paul and Barnabas were in Jerusalem, attending the Jerusalem Council. After the meeting, Paul and Barnabas began to plan another journey, this time to visit some of the churches started during their first trip. Barnabas suggested to Paul that they take John Mark with them. It was a *bad* idea. Paul would not even entertain the thought of having John Mark on his team again. In fact, in the King James Version of Acts 15:38, when Paul says that John Mark "departed" from them, the Greek word used for *departed* is *apostana*,[3] the root of the English word *apostasy*.[4] Interestingly, *apostana* is the same word used in the parable of the sower to describe the seeds that do not take root and "fall away" when persecution comes (Luke 8:13). Clearly, Paul had no sympathy for John Mark and viewed his leaving Pamphylia as a true abandonment, and he is adamant about not wanting John Mark to travel with him again.

The issues in Paul and John Mark's story remind me of the movie *300*, a fictionalized account of the ancient Battle of Thermopylae, when three hundred Spartans fought valiantly against a much larger and more powerful Persian army. At one point, the Spartan commander, King Leonidas, basically asks his men, "Who's not ready for this?"

With this question, Leonidas gives his soldiers an opportunity to back out of the fight and go home. He knows he is up against a tremendous challenge, and the only people he wants around him are those who share his vision, passion, commitment, and courage. He is well aware that having a halfhearted, intimidated soldier in his ranks is worse than having no soldier at all.

In the end, the formidable Persian troops suffer greatly for several reasons, but one of their biggest problems is that soldiers begin to desert the army, just as John Mark deserted Paul. In fact, many leave out of fear. In contrast, the Spartan army grows, and thirty thousand free Greeks join them, eventually stopping the Persian invasion of Greece. King Leonidas of Sparta knew exactly what Paul knew—that progress and victory of any kind depend on having the right people around you.

At the beginning of this book, you read Proverbs 13:20 in the epigraph: "He who walks with the wise grows wise, but a companion of fools suffers harm." The same principle is true with character qualities other than wisdom. The person who walks with strong people grows strong. The person who walks with faith-filled believers becomes full of faith. The person who walks with those who have confidence in God and in themselves becomes more and more confident every day. The people around you will so powerfully influence your character and your decisions that they will also impact your future in significant ways. Paul knew this, and that is why he didn't want to be around John Mark. Paul understood that God had called him to a great work, something more than a weak, jealous, insecure, frightened person could handle. He knew that in order to obey God and fulfill His plan, he needed the people around him to be strong, courageous, and mature.

Likewise, I believe God is calling you to something great. You may not start churches; you may start a business or a family. You may not write epistles to churches; you may write a classic novel or a song people will sing for generations. Whatever God has planned for you, it is a great work in His eyes, and the place where He is taking you will require faith and boldness. You will need people around you who inspire your faith with their own faith and who give you courage with their bravery. This is one of the biggest reasons relationships with people who shrink in the face of difficulty or fold under the pressure of challenges need to end. They do not necessarily have to end badly, as the relationship with Paul and John Mark did, but these people cannot go with you into your future even if they have been valuable in your past.

I have heard many stories from men and women who had big hopes and dreams but who needed support and encouragement. In some cases, these people were deeply disappointed and hurt because friends and coworkers who once encouraged them and seemed to be "for" them ended up deserting or distancing themselves at some point. Perhaps you have felt this way. Maybe you have had a John Mark in your life, and you believed that person would be with you for years, but now he or she has "gone back to Jerusalem." That's a painful experience. But from a positive perspective, if that person never was equipped to support you long-term, you are more likely to achieve your destiny without him or her.

In great relationships, you can reasonably expect people to get behind you and help you fulfill your dreams, and hopefully you can return the favor to them. True and lasting friends are not afraid to accompany you into your future. They will not run when pressure comes; they will support you through it, help you bear it, and continually remind you that your best days are ahead.

A relationship is going bad when you can no longer depend on someone who was once reliable.

In Acts 13:5, Luke describes John Mark as a "helper" or an assistant to Paul and Barnabas. The Greek word for *helper* is *hupereten*, which is translated, "under rower."[5] The word picture this term creates is that of a large vessel with three decks of oarsmen, or under rowers. These laborers were seated on the three decks underneath the main deck and could not see where they were going or what was happening around them. Their job was to provide power and momentum for the vessel, even though they did not know where they were headed. To use biblical language, they were rowing "by faith, not by sight" (2 Cor. 5:7). To do this, they had to trust the captain on the top deck to take them safely to their final destination. The captain had a drum at his side and would beat out each stroke they needed to take.

Boom! They took a stroke.

Boom! They took another stroke.

Boom! They rowed again.

The only sound the under rowers listened for was the beat of the captain's drum.

If we read the Greek correctly in Acts 13:5, we clearly see that John Mark was supposed to be an under rower. His only job was to listen to the "drumbeat" of Barnabas and Saul, to follow their lead and do what they requested. When they decided to go to Pamphylia, John Mark the under rower should have gone with them; that's what the beat told him to do.

The fact that John Mark deserted them upset Paul tremendously; the Greek indicates that he was furious![6] Apparently, John Mark's lack of faithfulness to the work of the Lord was extremely hurtful to Paul for quite a long time (Acts 15:37–38). In fact, I believe it was such a disappointment to Paul that he would later write that faithfulness is absolutely mandatory for the Christian life: "Now it is required that those who have been given a trust must prove faithful" (1 Cor. 4:2).

Do You Know John Mark?

Have you ever had an experience like Paul had with John Mark? Has anyone ever come into your life and been dependable for a season, then given up on you or abandoned you? Just as John Mark's actions were hurtful to Paul, the behavior of a friend, family member, or colleague may have disappointed you. I want to encourage you with this thought: You are working your way through a book that I pray is giving you new insights and fresh wisdom for the way you develop and handle your relationships from this point onward. As you ponder the insights and apply the lessons you have learned, you will increasingly make better choices about the people in your life. I do not want to imply that you will never be hurt or abandoned again; you may. Other people's choices are beyond your control. But I hope to inspire you, if you are still suffering over a relationship that has gone bad, to believe that great relationships are possible and to pursue them carefully, prayerfully, and with great faith.

I also know that sometimes, for your own good, you must bring a relationship to a close or allow the other person to walk away from it. Trying to do that with little instruction or experience can make the situation extremely painful for you and the other person, so I would like to devote the remainder of this chapter to some practical ways you can end a relationship when you need to do so.

Who Are You?

In order to determine if a relationship needs to end, the first step is to raise a critical question: Are you a Paul or are you a Barnabas?

The answer is important because it will help you determine your relational style and priorities. It will also clarify your motives toward the person from whom you need to separate.

You'll recall that before Paul and Barnabas's second trip, Barnabas asked Paul if they could take John Mark with them, and Paul responded with an emphatic "No!" (Acts 15:36–40). This clearly shows us the differences between the relationship philosophies of Paul and Barnabas.

For Paul, the ministry is too important and the work too demanding to lean on someone who has once been unreliable and could easily be unreliable again. For Barnabas, the work is a venue in which John Mark can receive the encouragement he needs, which is what Barnabas does best. In John Mark, Paul sees a liability; Barnabas sees potential. Paul is not willing to compromise the work for the sake of someone who has not been loyal, while Barnabas wants to risk supporting and encouraging John Mark and giving him a second chance. Paul's perspective on relationships can be summarized in the question, how can this person add value to where I'm going and what I'm doing? Barnabas's perspective on relationships is rooted in the question, how can I add value to this person?

A key point about the differences between Paul and Barnabas is that you can be like Paul in one situation and like Barnabas in another. Because every individual is special and unique, and because no set of circumstances is identical to another, you may need to play the role of Paul in some situations and the role of Barnabas in others. Some experiences may call for you to say, "No, I cannot risk investing in this relationship again. What I need to accomplish is too important to be jeopardized." Others may be good opportunities to give someone another chance while you provide needed support and encouragement. The important thing is to know which role to play in various types of situations.

What to Do When You Need to End a Relationship

Once you have decided whether to approach the end of a relationship from Paul's perspective or from Barnabas's, you will have some other matters to ponder and pray about. I would like to offer some advice on three important questions most people ask themselves when they have to part ways with someone who has been valuable in the past:

- "How should I *think* about this situation?"
- "What do I *say* when I actually bring closure to the relationship?"
- "How do I *respond to others* when they ask why so-and-so and I aren't friends anymore?" This also applies to business partners, ministry colleagues, and many other types of alliances.

How should I think?

I want to encourage you in two ways as you think about ending a relationship. First, be very clear about where God is leading you and why that requires the relationship to change. This understanding will give both you and the other person a clear rationale for ending a relationship, and the boldness to do it. Second, you must understand and believe that just as God brought the person with whom you are ending a relationship into your life, God will bring others into your life as well. Be patient, be prayerful, and be watchful, because He will bring you the people you need.

What should I say?

Let me suggest several things to consider if you have to tell someone you need to end a relationship.

- Be sincere. People know when someone is not being authentic.
- Be honest, but speak with love. The need for honesty does not give you the right to trample on anyone's feelings, so choose your words wisely.
- Be clear about where you are on your life's journey and what you need from a relationship. Clearly communicate why you need to make a change, using phrases such as, "Here's what I really need . . ."
- Do not assign blame. Take responsibility for your role in ending the relationship and avoid calling attention to the other person's flaws.
- Share what you have learned from the relationship and what you are grateful for. Be appreciative and thankful—and be specific.
- Create an opportunity for future reconciliation if appropriate. You never know what God may want to do later on, so avoid doing anything that would permanently prohibit the restoration of the relationship in some way at a later time.
- Let the person know you will continue to love him or her. The fact that a relationship is ending does not make the individual a bad person.

What do I tell others about the situation?

When you have been in a close relationship of any kind for a long time, whether personal or professional, people know it. When that relationship comes to an end, they will notice. The best way to respond if they ask about it is to say as little as possible, as positively as possible. For example, you could say something like, "Yeah, we don't spend as much time together anymore, but I think he's a great guy," or "Well, we needed to go different directions, but I sure did learn a lot from her."

Acknowledge the change, but make that a minor point, while majoring on the positive points about the other person. The principle of loyalty applies even after a relationship ends.

THE REST OF THE STORY

Are you wondering what happened to Paul, Barnabas, and John Mark? At the end of the story, Barnabas so believes in John Mark and wants to help him that he leaves Paul in order to do so. The two cousins go on to do effective ministry. Paul chooses as his new colleague a man named Silas, who ultimately will coauthor epistles with him, and who will be significant to Paul's next level of ministry. One way to look at this turn of events is to say that everyone involved ends up in the relationships they need to be in for their futures.

I also want you to know that something positive happens between Paul and John Mark at some point. No one knows exactly what took place, but they eventually reconciled. How can I be sure? Paul's own words in 2 Timothy 4:11 make it clear: "Only Luke is with me. Get [John] Mark and bring him with you, because he is helpful to me in my ministry." Enough said.

I pray and believe this will be the case for you—that you, like Paul and John Mark, will be able to move beyond good relationships gone bad and connect with people who will celebrate you, affirm you, and propel you into the future God has for you. If you are mourning the loss of a significant relationship, let me encourage you. The people in your life may change, but God's purpose for your life will not. Just as He sent Silas to Paul, in His grace, God will send you the right person for your future after you have had to let go of someone from your past—and you will go on to do great things!

RELATIONSHIP REMINDERS

- The fact that a relationship starts out well does not mean it will remain healthy or right.
- When someone who was once valuable in your life displays the following signs, you have strong clues that your relationship may need to end. This person (1) is not able to accept a change in the status or direction of your life, (2) is not loyal and stable under pressure or in the face of challenge, or (3) had once been dependable, but is now unreliable.
- When you have to decide whether or not to end a relationship, first ask yourself if you need to approach the situation as Paul would or as Barnabas would.
- When a relationship is ending, learn how to think about it, what to say to the other person, and how to speak to the people around you about it.
- Even relationships that seem to be over may be restored later.

RAISING YOUR RELATIONAL IQ

1. Have you ever encountered someone like John Mark, a person with whom you had a great relationship at first but who later abandoned you? How did you feel when that person left?
2. Do you see any signs that something is going bad in a current relationship in your life? What do you see?
3. Generally speaking, are you more like Paul or more like Barnabas? Do you tend to distance yourself from

people when they have disappointed you, or do you give them grace? Can you see the value in both ways of dealing with people under different sets of circumstances?

4. If you have reached a point where you need to discontinue a relationship that was once good and valuable, how can you do so in the kindest, most affirming, most loving way?

5. Why is it important to have the right people around you as you move forward into the future God has for you?

12

Kiss Orpah Goodbye

Recognizing Who Is in Your Life for the Long Term

BEFORE YOU START WONDERING WHY ANYONE would kiss Oprah Winfrey goodbye, take another look at the name in the title of this chapter. It's *Or-pah*, a biblical character mentioned in the book of Ruth. Maybe you are familiar with the story surrounding her (Ruth 1:1–17), but before I summarize it, I would like to make a point about something you may have experienced.

Have you ever enjoyed a nice cold glass of milk for a few days in a row, then gone out of town for the weekend and on Monday morning, stumbled to the refrigerator, poured yourself a bowl of cereal and milk, taken a bite, and spit it out in the sink because the milk was sour? The milk was fine before you took your trip. It served the purpose of providing you with calcium and other nutrients a week earlier, but now it tastes terrible and can make you sick.

Jugs and cartons of milk have expiration dates printed on them. Those dates let us know about how long we can expect the milk to be good. It should be good for a limited amount of time, but no reasonable consumer would expect it to remain fresh very long after that time expires.

As a pastor, I have encountered a number of people who cling to bad relationships when they need to let those relationships go because they have served God's purpose. Most of the time, the problem is that those relationships, like the milk, served a healthy purpose—both parties added value to each other at one time—but then reached a point where the relationship was no longer beneficial. Learning to recognize when a relationship has run its course is a skill that will keep you moving forward instead of trapped in relationships that have lost their value and purpose in your life.

RUTH, NAOMI, AND ORPAH

A man named Elimelech lived in Bethlehem, in the land of Judah. When severe famine threatened his life and the lives of his family there, he moved them to a nearby country called Moab. While they were there, Elimelech and his two sons, Mahlon and Kilion, died, leaving Elimelech's wife, Naomi, and the sons' Moabite wives, Ruth and Orpah, as widows.

In the wake of her losses, Naomi decides to return to her home in Bethlehem. In an emotional exchange, both daughters-in-law say they will go with her, and begin the journey. Along the way, Naomi tries to dissuade them, telling them to stay in their homeland, find husbands, and go on with their lives. Eventually, through tears, Orpah agrees to stay in Moab, but Ruth makes a powerful and passionate commitment to Naomi:

> Entreat me not to leave you, or to turn back from following after you; for wherever you go, I will go; and wherever you lodge, I

will lodge; your people shall be my people, and your God, my God. Where you die, I will die, and there will I be buried. The LORD do so to me, and more also, if anything but death parts you and me. (Ruth 1:16–17 NKJV)

Several important relational lessons can be learned from the story of Ruth, Naomi, and Orpah, but the one I want to focus on is this: some people are created and intended to be covenant partners in your life, while other people will only be halfway friends. Everyone who comes into your life is not supposed to be a best friend, a member of your inner circle, or someone you trust with your hopes and fears or your joys and sadness.

> *Some people are created and intended to be covenant partners in your life, while other people will only be halfway friends.*

God does bring long-term, deep, dependable friends into our lives. But He also causes us to intersect with people who come into our lives for a specific season or for a particular purpose. He sent Ruth into Naomi's life to be a lifelong friend and covenant partner. Orpah was only in Naomi's life because she married Naomi's son. When he died and no longer bound them together, her season with Naomi came to an end. Her behavior provides a stark contrast to Ruth's fierce loyalty. Orpah's eventual willingness to leave Naomi is one of several reasons she is a halfway friend, not a covenant partner.

Failing to understand the distinction between covenant

partners and halfway friends has brought great heartbreak and disappointment to many people. But if we can understand and honor God's seasons and purposes for each relationship, we and those with whom we relate can enjoy blessing and fulfillment within the context that God has ordained for our relationships.

WHAT IS A COVENANT PARTNER?

The word *covenant* is not uncommon in Christian circles, but because of its meaning and significance, it is also not one we should take lightly or use flippantly.

A covenant is much more than a promise or an agreement. It is a solemn, serious, unbreakable bond that can exist between God and an individual, as was the case with God and Abraham; between God and a group of people, as we read about in the Old Testament with Israel and with all believers; between two individuals, such as David and Jonathan; or between nations or groups of people, such as Israel and the Gibeonites in Joshua 9.

The first example of a covenant in the Bible is when God makes a covenant with Abraham. You can read the story in Genesis 15. The covenant ceremony through which God took Abraham is rich with symbolism, and like so many Old Testament stories and examples, it has a powerful New Testament application for you and me and all believers today.

The first thing we see in this covenant is the shedding of blood, which is why we sometimes hear the term "blood covenant." The highest, most powerful, most serious form of covenant is one sealed with blood—and the blood of Christ is what seals our covenant relationship with God today. The shedding of blood demonstrates the strength of a relationship. Throughout history, in some cultures, people shed their own blood to seal their covenant relationships. They make a small cut, perhaps on their palms, and place a small piece of dirt or something in it so it will form a scar when it heals. This physical mark becomes an outward sign of covenant relationship.

In biblical times, when people were in covenant, the relationship meant, "What's yours is mine and what's mine is yours," symbolized by the exchange of gifts. This applied to almost everything—to provisions and resources and even to friends and enemies. In other words, if one person lacked food or shelter, he could count on receiving those things from a covenant partner because of the intimate and binding nature of their relationship. Likewise, in a covenant relationship, both parties shared friends and enemies. If an enemy attacked one member of the covenant, the other responded as though the aggression had been personally against him. In the event of an attack, people knew their covenant partners would join forces with them and fight as though the battles were personal.

You may remember that David and Jonathan were covenant friends. This is why in 2 Samuel 9, David, the busy king of Israel, puts everything aside to search for any surviving member of Saul's family. He didn't have a covenant with Saul, but he did have a covenant with Saul's son Jonathan. So he asks, "Is there anyone still left of the house of Saul to whom I can show kindness *for Jonathan's sake?*" (2 Sam. 9:1, emphasis added). As was common in biblical times, the covenant relationship between David and Jonathan was so binding that it extended to their descendants (1 Sam. 20:14–15, 42). That's why David made such an effort to find Jonathan's son Mephibosheth, and move him, his family, and his servants from an uncomfortable life in a place called Lo Debar to his palace in Jerusalem. Simply because Mephibosheth was Jonathan's son and

Jonathan was David's covenant friend, "Mephibosheth lived in Jerusalem, because he always ate at the king's table" (2 Sam. 9:13).

Expressing the gravity and binding nature of biblical covenant is difficult in modern times, when everything from dishes to diapers is disposable. If we get upset with someone, we decide not to be friends anymore. In covenant relationships, entering into a relationship is an extremely serious process, and leaving is almost not an option. It is a situation that has many more benefits than liabilities, but it does require a high level of commitment.

A Spear for a Goat?

You may be familiar with the story of Henry Stanley, an American born in Wales, whose thirst for adventure and skills as a journalist combined to make him an ideal person for his employer, the *New York Herald*, to send on a search for the legendary medical missionary David Livingstone. Livingstone's mission to Africa was well-known, but people became concerned about him in 1869, because no one had heard from him in more than a year.[1]

One day during the search, Stanley came upon an especially powerful tribe who tried to stop his exploration. At a loss, Stanley asked his guide what to do. The guide replied that Stanley needed to "cut covenant" with the chief, which would require the shedding of blood and an exchange of gifts.[2]

Because Henry Stanley had health problems, he had a goat that traveled everywhere with him so it could provide him with milk. The chief wanted Stanley's goat as a gift, so Stanley gave it reluctantly, knowing he would not be able to continue his exploration if he did not. In exchange, the chief gave Stanley a copper spear, which did not seem very useful to Stanley—certainly not as useful as his goat.

With the covenant complete, Stanley continued his journey through Africa, looking for Livingstone. The first person he met along the way immediately bowed to him. Stanley then came to understand the copper spear was the symbol of the chief's authority and that when people in the region saw it, they knew that Stanley had the authority and the backing of the chief and his entire powerful tribe.[3] Stanley eventually located Dr. Livingstone in 1871. When he met the sick and exhausted missionary, he spoke words that have become well-known: "Dr. Livingstone, I presume?"

After he found Dr. Livingstone, Stanley remained in Africa because two newspapers, one American and one British, provided funds for his ongoing exploration of the continent.[4] As the story goes, Stanley ventured deep into Africa, cutting covenant more than fifty times.[5] His work was not always safe, as many African tribes he encountered had never seen a light-skinned person and could have been hostile to him. When new potentially dangerous tribes saw him, all he had to do was show the scars running down his arm (visual signs of covenant) and display some of the significant gifts received from other tribes. Needless to say, Stanley's exploration of Africa is widely considered a tremendous success.

Six Characteristics of a Covenant Partner

Now that you are coming to understand the power of covenant partnership, the question is, how can you identify people who have the potential to be covenant partners for you? Let's explore six key characteristics of a covenant partner from the story of Ruth, Naomi, and Orpah.

1. A covenant partner can accept change.

Orpah was fine as long as Ruth and Naomi stayed in Moab, a place that was familiar and comfortable to her. Before the two women had traveled very far out of Moab (a place representing sameness, not change, for her), she even said she would go with Naomi to Bethlehem. But when Naomi pressed her, she relented. When Orpah realized that Naomi was determined to get back to Bethlehem and back among the people of God and the things of God, she decided to stay with what was comfortable and familiar to her. With her husband deceased, she had fulfilled her duties as a daughter-in-law and had no obligation to go with Naomi.

A halfway friend will be fine as long as you keep doing what you have always done or stay where you have always been. This may mean that person stays with you as long as he or she is considered your "best friend," or as long as you give him or her enough time and attention. Or a relationship may be okay with someone as long as you have a certain job, position, or educational status. But when you decide to do something different, the other person becomes distant and disengaged. For example, some people may be satisfied in a relationship in which you provide for them financially, but may leave when you begin to insist that they take responsibility for their own finances. You may have a friend who seems loyal to you while you are both single, but when you get married, she is nowhere to be found. The same can be true when both people are married and one loses a spouse to death or divorce, or when both people are childless and one becomes a parent.

All sorts of scenarios for change exist, and in fact, many of the normal, expected changes people face over the course of a lifetime have the potential to alter relationships in some way. Let me encourage you to pay close attention to the way your friends and acquaintances respond when something changes in your life.

Those who cannot support you and rejoice with you are not destined to be with you in a long-term, purposeful relationship as a covenant partner.

2. A covenant partner does not run away during difficulty.

One of literature's greatest statements of unfailing devotion and unbreakable commitment takes place when Ruth says to Naomi, "Where you die, I will die, and there will I be buried" (Ruth 1:17 NKJV). Think about it: they have not even arrived in Bethlehem yet. Ruth has never seen the place they are going. She does not know anyone there except Naomi. Both the culture and the religion of their destination are completely foreign to her, yet with so much uncertainty ahead of her, she makes a lifelong commitment to Naomi. She says, "I am going with you and I will stay with you for the rest of your life. In fact, wherever you die is the place where I will live the duration of my days. When I die, I will be buried close to you." This almost unspeakably powerful commitment is an awesome example of the kind of unconditional love a covenant relationship requires and provides.

Ruth's no-matter-what devotion to Naomi sets a high standard for those of us who want to be covenant partners to others and to identify the covenant partners in our own lives. Ruth was determined to *stay*; she was not going to abandon Naomi or pull back from her, regardless of what happened.

Ruth was basically saying to Naomi, "Not even death itself will come between us. I am going to be with you during the good times and the bad times. Others may abandon you. Things may get messy, but when the dust settles, I will still be here."

A reality of life is that everyone goes through some type of trouble at some point. Nobody sails through life free from difficulty, and some people seem to face more than a fair share of heartbreak or tragedy. When difficulties arise, we need people who will stand by us, comfort and encourage us, support us, and refuse to leave us, no matter how bad things become.

Halfway friends will stick with you as long as doing so is comfortable and convenient, but will shrink back when you really need them. A covenant partner's approach to hardship is, "Okay, so this is what we're up against? Let's fight it together. I'm with you all the way!"

I encourage you to keep your eyes and ears open to the people in your life. When others experience pain or hardship, do they back off, or do they press in? Chances are, they will treat you the same way they treat others. When you have a bad day or suffer a disappointment, do they tell you to deal with it or do they offer compassion and encouragement? The way they treat you when some fairly minor problem occurs is a good predictor of the way they will relate to you when a major situation arises. If people step away, stop communicating, or seem unavailable when you are going through a challenging time, even though they may have a number of good qualities, they probably are not covenant partners for you.

3. A covenant partner trusts God.

Ruth says to Naomi, "Your people will be my people and your God my God" (Ruth 1:16). Ruth had been raised in Moab, a place that was not part of the promised land and regarded as hostile, enemy territory for God's people. We can only surmise that something happened in the course of the relationship between Ruth and Naomi that proved to Ruth that Naomi's God was the one true God. Whatever Ruth saw in Naomi's walk with God, she wanted. Something about Naomi's faith birthed faith in God for Ruth. In pledging her loyalty to Naomi and promising to go to Bethlehem with her, she also pledged her love and loyalty to Naomi's God and indicated a staggering willingness to trust Him.

Surely Ruth knew her new life with Naomi would not be easy. She was well aware that they were both widows, and she knew widows could not expect easy lives. She must have realized that they had little or no source of income, so they would have to depend on Naomi's God to provide for them. Ruth had a number of valid reasons to be afraid or concerned about her life with Naomi in Bethlehem, but she did not dwell on those negative possibilities. She simply declared, "Your God shall be my God."

When you, like Ruth, face many unknowns, when your faith is challenged and begins to waver, when you begin to doubt the things you normally believe firmly, or when you begin to fear the threatening uncertainties that lie ahead of you, you need someone around you to whom you can say, "Your God is my God!" You need someone who trusts God completely and who will pray for you and encourage you to trust Him too. A covenant partner is mature in faith and will remind you that God is faithful, that His Word is true, and that He never, ever fails.

I married a covenant partner, but I did not know it when we stood at the altar, all dressed up, and spoke our wedding vows. All couples profess their love and commitment to each other in some way when they get married, but today, when half of all marriages end in divorce, one person's passionate profession of love and commitment to another does not mean he or she is a covenant partner. It may simply mean that the other person is only seriously infatuated!

I discovered that my wife was a covenant partner fairly early in our marriage. As I mentioned previously, we moved from Florida to Birmingham, Alabama, in the fall of 2006 so I could accept a pastoral position at a prominent church in the city. In chapter 6 I explained that Ty made a tremendous sacrifice to do so.

Shortly after our arrival at the ministry in Birmingham, we experienced significant difficulty and drama we never anticipated. During the upheaval, the senior pastor recommended that I plant a new ministry because the situation involved considerable division among the church members. The shock of this suggestion left me speechless, partly because my wife and I had great love and commitment for him. She and I had both left significant positions and income to follow God to Birmingham. At that time, we still had our home in Florida plus a new home in Birmingham, so we faced the possibility of having no income while paying two mortgages! These were extreme changes, changes for which we had no way to prepare.

As I prayed and agonized about the uncertain future before us, I took comfort in my wife's love and support. One day after a sleepless night of prayer, talking to God about my fear of financial ruin and not being able to provide for my family because I would have no income for at least a year if I started a new ministry, my wife came to me and said, "Sweetheart, I want you to know that I think you should start the new ministry. I believe this is God's will for your life. And if we use every dollar we have and even lose our homes and ultimately have to eat beans out of a can, I am okay and will be with you every step of the way."

I knew at that moment, this woman I married was so much more than my wife in name only, she was a true covenant partner! She trusted God, she trusted me, and she did not run away during difficulty.

4. A covenant partner trusts you.

When Ruth says to Naomi, "Don't urge me to leave you" (Ruth 1:16), she's basically saying, "*Please*, don't force me to leave you and go home. *Please*, let me go with you!" In that plea, Ruth is sending a strong message: "Naomi, I trust you. I have been with you for ten years. I know your character, I know who you are, and I trust you."

A critical difference between covenant partners and halfway friends is that halfway friends do not *really* trust you. They will stick with you as long as they understand your behavior, as long as your actions are predictable, and as long as you are doing something they approve of and agree with. But the moment you do something that seems out of the ordinary, even if you are following God to do it (sometimes *especially* if you are following God), they begin to wonder what is happening to you. They may question your integrity, your faith, or your sanity. In the end, halfway friends will decide not to go with you.

A covenant partner is someone who knows you thoroughly, sometimes better than you know yourself. This person knows your heart, your integrity, and your walk with God. He or she may even know you well enough to know how you make decisions. Because of this deep knowledge and the close relationship you share, a covenant partner will not require an explanation when he or she does not understand what you are doing. This person may ask questions for information, but doesn't ask you to defend yourself. Your covenant partner trusts you and will say, "If this is how God is leading you, I'm in. Let's go!"

5. A covenant partner trusts himself or herself.

Ruth makes a tremendous statement when she says to Naomi: "Where you go I will go, and where you stay I will stay" (Ruth 1:16). The reason these words are so powerful is that Ruth had to trust herself immensely and have great self-confidence in order to speak them. A person who is willing to leave behind everything familiar and say, "I'm going with you, and wherever you choose to live, I'll live," has to be extremely secure. Ruth is saying, "Naomi, you don't have to worry about me. I can make it anywhere. I can take care of myself, and I can help take care of you. Wherever you want to go, I can thrive—and I can do it for the long haul."

This is significant because healthy relationships require both people to carry their own weight and walk on their own two feet. Each person must be capable of leading and managing his or her life financially, emotionally, physically, professionally, socially, and in every other way. When one person leans too heavily on the other, the relationship becomes unbalanced and unhealthy. If you are the one being leaned on, you will burn out and wear out after a while, because people get heavy when you have to carry them! If you find yourself with a needy person who continually requires your attention or time, move on. If it seems you are consistently pouring yourself or your resources into the person without return, love him or her, but move on.

While there may be appropriate times when you want to support your covenant partners in reasonable ways, these people do not need to be carried or empowered constantly. They have the internal and external resources to care for themselves, to conduct business or hold a job, and to live in a successful way without your intervention or assistance. Not everyone has these abilities, so when you are looking to identify covenant partners, keep these things in mind. Look for individuals who are confident and strong enough to trust themselves. They need to be secure enough to be who they are and live their own lives while walking with you appropriately.

6. A covenant partner will help you, not harm you.

When we read about how Ruth conducted herself once she and Naomi arrived in Bethlehem, we see that everything she did was intended to benefit Naomi. She did nothing to hurt Naomi. In fact, she did not even seem to do anything that was neutral. She was determined to be a blessing, not a hindrance or a burden, to her mother-in-law.

Sometimes people you may initially perceive to be covenant partners end up not being covenant partners at all. You discern that based on their behavior. As you try to identify the covenant partners in your life, watch carefully to see whether they help you or harm you, whether they move you toward your dreams and goals or steer you away from them. Look to see whether they encourage the important relationships in your life or try to separate you from the people who mean the most to you. Listen carefully to their words, then see if their actions affirm what they have said. If they say they support you but their actions are not supportive, that is a bad sign. If they say they love you but treat you disrespectfully and offer flimsy excuses for doing so, beware. And certainly, if their behavior causes any kind of bodily or emotional harm, part ways immediately and get help.

Sometimes people enter into covenant partnerships prematurely, before they *really* know the other person. They discover something they truly cannot live with for their own safety or well-being. For example, perhaps the person is physically, sexually, emotionally, or verbally abusive. Unfortunately, this happens far too often in marriages. Many times, heartbreak, heartache, and disappointment could be avoided if people had the skills and the patience to find out whether they were about to enter into a serious commitment with a true covenant partner or with a "pretend" covenant partner.

What a Covenant Partner Is *Not*

In the first chapter of the book of Ruth, we learn that Naomi, Ruth, and Orpah had all been together for about ten years—a significant amount of time. This teaches us that we can be in relationships with certain people for a long while before we realize they are not covenant partners but instead are halfway friends.

My colleague Susan told me about Michelle, a halfway friend in her life, and a person she *thought* was a covenant partner. The two women had been in close relationship for more than thirty years, since their families moved into the same neighborhood within several weeks of each other when Susan and Michelle were in fifth grade. Susan had endured and celebrated many changes in Michelle's life, such as marriage, the birth of children, and the changes those developments brought, while Susan had remained single and childless. Therefore Susan never had to ask Michelle to make the same adjustments she had made in their relationship.

Susan treated Michelle's children well—buying them gifts for special occasions, attending their ball games and recitals, and taking them to get ice cream once a week. In addition, Susan made time in her schedule to have lunch with Michelle every week. But when, at age forty-two, Susan met and fell in love with a wonderful man, she prioritized that relationship over all others. She was no longer able to attend as many special events for Michelle's children. She took the children for ice cream and had lunch with Michelle twice a month instead of once a week. When the great development in Susan's life meant adjusting the amount of time she spent with Michelle and her children each week, Michelle felt rejected and abandoned. She could not handle the change and overreacted to it by deciding not to allow her children to have ice cream with Susan at all and by completely discontinuing their lunches together. Susan soon realized that her longtime friend still had value in her life, but not as a covenant partner.

I share this story to make the point that longevity does not equal covenant partnership. The two friends in my story ate lunch together once a week and shared many details of their lives. This proves a point I have seen many times in my pastoral work with individuals who have problems in relationships: frequent communication and even a deep level of involvement in a person's life does not make a covenant partnership.

How do you know when someone is not a covenant partner for you? Let me offer some suggestions.

- Someone who simply gets excited about being your friend, especially when he or she benefits from the good things that happen to you, is not a covenant partner.
- Someone whose friendship is inconsistent is not a covenant partner.
- Someone who seeks to "ride on your coattails" or uses you for his or her personal gain or benefit is not a covenant partner.
- Someone who disappears when you are going through a tough time is not a covenant partner.
- Someone who lives and relates to you according to the ups and downs of his or her emotions is not a covenant partner.
- Someone who repeatedly and heavy-handedly tries to tell you how to live your life, run your business, or deal with other relationships is not a covenant partner.
- Someone who wants to separate or isolate you from friends and family is not a covenant partner.
- A person who is spiritually immature or who does not share your faith in Jesus Christ is not a covenant partner.
- A person who only calls on you when he or she is in need and does not ever offer to help or support you is not a covenant partner.
- Someone who needs excessive time, attention, or validation from you will become a burden and is not a covenant partner.

How to Handle a Halfway Friend

I want to call your attention back to the early part of Ruth and Naomi's story, when Orpah decides to return home, leaving just the two of them to journey to Bethlehem (Ruth 1:6–15). Notice Naomi's response. Naomi does not cling to Orpah; she does not beg her to stay; she makes no effort to try to talk her out of it or entice her to go with them. She probably does not even lose any sleep about the matter! The two women simply share a common, respectful parting gesture of their day (a brief kiss) and go their separate ways. Orpah goes back to Moab, and very little, if anything, is ever written about her again. Ruth and Naomi travel on to Bethlehem, and a great story of restoration and redemption unfolds for both of them.

When a halfway friend decides to part ways with you, let that person go! When you know he or she is not a covenant partner, when you know the season of relationship is over, then let the relationship come to a gracious and blessed end. You may want to acknowledge the positive aspects of your acquaintance and hopefully you will want to wish the person well, but do not try to hold on. In addition, avoid thinking about how you can restructure your relationship; do not try to "make" anything work. Cling to your covenant partners, but kiss your halfway friends goodbye when the time for closure has come.

Oh Yes, You'll Make It Without Them

When a relationship ends, one or both people involved may feel a bit unsteady for a while. Sometimes a halfway friend will play a mind game with you, saying, "I am going to leave," while also saying or insinuating, "and you'll never make it without me." You may reflect on the qualities you grew to like in your halfway friend and ask yourself if you will make it without him or her. I want to answer your internal question with a resounding Yes! While a period of adjustment may be necessary, you will not only survive without your halfway friend, you will thrive! The fact that a certain person walks out of your life does not mean you won't get the breakthroughs and opportunities you're longing for. Your destiny is not tied to your halfway friends; your destiny is connected to your covenant partners.

In fact, I have noticed that one of the ways God works is that He sometimes waits to bring a breakthrough or move you to your next level of success and destiny until your relationships are in proper order. He knows you need right relationships with the right people so you can receive all the blessings He wants to pour out in your life and be most effective in His service. So sometimes, before He *moves* you forward in His plan for you, He first *removes* people who will hinder or hold you back.

In Ruth and Naomi's story, we read that the two women arrived in Bethlehem *together* (Ruth 1:22), cooperating with each other, supporting each other, and encouraging each other along the way. They made their journey together and they came to their destination together. They made it to Bethlehem (which means, "House of Bread" or "Place of Provision") in Judah (the land of praise) together, to begin a new life that turned out to be wonderful. They found their way together to a place of great and unexpected provision. They had many reasons to praise God.

I believe with all my heart that one of the priorities of every Christian's life should be the development of covenant partnerships. Throughout Scripture, we see that relationships are vital to the walk of faith and to the fulfillment of God's purposes for our lives. Let me encourage you to be diligent to assess the relationships in your life. Begin to identify those people who may be covenant partners and those who may only be halfway friends. Take your time entering into a covenant partnership and go about it with much prayer. And when you find a covenant partner, do not let that person go!

RELATIONSHIP REMINDERS

- All relationships are not for life. God intends some relationships to be deep, significant, and long-term, but He designs others for specific times, purposes, and seasons.
- Don't try to hold on to an Orpah (a halfway friend) when that person decides not to move forward with you or chooses to go in a different direction. Bless and encourage your halfway friend, and keep pressing on as God leads you forward on your journey.
- Take your time as you think and pray about who your covenant partners are. Assess those people to see if they have the characteristics and qualities needed in such an important relationship.
- Seek God and ask Him who your covenant partners should be. Wait until you have confirmation and a settled peace in your heart before moving forward in such significant and solemn relationships.
- Don't quickly dismiss, walk away from, or let go of a covenant partner, because a covenant is a solemn and binding agreement before God. Because people are human and we live in a fallen world, rare occasions arise when two covenant partners may need to

separate. This should be done only with much prayer, wise counsel, and mature spiritual guidance—and when every effort for reconciliation has been exhausted.

RAISING YOUR RELATIONAL IQ

1. Who are the covenant partners in your life?
2. If you have a covenant partner, even if you've never applied that term to the relationship until now, what qualities in that person inspire your trust and desire for a lifelong relationship?
3. Is there anyone in your life currently who has the potential to become a covenant partner for you? Who is it? How do you know?
4. If you have a major disagreement or problem with a covenant partner, what relationship skills have you learned through this book or elsewhere that will help you successfully navigate and work through that difficult time?
5. Think about how much your covenant partners mean to you. How can you demonstrate or communicate to them in practical ways that you take their partnership very seriously?
6. In your own words, what is the value of having a covenant partner in your life?

13

When Helping You Is Killing Me

How to Have Healthy Relationships with Unhealthy People

A LOVING MOTHER, NOW RETIRED AND LIVING on a fixed income, allows her smart, healthy, thirty-four-year-old son, Derek, to live in her home rent-free, even though he makes no effort to get a job. She feeds him every day, cooks his favorite meal once a week, and does his laundry. But he does not appreciate anything she does. In fact, he complains when his favorite shirt is not clean and pressed.

Derek's mother knows he has a drug habit he refuses to give up, and she suspects he is the culprit every time a few dollars disappear from her purse. She never mentions it. She simply decides she does not really need the new medicine the doctor prescribed. She will wait until next month to fill the prescription, and she will skimp on birthday presents for her grandchildren. She wants to go on a weeklong mission trip with her church, but every time she saves some money, she cannot find it when she looks for it. Besides, she is uncomfortable with the thought of being gone for seven days. She is afraid to leave her house for very long because she fears Derek will have his friends over to visit. Who knows what they would steal from her?

When her older children or her friends mention the situation with Derek, she tells them exactly what she tells herself: "Derek and I both had a hard time when his father was sick. We both suffered such a loss when he died. I have to help him."

The unfortunate relational dynamics that exist between Derek and his mother are common in families, but not limited to families. For example, a bright, industrious CEO named Tom started a thriving business several years ago. The company would be a perfect acquisition for a larger firm—a deal that would enable Tom to live a comfortable life while pursuing some things he has always wanted to do: join his fellow church members building playgrounds in underprivileged areas of his city and spend more time with his family. But he is reluctant to sell his business because his chief financial officer, Allen, has not managed the fiscal aspects of the company well. The records are sloppy, and Tom knows several things have probably not been done correctly. The truth is that Allen was his college buddy who is now an alcoholic and refuses to seek help. Tom does not want the company financials under scrutiny because he does not want Allen to be exposed, knowing the publicity would devastate his family. After all, they were college roommates and fraternity brothers.

Derek's mother and Tom have something in common. In each situation, they are covering up for people close to them. Helping one person is, in a sense, "killing" the other one. Maybe you can relate because you have done what they have done, or something similar.

Right away, I want to make clear that my use of the word *killing* does not mean physical death. It means emotional death, the loss of life that happens when a situation literally douses your joy, drains your energy, steals your time, distracts you from God's purpose for your life, dampens your dreams, or robs you of your vitality and zest for life. I am talking about the kind of detrimental relationship that suffocates your heart. Deep down, on the inside of a person, that's a killer.

The Bible gives us a fascinating example of an emotionally deadly relationship in the account of Abraham and his nephew Lot. You may know their story, but I ask you to view it with fresh eyes as I walk you through it from a relational perspective so you can avoid making the mistakes Abraham made.

Even though Derek and his mother and Tom and Allen live centuries later than Abraham and Lot, the relational dynamics in this Old Testament account are as current as today's breaking news. In fact, they may be happening to you. They are common, but that does not make them benign. They may be killing you on the inside, but if you can recognize and understand them, you can save your life.

SHARED PAIN OR SHARED PAST

When two people realize they have something in common, that shared experience, ability, or desire often leads them to believe they should develop a relationship. But I say, "Not so fast!" Sometimes a shared experience does become a starting point for a relationship, but great relationships need to be built on much more than commonalities.

In the case of Tom and Allen, Tom was too protective of his fraternity brother turned employee. Their professional relationship was built on a common history—their college experience together—and that became detrimental to both of them. Derek and his mother shared the pain of losing Derek's father.

Abraham and Lot had both shared pain and a shared past. As family members, they certainly spent many days together. Abraham perhaps remembered when Lot was born, and Lot probably had happy memories of times spent with his uncle, Abraham. The two men were also bonded through a shared loss. In their case, it was the death of Abraham's brother, Lot's father. This is important because the fact that they were relatives and that they lost a loved one and grieved together became the foundation of a faulty relationship.

We read about Abraham's family in the book of Genesis. They lived in a place called Ur of the Chaldeans, where Abraham and both his brothers, Nahor and Haran, were born to their father, Terah. Unfortunately, Haran died in Ur while Terah was still living. With his remaining family, Terah set out for the land of Canaan, but stopped and settled before he got there. Some scholars believe Terah named the place where he lived Haran after his deceased son (Gen. 11:31–32). If this is true, it tells us that, in a symbolic way, Terah allowed the pain of loss to paralyze him. He could not move beyond the place of his pain.

Abraham, however, did move on because God told him to leave his country, his people, and his father's household and go to a land that He would show him (Gen. 12:1). So Abraham left Haran, headed to the place of God's choosing, and took Sarah and Lot with him (Gen. 12:4–5). Naturally, Abraham took Sarah on the journey because she was his wife, but notice this: God never told him to take Lot.

So why did Abraham allow Lot to go with him? I believe he did it for the same reasons many of us allow our relatives or old friends to stay close to us: because as family members, Abraham and Lot had a shared past and because they shared the pain of losing Haran. Genesis 11 is clear that when Terah went to Haran, he only took with him Abraham, Sarai, and Lot. This means Lot would have been left alone had he not gone with Abraham. I am sure Abraham hated to see that happen because, after all, Lot was family and the two of them had been through so much together.

Have you ever allowed a Lot to be part of your life simply because of shared hurtful experiences or because he or she has always been there? While similar experiences may serve as a bond between two people in a healthy relationship, shared pain or a shared past is not a good reason to develop a relationship with someone. If you have a relationship that is built on that kind of foundation, it may be toxic. I encourage you to take an honest look at the relationship and make sure it is based on more than common history or hurt. Otherwise that person may become to you what Lot was to Abraham—a big problem.

LOT HAS A *LOT* OF NERVE!

Abraham made a bad decision when he allowed Lot to join him on the journey toward the land God had promised him. Nowhere in Scripture do we ever read that Lot made a single positive contribution to the trip toward Canaan or to Abraham's life. He was nothing but trouble! He added no value to Abraham; he simply drained his uncle's time, resources, and energy.

During their travels, Abraham amassed considerable wealth as he acquired livestock, servants, gold, and silver (Gen. 12:16; 13:2). Because Abraham was blessed, Lot was blessed too; his prosperity was a direct result of his connection to Abraham.

Both men experienced so much increase that the land could not sustain both of them and their families, livestock, servants, and possessions.

What happens when a space is too small for so many people and so much stuff? A fight breaks out. The quarrel started not between Abraham and Lot but between their herdsmen. Abraham would not tolerate arguing, so he suggested to Lot that the two of them separate. He even allowed Lot to choose where he wanted to go and offered to take for himself the land Lot did not want.

I believe the most significant development in this part of Abraham and Lot's story is not the fact that they parted ways, but the *reason* they had to separate—the fact that Lot was ungrateful. Had he appreciated everything he gained because of his relationship with Abraham, perhaps he would have approached Abraham in a respectful way and said something like, "We are both so blessed, and I sure appreciate everything you've made possible for me. Our land is getting crowded, though, so would it be okay if I move a little bit in whichever direction you think would be best for me? That way, we'll both have enough space for all our tents and animals and servants." But he did not. He was eager to take what he considered the best land for himself and let Abraham have the leftovers.

Ungrateful attitudes are not limited to Old Testament times. Maybe you have shared your blessings with someone only to have that person gripe about them. Maybe you have gotten up early to give a coworker a ride to work only to hear complaints that your air conditioner is not very cold on a hot day. Or maybe you have allowed a relative to live in your home for a period of time only to have that person throw a pity party when you announce that you are selling your place because you are getting married or moving to a new city to accept your dream job.

Sometimes, when people do not appreciate the benefits we provide for them, we excuse their behavior with comments such as, "Well, she's had a hard life. I guess a little complaining is okay," or "At least now he's just ungrateful; he used to be drunk all the time!" The truth is, being ungrateful is similar in many ways to being selfish, and it is not acceptable in a healthy relationship. People who are blessed because of your generosity and then have the audacity to complain can be summed up in one word: *takers*. Sooner or later, relationships with takers become unhealthy and ultimately toxic.

One characteristic of a dangerous relationship with a taker is an ungrateful spirit, so be watching for it. For example, if you are considering a romantic relationship with someone, pay attention to the way he or she responds to a server when the two of you are eating in a restaurant. As the server delivers the meal or refills a beverage, does your date act as though it's the server's job to cater to his or her needs, or does your date stop talking long enough to say a quick, pleasant "thank you"? In addition, be aware of how people talk about others who provide benefits to them, even if they are grousing about a paycheck for which they have provided honest work. Do they have an air of entitlement and constantly say the pay is too low? Or do they appreciate having a paycheck at all?

The difference between a grateful person and an ungrateful one may seem minor, but it actually provides important insight into a person's character. The ability to appreciate good things is a positive quality that enhances a relationship. When you encounter someone who is thankful and gracious to others, you may want to keep moving forward with the possibility of a relationship. But when you see ungratefulness arising in someone, beware!

FOLLOW YOUR HEART

Because of Lot's ungrateful attitude and selfishness, being separated from him was the best thing that could have happened to
Abraham. Before we explore that point, let me say that we gain
great insight into the character of Abraham and Lot when we
examine the choices they made when they went their separate
ways. Genesis 13 records what happened: "So Lot chose for himself the whole plain of the Jordan and set out toward the east. The
two men parted company: [Abraham] lived in the land of Canaan,
while Lot lived among the cities of the plain and pitched his tents
near Sodom" (vv. 11–12). This passage does not mean much without a clear understanding of the symbolic importance of Canaan
and Sodom. Canaan was God's promised land, a place of His
blessing and abundance. Sodom was the polar opposite. It was a
city so full of evil, perversion, and degradation that God eventually destroyed it.

Remember, Lot "chose for himself" the land of Sodom. This
is significant because it reveals Lot's innate attraction to evil. His
heart was drawn toward immorality and wickedness; his character was so appalling that the things that offended God appealed
to him.

Abraham, on the other hand, had a heart to obey God. He did
not always behave perfectly, but God looked at his heart and saw
character that pleased Him. In Scripture, Abraham is even called
God's friend and is mentioned as a righteous person (2 Chron. 20:7;
James 2:23). Clearly Abraham loved God and was serious about
pursuing God's promise to him.

The relational principle we must understand from this part of
Abraham and Lot's story is this: people gravitate toward the situations and activities that represent what's in their hearts. When

assessing current or potential relationships, we must ask the question, "Does this person gravitate toward the same things I'm drawn to?" The question is not meant to figure out whether the two of you have identical emotional DNA; it is intended to help you discover whether or not the two of you are walking in agreement in values, convictions, matters of character, and priorities—a subject covered in chapter 3.

We must be aware of the things to which people gravitate, because that gives us tremendous insight into the heart of a person. In relationships, we operate on the level of the heart whether we realize it or not. We do not relate to people based on what they say, think, or do. Instead we relate to who they are in their hearts, because everything else comes from that place (Prov. 4:23). When emotional poison is in the heart of a human being, he or she has nothing but toxicity to offer a relationship.

THE SILENCE IS DEAFENING

An interesting thing happened to Abraham while he was dealing with Lot: he not only suffered damage emotionally, he also began to "die" spiritually because he could not hear God's voice for a period of time, and God's voice had always been a source of life and strength for him. Nothing is as encouraging, as powerful, or as comforting as hearing God's voice. And nothing is as frustrating as feeling that God is distant or uninterested in you because you can't sense His presence or His leading in your life. If you have ever experienced this, you know how difficult it is, and you know how Abraham felt when it happened to him.

One of history's most vivid, powerful instances of God's speaking to a human being occurred when He said to Abraham:

Leave your country, your people and your father's household and go to the land I will show you. I will make you into a great nation, and I will bless you; I will make your name great, and you will be a blessing. I will bless those who bless you, and whoever curses you I will curse; and all peoples on earth will be blessed through you. (Gen. 12:1–3)

To say the least, this encounter with God was a defining moment for Abraham. It gave him hope, purpose, and direction. He did not know exactly what God would do, but he had a promise he could build his life upon—a promise that could guide his decisions. Abraham knew God's voice intimately. He had heard God speak about the situations that mattered most to him, making him a promise that exceeded everything he could imagine.

And then, silence.

God did not speak to Abraham again until after he and Lot separated (Gen. 13:14). This is a stunning illustration of a crucial principle to live by as you enter into new relationships and grow in existing ones: having the wrong people in your life may not only damage you emotionally, it can keep you from hearing God's voice and receiving His guidance. Being involved in a toxic relationship can put you in a holding pattern, unable to fulfill your destiny. This is a strong statement, I know, but Scripture affirms it, and I have seen it happen time after tragic time in people's lives.

Being involved in a toxic relationship can put you in a holding pattern, unable to fulfill your destiny.

In fact, one of my colleagues once reached a point when his entire life came to a complete stop and he seemed on the brink of losing everything. When he prayed about his circumstances, he realized he had to sever a significant personal and professional relationship. Soon, God began to open astounding doors for him. Within a few short months of walking away from this toxic relationship, God miraculously brought not one, but *two* lifelong dreams to pass for him. I cannot overemphasize the fact that having the wrong people around you can prevent you from fulfilling God's plans for your life. The presence of even one individual who should not be with you can keep you from reaching your destiny and hinder the fulfillment of your overall purpose.

Lot knew Abraham's purpose—to get to Canaan and experience the blessings God promised him there. He saw God's hand of blessing and favor on Abraham, and I believe that is why Lot left everything to go with him. But remember, God never told Abraham to take Lot with him, and Lot became a hindrance to God's purposes in Abraham's life.

You know by now that relationships are not neutral; they either help you or hinder you. People either cheer you on and push you forward in God's plans, or they drain your energy and hold you back. They are either assets or liabilities. Having a Lot in your life will drive a wedge between you and God, separate you from your purpose, and cause you to stumble as you try to pursue what God has for you. If that won't kill you emotionally, I don't know what will.

At the end of this chapter is a list of characteristics of toxic relationships. All of them are based on Lot's unwise actions or his negative influence on Abraham's life. I encourage you to use these eight indicators to determine whether you have a Lot in your life, and if you do, do yourself a favor and separate.

THE OTHER SIDE OF OBEDIENCE

The last verse of Genesis 13 is the climax of the story of Abraham and Lot's separation: "So [Abraham] moved his tents and went to live near the great trees of Mamre at Hebron, where he built an altar to the Lord" (v. 18). This tells us Abraham realized God had more for him than he was presently experiencing, and he needed to pursue it. He had left the burden of relationship with Lot behind him, and he refused to stay settled in an old place. He was finally free to go after God's best, and he knew he could have it.

The thought of separating from someone who has been significant in your life can be daunting. We can easily infer from Abraham and Lot's story that leaving Lot behind was emotionally taxing and difficult for Abraham. But the important point is that what comes after separation can be amazing. Ephesians 3:20 tells us, "God can do anything, you know—far more than you could ever imagine or guess or request in your wildest dreams!" (MSG). He has great things in store for us, but we can only access them if we hear and obey His voice, and that includes following Him as we make good relational decisions.

God always has something good on the other side of obedience; He always offers us more. In Abraham's case, his separation from Lot caused his life and his faith to expand in tremendous ways. After Abraham left Lot, he *saw more* in terms of having greater vision for his life; he *believed more* in God's love and ability to bring impossibilities to pass; *he realized God wanted more* for him than he had ever experienced; and he *worshipped more.*

I hope these lessons from Abraham's life will give you the courage to make the relational decisions you need to make. Remember that the most important relationship of all is your relationship with God, so do whatever it takes to be in a position to hear His voice and obey. You will be amazed at the great things that unfold for you! I promise.

DECISIONS CAN BE DANGEROUS

While Abraham moved forward, enjoying God's blessing, Lot remained in the evil environment of Sodom. We must remember that Sodom was the location Lot *chose*; no one forced him into that bad place. When people around us want our help in significant ways, we are wise to ask ourselves how many of their problems they have brought on themselves through their choices. I realize people sometimes make choices without understanding how severe the consequences may be. I also know that sometimes people make good choices but still somehow end up with bad results through no fault of their own. The fact remains that one person's decisions almost always affect others. Sometimes that turns out positively, and sometimes it is negative or even devastating.

Thankfully Lot's bad decision to move to Sodom did not devastate Abraham, but it could have. When rebel armies invaded the city where Lot chose to live, he found himself in danger. He needed someone willing to undertake a high-risk rescue mission for him after he fell captive to the armies of a warring king and lost all his possessions (Gen. 14:1–15). Who rescued him? Abraham.

When Abraham heard about Lot's plight, he gathered 318 trained men and devised a strategy to save his nephew. Genesis 14:14 teaches us that these 318 men were born in Abraham's household, meaning that they were not hired guns. They were men Abraham knew, men in whom he had invested. He'd practically raised them. Moreover, at this time, Abraham had a promise from God that he would have an heir, but he had no biological children.

He may well have believed one of these men would be his heir. He not only risked the lives of these men who were close to him, he had no way of knowing whether he was also jeopardizing the life of his potential heir and the chance to see God's promise come to pass.

In the end, Abraham and his men did rescue Lot, and the decision to do so was exceedingly courageous. Abraham risked everything to save the nephew who did not share his values, did not appreciate him, was not loyal or respectful to him, and had caused him great trouble. Lot's unwise, ungodly decision ultimately endangered Abraham and 318 other men. Being involved with Lot could have killed Abraham, literally!

If you are suffering because of other people's bad decisions, you may need to find a new set of friends. Know this: healthy relationships are not dangerous to you or to the people around you. For example, if you are a single mother who desperately wants a husband, the right man for you will not gaze lustfully at your teenage daughter when you are not looking. He will not "talk tough" to your son. He will not ask to borrow your money, and he will not treat you physically in ways that are not respectful. If you are an employee, a healthy relationship with your boss will not include intimidation. If you are a true friend of someone, the relationship will not involve control or manipulation. All these dynamics are unhealthy and may become unsafe in a relationship. They make relationships toxic, and toxic relationships will kill you emotionally.

HE SACRIFICED HIS OWN DAUGHTERS!

The more we read about Lot, the more we see that he did not value other people and he did not value relationships. This was most clear when the men of Sodom came to his house wanting to have sexual relations with the angels who were his houseguests. Instead Lot offered them his two virgin daughters (Gen. 19:1–8).

Had Lot never done anything else bad, this one action alone would have demonstrated his perverse character. But then again, Lot did not tend to act righteously. He made one wrong choice after another, clearly revealing his base, immoral nature. We learn from this story that people will show you who they really are through their actions and decisions. Pay attention: if they do not value other significant relationships in their lives, they are not likely to value a relationship with you, and that will eventually do you great harm.

Maybe Abraham thought Lot valued their relationship as much as he did. But if Lot would sacrifice something as precious as his daughters' virginity to a band of perverse men, he would sacrifice Abraham too—probably in a quick, decisive way. Frankly, Abraham had no reason to believe Lot was loyal or seriously interested in a healthy relationship, but he continued to invest in it anyway.

One of the most painful realizations in life is that you are in a relationship that does not mean as much to the other person as it does to you. I will address this at length in chapter 15, but the important point for now is this: one-sided relationships are doomed to fail. On the way to failure, there will be dysfunction, disappointment, and frustration. These relationships are unhealthy and detrimental, just as Abraham's relationship with Lot was. It's just a matter of how long you want to extend the agony.

LEAVE SOME THINGS BEHIND

Anytime two people enter into a purposeful relationship, one or both of them may have to let go of some things from the past.

Abraham had no problem leaving things behind. When God told him to leave his father's house, his homeland, and everything familiar to him, he did it without looking back. That's what people do when they love God and want to pursue God's promises and purposes. They will leave anything and everything to follow Him.

Lot, on the other hand, had a problem releasing certain things. He did not let go easily. Even when he knew God was about to decimate Sodom, he lingered (Gen. 19:14–16). Most people, realizing the wrath of God is about to destroy a place, would run as fast and as far as possible. Not Lot. First, he hesitated to leave, and an angel had to grab his hand and pull him away to safety. Then, when the angel told him to take his family and run to the mountains to escape certain death, Lot said no. Instead, he wanted to settle in a small town as close to Sodom as he could get (Gen.19:17–20).

People who may draw you into emotionally deadly relationships are unwilling to leave unhealthy or sinful places in their lives in order to have something better. Some are willing to leave, but like Lot, they want to stay close to their sin, addictions, bad habits, or negative influences. Those who will not let go of the past or allow themselves to be too far removed from it cause trouble in relationships. No matter how many people believe in them, help them, or think they can change, the fact is they will not do so unless they decide to walk away from old patterns.

The idea of being willing to leave some things behind applies to many areas of relationships. Think of a newlywed couple. Many times one spouse is eager to "leave and cleave" and begin a new life together, but the other will not leave parents or old friends behind. Or consider a young employee who has been promoted to a new position in a company. His superiors realize he has the skill to thrive in a leadership position, and they give him the opportunity to do so. His problem is that he cannot relate to others as a leader because those who now work for him were his basketball buddies last week and he does not want to lose his camaraderie with them.

A God-ordained relationship can be one of the best experiences of your life, but it may involve the need to leave some things in the past. Each person in the relationship may need to demonstrate a willingness to let some things go in order to move forward with the relationship. I encourage you to be willing to release things that need to stay in the past so you can have great relationships in the future. At the same time, assess whether others are willing to give up what they need to leave behind in order to be in relationship with you.

It Keeps Going . . . and Going . . . and Going . . .

I believe the most heartbreaking part of Abraham and Lot's story takes place not between the two of them, but in future generations. Lot's daughters become as perverted and unrighteous as he is, and because he is old and they are still unmarried, both of them sleep with him and become pregnant. One gives birth to Moab, who becomes the father of the Moabites. The other bears a son named Ben-Ammi, father of the Ammonites (Gen. 19:37–38). Years later, the Moabites and the Ammonites will become fierce enemies of the children of Israel. Lot ends up becoming the father of the antithesis of God's promise to Abraham. Helping Lot really does end up killing Abraham's seed.

For various reasons, people still try to connect or stay connected with those who not only hinder God's plans for their lives but actively oppose those plans. We try to stay friends with people who are enemies of God's purposes for us. We rationalize these relationships by downplaying the influence our friends have on us or by saying we are merely trying to help them. We need to understand that we are not the only ones affected by our relationships. Our families, friends, and coworkers may be affected too.

In the years to come, Abraham's future generations will be wounded and killed at the hands of Lot's descendants. One dysfunctional relationship between two relatives will affect many people. Dysfunction still works that way today. I urge you to take seriously each relationship in your life. Seek God earnestly to know which relationships He has for you and which ones are not part of His plan. Don't let your desire or ability to help another person damage you emotionally or kill God's purpose for your life.

Eight Indicators of a Toxic Relationship

Helping someone you do not need to help, as Abraham did for Lot, truly can be detrimental to your life. While it may not kill you physically, it can definitely kill your heart. I know many people who will affirm the fact that this kind of relationship can be as dangerous to your well-being as drinking a sip of poison every day. A toxic relationship

- is based on a shared past or shared pain.
- is unbalanced because one person benefits from the other without being grateful or appreciative.
- is strained because one person is pursuing God's purpose and promises while the other person is headed in a different direction.

- causes one person to cease to hear God's voice or lose momentum in following Him.
- jeopardizes not only the parties directly involved but family and friends too.
- is not of equal or similar value to both parties.
- cannot move forward because one individual cannot leave certain things behind.
- suffers long-term damage because one party produces "enemies" to the other person's life or destiny in God, in some cases affecting future generations.

SET SOME BOUNDARIES

One of the best ways to effectively deal with people who are killing you emotionally is to establish healthy boundaries. When God divided the promised land and gave a portion of that territory to each of the twelve tribes of Israel, He did so by establishing boundaries, often using geographical features such as rivers or mountains.

When you set boundaries in relationships, you set limits that will keep you healthy and keep other people from taking too much of your time, energy, or resources. Boundaries help people understand how far they can go with you, and communicate what you will and will not allow. People who are like Lot and have tendencies to use or take advantage of others to the point that it damages them will not set boundaries for you. You have to set them for yourself and let people know where your limits are. I would like to suggest some boundaries for you to consider. You may want to establish others based on your personal circumstances.

- Limit the amount of time you will spend each week with the person who could kill you emotionally.
- Limit the activities you will facilitate for this person. For example, you could say something such as, "I will take you to your AA meetings; I will not take you to the liquor store."
- Do not feel guilty if you must change plans occasionally with an unhealthy person. For example, if you are sick and need to stay home instead of taking her grocery shopping, simply let her know. Then take some medicine and go to bed!
- Clearly communicate to this person that you are not his or her go-to friend, family member, or coworker when he or she makes bad decisions.
- In an appropriate way and with wise boundaries, share the focus and direction of your life with this person; clearly state that you will not tolerate or support actions or behaviors that distract you from the direction in which you are heading.
- Set clear expectations for values and behavior that must be respected when you spend time with this person.

I hope this chapter has helped you identify people with whom you could be in toxic relationships and to understand how important it is not to allow them to damage you emotionally. God has awesome plans for your life. Keep your heart fully alive so you can enjoy them!

RELATIONSHIP REMINDERS

- When God calls you to help someone, be obedient but be wise.

- Don't allow yourself to help people God doesn't assign to you because, emotionally speaking, helping them could "kill" you.
- Don't be afraid or reluctant to leave a relationship if it becomes unhealthy. Don't let feelings of misplaced guilt or sympathy keep you from making a good choice for yourself.
- Stay away from relationships that could hinder your pursuit of God's purpose or keep you from fulfilling your destiny.
- Realize that every relationship you have affects other people in your life, and that the relationships they have affect you.

RAISING YOUR RELATIONAL IQ

1. Have you found that trying to help someone was good for that person but detrimental to you? What did you learn from that experience?
2. Which relationships in your life are based on shared pain or a shared past? What do you share, and why is it so powerful?
3. In your relationships with people who share your past or your pain, do you see signs that any of these relationships are or could become toxic? What do you see?
4. Are you currently helping anyone who does not appreciate your assistance? Why is a lack of gratitude a bad sign?
5. How do you think wrong relationships actively interrupt or oppose God's plans for your life?

6. Is someone in your life right now displaying any of the eight indicators of a toxic relationship? How can you begin to set limits and keep that person from hurting you emotionally?

7. What kinds of boundaries do you need to set with certain people in order to protect yourself emotionally and to stay on the path of destiny God has laid before you?

P A R T   3

Essentials of Great Relationships

AT THIS POINT IN THE BOOK, YOU HAVE BEEN exposed to the critical laws of relationships, learned to identify relationships that need to come to an end, and gained skills for drawing those relationships to a close wisely and lovingly.

In part 3 of this book, I want to explore some additional ideas, principles, and truths necessary for great relationships. You realize by now that great relationships do not appear quickly on the landscape of your life. They require time, effort, and skill. They also require a deliberate process, one that the story of Elijah and Elisha will make clear in chapter 14. The process of great relationships is not always easy, but it is worth the investment it requires.

Another essential ingredient of great relationships is being healed from the pain of bad relationships. One of the most hurtful relationships anyone can endure is to be spurned or rejected by someone significant. The Song of Songs offers tremendous insights into ways a person can be healed of a lovesick heart, avoid painful situations of unrequited love or unappreciated interest in the future, and find the only lasting love worth having.

14

The Journey Matters

UNDERSTANDING THE PROCESS
OF GREAT RELATIONSHIPS

IF YOU WERE TO ASK ME TO LIST THE BIGGEST relational mistakes I hear about in pastoral ministry, I would have to include this: "I gave too much too soon." I know what that means, and I am sure you do too—perhaps from personal experience. It means someone moved too fast and gave too much time, too much information, too much energy, or too much of his or her heart to a person who did not prove trustworthy. This happens when junior high school students fall into puppy love for the first time (or when people who haven't seen junior high for years meet someone who sweeps them off their feet). It also happens when eager employees finally land dream jobs, or when mothers of infants or toddlers are hungry for adult conversation and meet new friends with young children. And it takes place when business owners identify promising new clients or when committee chairs find people who are eager to serve.

I have had several experiences involving giving or being tempted to give too much too soon. One was particularly disappointing. I remember my great excitement and high hopes when a man named Robert agreed to join my staff. His credentials were excellent, and I was happy and thankful to know he was qualified to take some of the responsibilities I carried at the time, freeing me to focus more intensely on the areas to which I felt called in that season of ministry. Everything I had heard about Robert, my interview with him, and the correspondence we had exchanged indicated he would be ideal for the position I needed to fill. I also felt that the working relationship would not only be positive but synergistic.

Almost immediately when Robert came to work, he wanted access to my family and knowledge of every area of my life. By this time, I had learned the hard way that I had to protect my family and myself from people who had not earned my trust. I was kind but firm as I refused to allow him what he wanted. I tried to give him the benefit of the doubt, thinking, *Maybe he's acting this way because he's new in town and he doesn't really know anyone yet. Maybe he doesn't understand that I am his boss, not his buddy. And maybe he doesn't realize that I am very careful about exposing my wife and children to people I don't know well.*

In the earliest days of our association, I was not completely comfortable with Robert because I felt he wanted too much too soon from his association with me, but I hoped we could resolve that and find our way to a healthy professional relationship. As we worked together, I soon noticed that he mishandled every single situation I delegated to him. Still, over a period of months I was willing to try to develop a positive relationship that would enable Robert to fulfill his potential and live up to the hopes and expectations I had of him.

Suddenly, one day, Robert resigned his staff position and left the relationship. The reason? It was not a disagreement over pay or hours or job description. He left because he was so frustrated that I refused to become his best friend overnight and I did not give him immediate access to my family and to all areas of our ministry. My disappointment was almost indescribable when I realized that he had never intended to serve the ministry, support me, or bless the people to whom our ministry is dedicated. He had only wanted to ride my coattails.

I am thankful I did not give Robert what he wanted. By that time in my life, I had learned a vital lesson about relationships: the journey matters. We *must* go through some things with people in order to develop authentic relationships with them and know who they really are. Great relationships are not born overnight. They take time, but they are worth it.

> *Great relationships are not born overnight. They take time, but they are worth it.*

A Word and a Person

Ever since the beginning of time, when God has wanted to accomplish something, He has consistently used two critical components: His Word and a person. If you take a close look at Scripture, you will see that everything God has done from creation onward, He has done through His Word and a human being. Consider these significant works of God throughout history:

- preserving humanity and animals in the Flood through Noah

- the birth and growth of God's people through Abraham
- freeing His people from Egyptian slavery through Moses
- leading His people into the promised land through Joshua
- the rebuilding of the walls around Jerusalem through Nehemiah
- bringing salvation to the Gentiles through the apostle Paul
- redeeming humanity through Jesus Christ

The principle of the partnership between God's Word and a person is well established in Scripture. It means that whenever God wants to bless one person's life (including yours), He will do it through His Word and a person. God will intentionally place people in your life for the sole reason of blessing and elevating you, just as He has done for generations. Think about it: Jacob was blessed because of Isaac, Joseph was blessed because of Pharaoh, Joshua was blessed because of Moses, Samuel was blessed because of Eli, and David was blessed because of Jonathan. Each of these relationships has its own fascinating story, but I simply want to emphasize the point that in each one of them, the people had healthy relationships with each other. The relationships were not casual—they were deep. They were not always easy, but they were real. In order for people both in biblical times and today to enjoy healthy relationships, certain characteristics and attitudes must be present and a process must be allowed to unfold.

A Prototype for Healthy Relationships

God wants to bless and promote you through people He sends into your life—people who are destined to elevate you. For the increase He desires to become a reality, your relationships with these people must be healthy. They cannot be casual. They cannot be built on false pretenses or include pockets of dishonesty or disrespect on any level. The associations that will take you to the next level in your life have to be pure, solid, deep, and full of integrity.

Many people have missed the blessings and the great things God wants to do in their lives because they are not willing to establish the right relationships with the right people in the right ways. Cultivating these kinds of associations with people requires a combination of attitudes and actions that lead to relational health and ultimately to personal growth and advancement.

Scripture provides us a tremendous example of two people who developed and sustained a healthy relationship. In 1 Kings 19 and 2 Kings 2, we see that the young prophet Elisha wants to establish a relationship with the older and more experienced prophet Elijah. This relationship will be critical to Elisha's future. He will end up being blessed in extraordinary ways because of Elijah. During the course of his ministry, he will perform twice as many miracles as Elijah and enjoy the "double portion" he requests. But this relationship that so blesses Elisha's life requires several things of him: commitment and respect, desiring the best for his mentor, an active involvement in something positive, a capacity for healthy relationship, a willingness to deal with unpleasant situations, and the willingness to sacrifice for something new and different. Likewise, the relationships that will raise your life to a new level and usher you into great blessings will require some investments of you.

Great relationships require you to prove your commitment and respect.

The significance and benefit of the relationship between Elijah and Elisha is revealed in a powerful conversation between the two men. Elijah asks, "Tell me, what can I do for you before I am taken from you?"

Elisha immediately makes a huge request: "Let me inherit a double portion of your spirit" (2 Kings 2:9).

Elijah does not say okay right away. Instead, he answers, "You have asked a difficult thing . . . yet *if you see me* when I am taken from you, it will be yours—otherwise not" (2 Kings 2:10, emphasis added).

What does Elijah really mean when he says, "If you see me when I am taken from you"? Does he mean, "If you just happen to be around when I die, you can have the double portion"? I don't think so. He is saying so much more. He means, "If you are around me at the end of my life because you have walked with me over the years, because you have made a habit of spending time with me, because being together is a priority in your life, because we have had a deep, solid, genuine, healthy relationship for a long time, then no doubt you will be with me in the end. If you are still there, if your loyalty remains strong, if you are still watching me, you will be with me when I leave this earth, then what you ask can happen. You will be in position to receive the double portion."

Elijah understands the power of commitment, and that is what he is communicating when he says, "If you see me." He knows Elisha's best chance to "see him" when he dies is to stay faithful and committed as a friend until the very end. Similarly, the healthy relationships in your life will involve a significant element of commitment. That will mean staying in relationship when doing so is easy and when it is grueling. It will require the refusal to abandon or forsake a friend, spouse, family member, or colleague in the moments when you really want to run from the relationship. I do not ever recommend staying in a relationship that is abusive, but I do understand that all relationships have seasons of difficulty. One mark of a healthy association is the ability to stay committed through tough times. Great relationships are not built on good times alone, and they do not develop quickly. They take time, and that time needs to include challenges because challenges are incubators for growth, strength, and trust. A substantive, healthy relationship will weather storms and trials, and it will stand strong over a long period of time because everyone involved is committed.

Sometimes people stay committed in relationships for the wrong reason. They know they can benefit from another person, so they contrive a false kind of loyalty designed to get them what they want. This is both wrong and unhealthy. In a healthy relationship, commitment is based on respect.

A truth about great relationships is that one person cannot disrespect another and also expect to receive from that person. Disrespect, dishonor, and disregard have a way of canceling any potential benefit of a personal or professional association. The only way to receive from people is to respect them.

Great relationships require you to want the best for the other person.

When Elijah speaks to Elisha about his departure from his mortal life, he refers to it as being taken up from him. Literally, Elijah "went up to heaven in a whirlwind" (2 Kings 2:11). Sometimes in relationships, one person is "taken up" or elevated, figuratively speaking. Perhaps one coworker gets a raise or promotion that someone else wanted; maybe one spouse gets a great opportunity or chance for visibility while the other one must stay behind the scenes. Maybe someone's child gets a full scholarship to college while other parents must work hard at difficult or low-paying jobs to fund their child's education. Life is full of opportunities for increase in every arena. Unhealthy relationships may crumble under the pressure of promotion, but as I mentioned in the chapter on Paul and John Mark, healthy ones survive and even thrive in the wake of it.

The key to maintaining a healthy relationship when one person has something wonderful happen and the other does not is to refuse to be jealous. If you are the one who feels left behind when a spouse's, colleague's, or friend's dreams come true (especially if you have those same dreams), then fiercely resist the temptation to envy. Instead, even if it stings a little, bless, encourage, support, and cheer for the other person. Celebrate his or her victory and determine to continue walking closely with that person. Don't be untrue to yourself by denying your disappointment, but do not jeopardize an otherwise great relationship by letting something as petty as jealousy come between you and another person.

I have seen numerous people absolutely destroy good relationships by allowing jealousy to take over their hearts. In healthy relationships, both people can be mature enough to be champions for the other, to spur each other on to greatness, to rejoice in the good things that happen to each other, to realize that God is moving both people forward (just maybe on different schedules), and to enjoy the favor of God together when it comes to one of them.

Great relationships require you to be actively engaged in something positive.

Most of the time, people who have healthy relationships also have active, healthy lives. They do not sit around hoping for a dream job, a great opportunity, or for Mr. or Ms. Right. They refuse to delay their lives passively by waiting for something wonderful to happen; they get busy making things happen. They invest their time in things that are fruitful and productive, making the most of every minute.

There was a time in Elijah's life when he was tired and a bit discouraged. God speaks to him in his weariness and despair, directing him to "anoint Elisha son of Shaphat from Abel Meholah to succeed you as prophet" (1 Kings 19:16). Elijah soon finds Elisha and throws his cloak on him, a gesture indicating that he has chosen Elisha as his successor. At the time he receives Elijah's cloak, or mantle, Elisha is active and engaged in the positive work of plowing a field.

We see this principle of people being busy and occupied with valuable work when God calls them in Moses, Gideon, Jesus' disciples, and others throughout Scripture. So many people who have been called into greatness have been summoned to it while doing what they needed to do.

Most people want a lot out of their relationships, but many have adopted a passive posture. One of the keys to being able to enter into a strong, healthy relationship is to be actively engaged in your life before the relationship you desire comes along. Scripture affirms that God's blessing and favor tend to connect with people who are moving forward, not those who are sitting still. Naturally speaking, the same is true. Often, people do not want to get involved with those who are not making progress in their lives. God and others need to see that your life is advancing and that you are busy doing what you know to do. God and the people around you are looking to see that you are living the kind of life worth investing in and that you can be trusted to act and obey when He calls you into your next synergistic relationship.

Great relationships require you to demonstrate the capacity for healthy interaction.

Do you see what Elisha is doing when Elijah finds him and throws his cloak on him? He is plowing with twelve yoke of oxen and he himself is driving the twelfth pair. That's hard work! But more than being a wearisome task, driving a yoke of oxen is a humble job. Elisha is not out in front, nor is he overseeing the plowing efforts; he is doing manual labor behind the oxen and doing it in such a way that no one will notice him. He calls no attention to himself; he simply does the work he needs to do. This tells us Elisha can accept not being in the spotlight; he is content to let Elijah shine and succeed. Even though he will go down in Christian history as a mighty prophet, he has no need for visibility and acclaim.

We can all learn from Elisha's example. Just as he was comfortable in Elijah's shadow and sought no publicity for himself, if we are going to have healthy relationships, we, too, must be content to stand in the background or to walk steadily beside others, not needing attention or applause. In great relationships, people really are not interested in competing with one another, and there is not much room for ego.

Great relationships require you not to mind getting dirty.

Can you imagine what it was like to walk behind a team of oxen in the dusty muck of a field? The fact that Elisha seems comfortable plowing behind farm animals leads us to believe he must also have been accepting of the fact that sometimes people have to work through a mess. This is true physically but it is also true relationally. Relationships are not perfect because people are not perfect. Every relationship has its challenges, misunderstandings, hurt feelings, and crises. Even healthy relationships will not be perfect. They may be healthy, but the people involved will have to work hard and deal with unpleasantness at times.

The important thing to do when relationships encounter difficulties is to learn to distinguish between healthy messes and unhealthy messes (see the section titled, "You Can't Run on Empty" in chapter 2). I have heard many stories about people who rob themselves of great relationships because they stop pursuing people as soon as they encounter minor misunderstandings or surface-level problems. This happens often in dating relationships and friendships. It is somewhat less common in work relationships because people cannot always walk away from their professional colleagues easily.

We need to learn to give people a chance. We must understand that we will never be able to develop healthy relationships if we allow insignificant incidents to push us away from others. Unless we are dealing with major character flaws, things that are illegal or immoral, or serious issues, staying in relationships long enough to truly get to know people is important. Every relationship will have bumps in the road; some of them will be huge, but others will be fairly minor. As the old saying goes, we can't sweat the small stuff.

Next time you are in a new relationship and the other person does something that annoys you, take a deep breath and decide to stay in the relationship a little longer. See if you can look beyond that one situation and discover a great person on the other side of it.

Great relationships require you to be willing to sacrifice for something new and better than anything you have known before.

When Elijah throws his cloak on Elisha, Elisha runs to him and says, "Let me kiss my father and mother goodbye . . . and then I will come with you" (1 Kings 19:20).

Elijah has a surprising response, "Go back . . . what have I done to you?"

This exchange may seem strange, but Elijah has a reason for telling Elisha to go back. He realizes the importance of questioning Elisha's motives. He wants to verify that Elisha is pure-hearted and committed to going with him for the right reasons.

Elijah understands that no one can be in a healthy relationship and please everyone else simultaneously. Healthy relationships require time, energy, focus, and other qualities to be allocated smartly. This is a reality because no one has unlimited resources. People who are serious about strategic relationships simply do not have enough of anything to be able to give boundlessly to every single person who wants their attention. When Elijah speaks to Elisha about going "back," he is really asking, "Do you want what you've always had [represented by Elisha's father and mother], or are you open to the potential of something new [represented by a relationship with Elijah]?"

Elisha quickly proves his commitment to his new alliance with Elijah and to all the possibilities that relationship holds. He deals swiftly and decisively with the symbols of his earlier life, effectively making a return to the past impossible. He slaughters his oxen; he burns his plowing equipment, and then, according to 1 Kings 19:21, "he set out to follow Elijah and became his attendant."

Just as Elisha was willing to make significant sacrifices and let go of his past so he could embrace his future, you will also have opportunities to move ahead in life via new relationships; or you can stay in your past by choosing not to align with certain people. When God wants to do something tremendous in your life, He will use a word and a person, just as He always has. The question is, when that word comes to you and when that person enters your life, will you leave behind everything old and move into something new and great?

"OH, THE PLACES YOU'LL GO!" (THANK YOU, DR. SEUSS)

In 2 Kings 2, Elijah and Elisha take a final journey together before Elijah goes to heaven. Each place they go is highly symbolic, representing a necessary and vital aspect of all healthy relationships. If you want your relationships to be healthy and mature, you can also expect to go through the situations these places represent. In fact, I would go as far as to say that if a relationship is going to be strong and healthy, it *must* follow the same course, metaphorically, that Elijah and Elisha traveled. If we were to track their journey on a map, we would see that they travel together to four places in 2 Kings 2: Gilgal (v. 1), Bethel (v. 2), Jericho (v. 4), and the Jordan River (vv. 6–8). These places are familiar to most Bible readers because of their historical significance, but they also represent significant experiences in our relationships.

Gilgal

When Joshua led the Israelites into the promised land years before Elijah and Elisha lived, the first place they came to after crossing the Jordan River was Gilgal (Josh. 5:1–9). This was the location where Joshua observed the covenant ritual of circumcision for the Hebrew males who were not circumcised prior to entering the promised land, so Gilgal is a place that symbolizes the cutting of flesh.

In every healthy relationship, the blade of truth and honesty must be applied at times. If two people cannot have honest communication that sometimes hurts, the relationship will be superficial at best. We have heard that "the truth hurts," and sometimes it does. But when the truth is delivered with love, even painful honesty leads to relational health and strength.

This is true for romantic and platonic relationships, and it is also true in the workplace and in families, churches, and social organizations. It also applies to a believer's relationship with God. Scripture is clear that He chastens those He loves (Heb. 12:6). No matter what the arena or context of a relationship, if it is going to be genuine and healthy, it will have its uncomfortable moments when both parties must face truth.

Bethel

Throughout Scripture, Bethel is known as a place of prayer and worship. Any healthy relationship will stretch you and push you to prayer and worship through its challenges and its joys. I think any believer who is part of a strong, healthy marriage would admit to going through some difficult situations in which one or the other, or both spouses, had to take the circumstances to God in prayer. There are times in such an intimate relationship that two people need divine help and intervention, and the only way to ask for it is through prayer. There are also times in marriage when the relationship is strong and blissful, and the only way to respond is to thank and worship God.

I do not mean to imply that marriage is the only relationship in which prayer and worship play a vital role. If you are a believer, you can pray and worship your way through every relationship you have, but it is also important to realize that certain situations will call for fervent prayer and intense worship.

Jericho

The city of Jericho has long been known as a fortified city of thick walls and strongholds, which symbolize the walls we erect around ourselves. We may build walls to keep others from getting too close to us or to keep us from giving too much of ourselves to others in relationships. Sometimes knowing others deeply and allowing ourselves to be deeply known can cause us to feel vulnerable; we feel more secure if we refuse to let it happen.

A healthy relationship is only possible with a person who will not allow you to hide behind those walls or remain entrenched in strongholds. Whether you help others climb out from behind their walls or whether you allow someone to draw you out from behind yours, being honest, vulnerable, and transparent is vital to a healthy relationship. One way to begin to assess whether a relationship is healthy or not is to ask yourself, "Am I allowed to hide from this person or not?" If the answer is no, meaning that relationship pulls you away from your strongholds and defense mechanisms in a loving and honest way, you have a vital ingredient for a healthy relationship.

The Jordan River

Do you know that the Jordan River flows into the Dead Sea? The sea into which the Jordan River flows is called "dead" because it does not sustain life. Nothing lives in the Dead Sea; plant and sea life that flow into it die quickly. Symbolically, the last place Elijah and Elisha visit together speaks to death. One of the most foundational truths of healthy relationships is that they are impossible unless both parties involved are willing to die to themselves. They must be willing to lay aside their rights, agendas, and goals, doing what Romans 12:10 says to do: "Be devoted to one another in brotherly love. Honor one another above yourselves."

If you have ever been a part of a relationship in which both people die to themselves, you know that the most amazing thing happens as a result: two individuals willingly put to death their personal preferences and aspirations and a great relationship comes to life.

EMBRACE THE PROCESS

In a world that seems to be spinning faster and faster, certain things still just take time and require a necessary process. For example, we cannot rush the gestation period of a human being, we cannot push the earth to rotate on its axis any more rapidly, and we cannot speed up the passage of time. Likewise, no one can successfully rush the development of a healthy relationship; it takes hours, days, weeks, months, and years.

Healthy relationships take time to build because they must undergo certain situations and be tested in the crucible of circumstances. Relationships are forged in all sorts of ways, and while the specifics may vary, the need for the process remains constant.

Strong relationships are worth the investments of time and energy they require. I encourage you to position yourself for the best relationships you have ever known by understanding the process they must go through and devoting yourself to it. Study the lives and relationship of Elijah and Elisha, learn from them, and allow the kinds of blessings that came to them centuries ago to manifest in your life today.

RELATIONSHIP REMINDERS

- Pay attention when you notice that a word and a person have come into your life at a certain time. It's possible that God may be getting ready to do something great!
- Be looking for opportunities to prove your commitment and show your respect for the people in your life who may be candidates for healthy relationships. Act on those opportunities.
- Let go of any jealousy or competitiveness in your heart. Let people know that you are content to be in the background and that you are happy to see them shine.
- Don't sit around waiting for something wonderful to happen to you or for a great relationship to find you. Get busy doing something positive!

- Be sincere about wanting the best for every person in your life and help them achieve it.
- Resist the temptation to walk away from a relationship too soon because a person misspeaks, makes an innocent mistake, or does something you view as negative but really is insignificant or minor. Give people a chance!
- Every relationship is a journey. It must go through certain places and learn from certain situations in order to be healthy. Resist the desire to try to skip or race through any set of circumstances necessary for a great relationship. Even if it is painful, embrace it, knowing that it serves a good and healthy purpose in the big picture of a relationship.

RAISING YOUR RELATIONAL IQ

1. In your life right now, who are the candidates for great relationships? Why?
2. Are you content to be in the background or do you prefer the spotlight? If you want to be the center of attention in your relationships all the time, what good things might you miss by not allowing the other person to shine at times?
3. Why are jealousy and competition so destructive in relationships?
4. In what practical ways can you show the people who are important to you that you really want the best them and will help them achieve it?
5. Have you ever made a hasty decision and bac

away from a relationship before really giving someone a chance? Did you later regret it?

6. Do you consider yourself patient with others or do
   you tend to react too quickly when they make mistakes, say something wrong, or do something you
   don't like?

7. In your own words, why is it necessary for relationships to go through certain things if they are going
   to be strong, healthy, and valuable to both parties
   involved? What benefits can people reap from the
   process and journey of relationships?

15

Lovesickness and Its Cure

THE VERTICAL FACTOR

CHARLES SCHULZ'S COMIC STRIP, *PEANUTS*, features a cast of memorable characters: Lucy, Linus, Snoopy, Woodstock, Pigpen, and others—including a girl named Peppermint Patty. Peppermint Patty has a *serious* crush on Charlie Brown. In fact, she is obsessed with him. She works so hard to get him to return her affections, but he simply is not interested. While romantic notions of Charlie Brown fill her thoughts, the boy with the curl on his forehead and the zigzag across his shirt can only sigh and say, "Good grief."

Peppermint Patty is lovesick.

Peppermint Patty is in good company. She is part of an enormous throng of people who have been madly in love with someone who can only say, "Oh, good grief. Go away." Classic works of literature, from *Wuthering Heights* to *The Great Gatsby* to a host of modern-day books, tell the stories of hope-filled romantic pursuits that fall flat. Movies such as *Gone with the Wind*, *Sabrina*, and *My Best Friend's Wedding* have presented tales of spurned passion on big screens for years. Most of us, regardless of age, can recall the

soulful lyrics of songs about unfulfilled yearnings for love by art-
ists such as Patsy Cline, Elvis, Bonnie Raitt, and Radiohead.

In the 1600s, English poet Abraham Crowley perfectly cap-
tured the torment of loving someone who does not love in return
when he wrote, "A mighty pain to love it is, and 'tis a pain that pain to
miss. But of all pains the greatest pain, It is to love, but love in vain."[1]
Some three hundred years later, people were still writing about it.
Joyce Carol Oates succinctly observed, "The worst thing: to give
yourself away for not enough love."[2]

The fact that so much creativity in our culture has focused for so
long on unrequited love tells me it is an enormous issue. Unrequited
love is one of the most frustrating, agonizing experiences in life, but
it is also quite common and has plagued human hearts for thousands of years. Maybe you know firsthand how Peppermint Patty
and the people in books, movies, and music felt. Perhaps you, too,
have longed for a relationship with a certain person who never
seemed even the least bit interested in you. This happens often in
romantic relationships but also in friendships (just ask a junior high
student who cannot seem to find acceptance with the popular crowd
at school). It even happens in corporate settings, when people will
do almost anything to try to secure certain jobs with prestigious
companies only to be rejected time and time again.

This widespread and painful problem of unrequited love or
interest must have an answer, and I believe it does. We start the journey toward the solution with one question: How did this happen?

How Did This Happen?

When people catch a cold or the flu, telltale symptoms arise: sneez-
ing, coughing, runny noses, fever, and body aches, to name a few.

One of their first questions is often, "Where did I get this?" We know such conditions are highly contagious and can be caught in all kinds of public venues.

The condition of lovesickness is different. Its symptoms include the inability to think clearly, excessive focus on one individual, emotions that go haywire, forgetting important things that need to be done, poor judgment, perhaps even butterflies in the stomach, and a heart that is deeply troubled over unrequited love. We do not contract lovesickness because other people have it and spread their germs; we get it because of the decisions we make. If we can understand how we get sick, we can learn to get better.

The Bible contains an ancient love story, the meaning of which people have debated for years. Some scholars suggest it is nothing more than a true account of an actual romance between two people. Others contend that it is an allegory in which the lover represents Christ and his beloved represents believers. For our purposes in this book, I will approach the story as an allegory. Let me share it with you.

Lover: I have come into my garden, my sister, my bride; I have gathered my myrrh with my spice. I have eaten my honeycomb and my honey; I have drunk my wine and my milk. . . .

Beloved: I slept but my heart was awake. Listen! My lover is knocking: "Open to me, my sister, my darling, my dove, my flawless one. My head is drenched with dew, my hair with the dampness of the night."

I have taken off my robe—must I put it on again? I have washed my feet—must I soil them again?

My lover thrust his hand through the latch-opening; my heart began to pound for him. I arose to open for my lover, and my hands dripped with myrrh . . . I opened for my lover, but my lover had left; he was gone. My heart sank at his departure.

I looked for him but did not find him. I called him but he did not answer. The watchmen found me as they made their rounds in the city. They beat me, they bruised me; they took away my cloak, those watchmen of the walls! O daughters of Jerusalem, I charge you—if you find my lover, what will you tell him? Tell him I am faint with love. (Song 5:1–8)

The first eight verses of Song of Songs 5 hold significant clues to the reasons people become lovesick. The lover is lovesick for three primary reasons we can easily see: his beloved is not awake; she is not willing to be inconvenienced for a relationship; and she does not value his interest in her or his presence in her life at that moment.

She's Asleep

Can you see what happens in the beginning of Song of Songs 5? A lovesick man stands at his lover's door, but the woman is in bed, sleeping. They are supposed to be in the relationship together, equal participants, but in reality they are not. The lover is much more engaged in the relationship than his beloved is. When he knocks at her door and she replies, "I slept but my heart was awake," we can see that her heart is in one place doing one thing, while her body is in another place doing something different. This means she has not given all of herself to this relationship; she is not all in. This causes her already lovesick lover to feel a little sicker.

You see, lovesickness happens when one person in a relationship is completely focused on the other person, who is not focused on the relationship at all. Maybe you know how that feels because you have been thoroughly infatuated with someone who hardly seemed aware of your existence. In a healthy relationship, both participants focus equally on the other. They both understand the relationship and want to give themselves to it to keep it from being one-sided. In a lovesick situation, one person gives excessive time, attention, and energy to pursuing the other, while the other does not invest much of anything. When this kind of unbalanced attention and focus takes place, I like to say the principle of magnification is at work. This means that whatever we focus on becomes bigger and bigger in our minds.

> *In a healthy relationship, both participants focus equally on the other. They both understand the relationship and want to give themselves to it to keep it from being one-sided.*

Think about the principle of magnification this way: Let's say you really, really like chocolate cake. One day, the thought occurs to you, *I really want a piece of chocolate cake.* Unless you have a phenomenal amount of willpower or a medical reason not to eat cake, your thoughts will cause you to focus more and more on that piece of cake until you get it. It becomes increasingly important to you until you finally satisfy the craving.

Feeling this way in relationships works like wanting that chocolate cake, but to a greater degree. When you focus intensely on someone else, that person and the idea of a good relationship occupy a large place in your life. In an unbalanced relationship, no matter how big a place someone holds in your heart and mind, you hold a small place in his or hers. This happens most frequently in romantic associations, but applies to various other types of relationships as well.

In the story of the lover and his beloved, he is obviously focused on her in a major way. She is not awakened to the strength of his feelings; she is not nearly as eager to participate in the relationship as he is. He clearly does not occupy her thoughts the way she fills his.

If you fail to deal properly and honestly with the way someone feels about you when that person is less interested in a relationship than you are, it will make you lovesick. To stay relationally healthy, do your best to assess clearly how others feel about you. If you have a strong interest in a person or a group, let that be known and evaluate the response. If the other entity is similarly enthusiastic about a relationship with you, keep moving forward. If not, realize that the relationship may not hold as much potential as you had hoped. Be honest about that, accept it, and move on to a situation that will be less frustrating for you.

SHE DOES NOT WANT TO BE BOTHERED

Once her persistent lover's knock awakens the beloved and she realizes he wants to see her, she says, probably groggily, "I have taken off my robe—must I put it on again? I have washed my feet—must I soil them again?" (5:3). In other words, "I have just gotten comfortable and cozy in my soft, warm bed, and you want me to get up and get dressed? I have just gotten clean and you want me to get my feet dirty again? I don't think so!"

To assess the beloved's response bluntly, she really is not interested in seeing her lover. She does not want to be uncomfortable or inconvenienced, while he is up late at night making an effort to see her. She has no idea how much he loves and longs for her; she just wants to stay in bed. She does not want to leave her comfort zone and she has no idea how hurtful that is to the man so persistently pursuing her.

French philosopher Blaise Pascal said, "The heart has its reasons, which reason does not know."[3] This means love causes people to do things they normally would not do. Love causes people to go out of their way, to sacrifice and stretch on behalf of the other. In a healthy relationship, both people involved go to great lengths for the other. Lovesickness occurs when only one person is willing to make such effort, while the other person is unwilling to be inconvenienced or made even a little uncomfortable.

When my coworker Belinda worked in the public relations field, she had a project on a particularly tight schedule. She and her team worked feverishly and frantically to finish a promotional piece in time for a big event where her client was scheduled to appear. For her client, a rising star in his field, this opportunity could significantly raise his visibility and credibility within his market. When the piece was just moments away from completion, someone raised an important question about some of the facts and figures it included. When Belinda called the client, needing immediate clarification, the client responded nonchalantly, "Hmmm. I don't really know about that without looking it up. Right now I'm watching my favorite TV show. I'll get back to you later this afternoon."

Numerous people had sacrificed and truly gone the extra mile to make sure the client had his advertising piece for his event. The tight schedule did not allow for an extra few hours on the day it needed to go to production; it did not even allow for an extra thirty minutes. The team needed their answer right away in order to finish the job and not miss the event, but the client did not want the inconvenience of interrupting his television show.

Though the public relations team and Belinda certainly were not "in love" with their client, they had invested a tremendous amount of creativity and energy to satisfy him. When they realized they seemed to care more about meeting his deadline than he did, they regretted working so hard and sacrificing so much on his behalf. Their story teaches us an important lesson: when we really believe in something or really yearn to have people in our lives, we need to pay attention to their responses to us, especially if we sense that our efforts to build relationships are inconvenient for them. People who qualify for great relationships are glad to accommodate us whenever they can. We will feel comfortable, welcome, and valued in their presence.

She Does Not Value Her Lover's Interest or Presence

When the beloved finally gets out of bed and goes to the door, something surprising has happened. She says, "I opened for my lover, but my lover had left; he was gone." Yes, her lover, who had been patiently knocking and waiting for her, finally had enough. By the time she decides to respond to him, he is gone. She does not value her lover, nor does she value his interest in her at that time. In addition, she does not value his presence as he longingly tries to see her. He makes a serious effort for her, but she has no enthusiasm for him. Eventually, he gives up on her.

Remember, lovesickness happens because one person has been giving everything to the relationship while the other person has been withdrawn or unwilling to be inconvenienced. Often a funny thing happens within a lovesick relationship. After the person who gave so much decides to "check out" emotionally or leave because his or her feelings have not been reciprocated, that seems to be the moment the other one is finally ready to respond. The problem is, by that time it is usually too late.

We have heard the phrase "timing is everything." That also applies to relationships. In fact, timing is one of the most important components of any relationship. Everyone involved in relationships needs to understand that people will not pursue others without limits; after a while they will move on. People need to understand that others will not pursue them infinitely; they will eventually find someone else. We need to be respectful of other people's feelings; that includes being respectful of the timing of their emotions and realizing that at some point, whatever the situation is, the clock will run out.

In the early days of my ministry, I did a lot of biblical relationship counseling. Troubled couples often shared with me situations in which one person had wholeheartedly poured himself or herself into the relationship and had given everything possible to the other person, who did not seem to notice. When the one who invested so much finally became exhausted and gave up, the other one seemed to snap to attention and be ready to make meaningful investments in the relationship. The problem was, the timing was bad. The other person had already spent so much time waiting and investing in the relationship that he or she was out of patience. It was not the right time to reinvest. The right time would have been months or years earlier. The emotional and relational dance that takes place in situations such as these is dizzying. When you are ready, the other person is not ready. When the other person is ready, you are not. Back and forth. No wonder it makes a person lovesick!

If you have ever been in a relationship in which you give your love, your heart, your time, or your energy to someone who does not reciprocate, you can probably understand why the lover in Solomon's story and the people I counseled gave up after a while. The fact is, pursuing someone can be exhausting! If you have ever pursued another person and been resisted or rejected, you can understand why the lover left. When someone does not value your presence, you have to decide whether to keep trying to make a relationship work or to walk away. Most of the time, continuing to put your heart and soul into that endeavor becomes counterproductive.

Because the beloved did not value her lover's presence, she did not receive everything he could have given her. She says, "My lover thrust his hand through the latch-opening" (5:4). That tells me she only got a small part of him. She saw only his hand when she could have had so much more. When people do not feel valued, they begin to withhold parts of themselves from relationships. Maybe you have done that. Maybe you know how terrible it feels to know you are not a priority in the life of someone who is extremely important to you. That's how the lover felt, and his feelings, like yours, were understandable.

Perhaps you have read this entire book wishing the lessons you have learned would work in a certain relationship in which you feel hurt and devalued. Those emotions are reasonable and understandable. The desire to be valued is healthy and normal. Being frustrated when you feel you are exhausting yourself for someone is also perfectly acceptable. Everyone has legitimate, God-given needs, and relationships are designed to meet those needs. But those needs are only met in fulfilling ways as we allow God to meet the needs He is supposed to meet and allow others to meet the needs they are supposed to meet. With God's help, your heart can heal from the pain of not having important needs met, and you can develop healthier relationships in the future.

THE CURE FOR LOVESICKNESS

The betrayed ex-wife of South Carolina governor Mark Sanford told Dr. Phil McGraw in May 2010 that she would be open to another romantic relationship, as long as she picked a man who could "love me back."[4] How many people have that attitude? And how many people fail to feel "loved back" because they themselves have never been taught how to have healthy relationships? The truth is, no boyfriend, girlfriend, or marriage partner can meet the relational needs that God alone can fulfill.

We usually attribute the pain of being lovesick to the relationship between a man and a woman. We need to understand that the fifth chapter of Song of Songs, as an allegory, is also a picture of how God feels about us. He is lovesick for us! These verses are about much more than a love relationship between a male and a female; they have profound spiritual and relational significance for us.

Revelation 3:20 paints a picture of another Lover standing at a door and knocking. Christ is the Lover, and the door represents the human heart. Revelation 21:9 reveals that those who believe in Jesus Christ are, collectively, His bride. No matter who we are or what we have done, He is patiently wooing us, asking us to allow Him into every area of our lives, and longing to enjoy a deep and personal relationship with us. Unlike the lover in Song of Songs, Christ will never grow weary of pursuing us. He will knock and wait until we answer. When we do open our hearts to Him, He will give us a quality of relationship no human being can ever provide, and He will bless in ways we could never imagine.

THE VERTICAL FACTOR

One benefit we receive from God is genuine, unconditional love. He loves us perfectly and accepts us completely. This is the vertical aspect of relationship; it goes up and down, between God in heaven and us on earth. We can gain great insight into the way God sees us by looking at the way the lover addresses his beloved. He says, "Open to me, my sister, my darling, my dove, my flawless one" (Song 5:2). *Sister, darling, dove,* and *flawless one* each reveal something important about our vertical relationship with God and something specific about the way He feels toward us.

My Sister

The word *sister* represents family. In God's family, which includes all believers, male and female, He is the Father and we are His children. According to Romans 8:15–16, He has adopted us as His own sons and daughters: "You received the Spirit of adoption by whom we cry out, 'Abba, Father.' The Spirit Himself bears witness with our spirit that we are children of God" (NKJV).

If you have a wonderful biological family, you may be able to easily understand and embrace the family of God. If your earthly family was or is filled with strife, disappointment, or pain, you can take comfort in knowing that God's family is a place where you are wanted—a place of love, hope, healing, and strength. He is a perfect Father, and His desire is to surround you with love, approval, and unconditional acceptance.

My Darling

The word *darling* connotes deep affection and intimacy. It is a term of endearment—one that conveys great love. God is so in love with you, and you are so important to Him, that you are the apple of His eye (Psalm 17:8) and He has your name engraved on the palm of His hand (Isa. 49:16). As author Max Lucado says in this familiar quote, "If God had a refrigerator, your picture would be on it."[5]

The prophet Zephaniah crafted a beautiful word picture about God's love when he wrote: "The LORD your God is with you, he is mighty to save. He will take great delight in you, he will quiet you with his love, he will rejoice over you with singing" (3:17). In Hebrew, these words evoke the image of God dancing and spinning with joy over the people He loves. That includes you!

My Dove

The dove is a well-known symbol of peace. Maybe you have received Christmas cards featuring drawings of doves and including the words "Peace on Earth." Or maybe you know that in military and political circles, a "hawk" is a person who is eager to go to war, while a "dove" is a person who prefers and pursues peace.

The beauty of being loved by God is that He brings perfect peace to your life. That God sees you as His dove is extremely powerful if you think about its ramifications. I know you are aware that relationships can be the sources of tremendous hurt and frustration. Sometimes being in a certain relationship feels like living in a war zone every day. The drama some people can bring into your life can be staggering. God is completely drama-free; He brings peace, not turmoil, into every situation. He settles things down instead of stirring them up!

Relationships can also involve a good bit of unpredictability and uncertainty, and that can keep you uptight. God will never stand you up, and He will never let you down. He never changes; He does not act one way one day and another way the next. Hebrews 13:8 says, "Jesus Christ is the same yesterday and today and forever." That means you can absolutely count on Him, and you can count on His love to be constant and strong all the time. That steadiness infuses your life with peace.

If you feel your life is spinning out of control, continually presenting you with unexpected challenges, or filled with drama, the one relationship that will calm your internal storms is your relationship with God. If you focus on growing your relationship with God, not only will your other relationships improve, but an unprecedented sense of peace will blanket your life.

My Flawless One

Have you ever thought of yourself as flawless? Some people think of themselves as perfect from a worldly perspective, and that often leads to arrogance and gets them in trouble. Other people cannot imagine considering themselves to be flawless because they are painfully aware of their many faults and short-comings. People who think they are perfect in a worldly sense and those who believe they are terribly flawed are both wrong. The truth is, we all sin, we all make mistakes, and we are all works in progress—and works in progress can be messy before they become beautiful.

Regardless of your mistakes and your messes, God calls you His "flawless one." He is not focused or fixated on your sin; He sees you as absolutely perfect. He sees you that way not because of anything you have or have not done, but because the shed blood of Jesus Christ wipes away every sin and fault. His sacrifice makes you righteous, acceptable, and perfect in God's eyes.

A real, vibrant relationship with God is the vertical factor that will empower all the horizontal realities in your life. Knowing and believing you are loved, forgiven, and accepted by God will give you the fuel you need and the security you desire in order to have healthy relationships with the people around you. Even if someone fails to love you the way you love him or her, knowing that God's unconditional love is a constant reality in your life will forever make the difference for you, no matter what!

RELATIONSHIP REMINDERS

- Lovesickness is not a physical illness. It is something that afflicts the heart of a person who is madly in love with or completely focused on someone else who does not acknowledge interest or return affection.
- Lovesick people often find that the ones they love are not awakened to the way they feel about them or simply do not care how much they long for them.
- Lovesick people need to realize that people who do not want to be inconvenienced or who are uncomfortable in relationships do not qualify as good candidates for great relationships.
- Lovesick people need to understand that they may need to walk away from people who do not value their presence.
- A relationship with another human being will never be an antidote for lovesickness. The only way to cure a lovesick heart is through a deep, personal relationship with God.
- God is lovesick for you. You are His sister, His darling, His dove, and His flawless one.

RAISING YOUR RELATIONAL IQ

1. Have you ever been lovesick? What was that experience like?
2. If you are lovesick now, is it time to walk away from the relationship you have been so strongly pursuing?
3. Have you ever thought about God in terms of a Lover

pursuing you, His beloved? How do you feel when you realize He is longing for you?

4. What does it mean to you personally to know you are part of God's family?

5. How does the fact that you are God's darling impact you?

6. How do you feel when you realize that God wants to bring peace to every area of your life?

7. In your own words, express what it means to you to be flawless before God.

Acknowledgments

Beth Clark: we make a great team!

John Eames: thanks for believing in me.

Brian Hampton: I greatly appreciate your willingness to take a risk on a new author.

Kristen Parrish, Janene MacIvor, and the Thomas Nelson editorial and production teams: thank you for shepherding this book through the publishing process.

Chad Cannon, Katy Boatman, Emily Lineberger, and the Thomas Nelson marketing and sales departments: thank you for your efforts to promote *The People Factor*.

My Cabinet: thank you for your faithfulness, hard work, support, and prayers.

To all my family and friends who offered prayer, support, and encouragement for this project: I am grateful!

Notes

Foreword

1. *Seth's Blog*, October 9, 2012, http://sethgodin.typepad.com/seths
   _blog/2012/10/association.html.

Chapter 1

1. Jay Worth Allen, "The Meaning of Sincerity," *Freed in Christ!*
   (blog, August 16, 2010), http://drjaymissdiana.com/WRITINGS
   /Other%20Writings/Meaning%20of%20Sincerity.htm.
2. *Oxford Dictionaries*, s.v. "hypocrisy," accessed July 11, 2013,
   http://oxforddictionaries.com/definition/english/hypocrisy
   ?view=uk.
3. Google, http://www.google.com/search?client=safari&rls=en&q
   =definition+of+vulnerable&ie=UTF-8&oe=UTF-8.
4. John Donne, "XVII. Meditation," in *Devotions upon Divergent
   Occasions: Together with Death's Duel* (Middlesex, UK: Echo
   Library, 2008), 97.
5. Gary Smalley, Michael Smalley, and Robert S. Paul, *The DNA of
   Relationships* (Carol Stream, IL: Tyndale House, 2004), 42.

Chapter 3

1. Julie Creswell and Landon Thomas Jr., "The Talented Mr.

Madoff," *New York Times*, January 24, 2009, http://www.nytimes
.com/2009/01/25/business/25bernie.html?pagewanted=all.

2. Colleen Long and Tom Hays, "Mark Madoff Suicide: Bernie
Madoff's Son found Hanged in NYC Apartment," *Huffington
Post*, December 11, 2010, http://www.huffingtonpost.com/2010
/12/11/mark-madoff-suicide-hanged_n_795342.html.

Chapter 6

1. Susan Scott, *Fierce Conversations* (New York: Berkley, 2002), xiv.
2. T. D. Jakes, *Let It Go* (New York: Atria, 2012).

Chapter 10

1. Marvin Vincent, *Vincent's Word Studies in the New Testament*,
vol. 1, 2nd ed. (Peabody, MA: Hendrickson Publishers), 98.

Chapter 11

1. Answers, s.v. "Marvin Gaye," http://www.answers.com/topic/
marvin-gaye.
2. Jim Collins, *Good to Great* (New York: HarperCollins, 2001), 41.
3. *Vincent's Word Studies in the New Testament*, 528.
4. The NIV says John Mark "deserted them" and *The Message* says
he "jumped ship."
5. Spiros Zodhiates, ed., *The Complete Word Study Dictionary New
Testament* (Chattanooga, TN: AMG International, 1992), 1418.
6. Vincent, *Vincent's Word Studies of the New Testament*, 528.

Chapter 12

1. BBC History, "Henry Stanley," http://www.bbc.co.uk/history
/historic_figures/stanley_sir_henry_morton.shtml.
2. For a biblical example of exchanging gifts as part of a covenant
ceremony, see the story of Abraham's offering to God and God's
promises to Abraham in Genesis 14:18–20; 15:5–10; and 22:1–18.
3. Tim Bagwell, *When I See the Blood* (Hagerstown, MD: McDougal
Publishing, 1998), 73–74; www.mcdougalpublishing
.com, http://www.sermonillustrator.org/illustrator/sermon10
/cutting_the_covenant.htm.

4. BBC History, "Henry Stanley."

5. Richard Booker, *The Miracle of the Scarlet Thread* (Shippensburg, PA: Destiny Image, 1981), 30.

Chapter 15

1. Abraham Cowley, "Gold," in *The Poems of Abraham Crowley*, ed. A. R. Weller (n.p.: Nabu Press, 2011), 55.

2. Joyce Carol Oats, *The Collector of Hearts* (New York: Plume, 1999), 45.

3. Blaise Pascal, *Pascal's Pensees* (Teddington, UK: Echo Library, 2008), 276.

4. "Alienation of Affection," *The Dr. Phil Show*, May 13, 2010, http://www.drphil.com/shows/show/1458.

5. Max Lucado, *A Gentle Thunder* (Nashville: Thomas Nelson, 1995), 122.

About the Author

Photo courtesy of The Worship Center Christian Church

The compelling, insightful voice of Pastor Vanable H. Moody II, affectionately known to thousands as "Pastor Van," has been heard on secular and gospel music radio stations, at the Vatican (as part of Pope John Paul II's Pontifical Council for Promoting Christian Unity), in the classrooms of Harvard and Oxford Universities where he has furthered his education, in the World Council of Churches (as part of the Decade to Overcome Violence in Berlin, Germany), as part of the thirtieth anniversary of the March on Washington, at the Black Women in Church and Society (BWCS) Think Tank, and most frequently in the pulpit of his dynamic church, the Worship Center in Birmingham, Alabama.

Comfortable and enthusiastically received by a variety of audiences, Pastor Van is an engaging communicator, gifted visionary, compassionate pastor, strong leader, and skilled administrator. He was led to establish the Worship Center ministry in March 2006. Since that time the Worship Center has grown at an astounding pace.

Pastor Van; his wife, Ty; and their children, Eden Sydney and Ethan Isaiah, live in Birmingham, where his vibrant ministry is at the forefront of a fresh and exciting movement of God.

CPSIA information can be obtained at www.ICGtesting.com
Printed in the USA
LVOW07s1416190214

374363LV00010B/82/P